A STRANGER AT MY TABLE

A Stranger
at My Table

Ivo de Figueiredo

**Translated by
Deborah Dawkin**

DoppelHouse Press | Los Angeles

A Stranger at My Table
By Ivo de Figueiredo
Translation © 2018 Deborah Dawkin

En fremmed ved mitt bord
© 2016 Ivo de Figueiredo
Published by agreement with Copenhagen Literary Agency ApS, Copenhagen.

All photographs and documents are taken from family albums and are courtesy of
Ivo de Figueiredo, except the images of Rita Tushingham, p. 135, and Paul Danquah,
p. 136, which come from the 1961 film *A Taste of Honey* © British Lion/ Woodfall/
The Kobal Collection.

The DoppelHouse Press publication of this translation has been made possible
through the financial support of NORLA, Norwegian Literature Abroad.

COVER DESIGN: Janet Lê with Carrie Paterson

PUBLISHER'S CATALOGING-IN-PUBLICATION DATA
Names: Figueiredo, Ivo de, 1966-, author. | Dawkin, Deborah, translator.
Title: A Stranger at my table : the post-colonial story of a family caught in the half-life
of empires / by Ivo de Figueiredo; translated by Deborah Dawkin.
Description: Includes bibliographical references. | Los Angeles, CA: DoppelHouse
Press, 2019.
Identifiers: LCCN 2018959796 | ISBN 9780999754474
Subjects: LCSH Figueiredo, Ivo de, 1966-. | Figueiredo, Ivo de, 1966- --Family.
| Fathers and sons. | Children of immigrants--Norway--Biography. | Families. |
India--Emigration and immigration. | Goa, Daman and Diu (India)--History. |
Decolonization--Africa. | BISAC BIOGRAPHY & AUTOBIOGRAPHY / Personal
Memoirs | BIOGRAPHY & AUTOBIOGRAPHY / Cultural, Ethnic & Regional /
General
Classification: LCC JV8218 .F55 2019 | DDC 325.481/09--dc23

DoppelHouse Press
Los Angeles, California

Printed in Canada

Home was something in my head. Something I had lost.

V.S. NAIPAUL, *A Bend in the River*

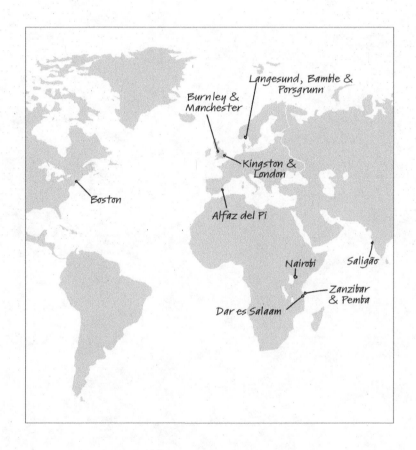

Oslo, July 2011

I'VE NOT SEEN OR TALKED TO DAD for over five years. I believe I sent him an email on his seventieth birthday out of a sense duty. Beyond that, we no longer have any contact. As the years have passed I've come to think of him as a stranger, some guy who lived with us for a few years, and then disappeared. In the picture below he stands outside Grandpa's workshop in Bamble. An Indian in the Norwegian snow.

Dressed for the city in a snowdrift in the middle of the forest. For years I've looked at this picture and felt it safest that he stay there, at a distance, frozen, tranquil, before the snow melts and stirs everything into motion.

The snow has begun to pile up in my own life now. I can't leave him standing there any longer. I need to know how he came to be there, how it all began, and why everything went so dreadfully wrong between us. I need to know this now, before everything freezes again.

For the last eight or ten years Dad has lived in Alfaz del Pi on the Spanish Costa Blanca, surrounded by people I've never met and don't know. I could visit him there, but I don't. Not yet. I'm not ready. Instead, I take a plane to the United States, to Boston, where his sisters live. We sit around the dining table in an old apartment building on Mass Avenue. The apartment is arranged around a long, dark corridor with doors that lead to a series of rooms that all face out toward the traffic. The floors are warped with age. The thin windowpanes keep neither the noise nor summer at bay. The air is heavy with heat, except in the dining room where an air-conditioner roars.

My aunts look at me with the same gentle, empathic gaze I remember so well from their visits to Langesund when I was a child; it's as though everything I tell them, any feelings I express, become etched in their faces. Though, in fact, they speak with their whole bodies, the way Indian women do. The many years they have spent in the United States have undoubtedly wrought changes in them, but not in their body language; heads that sway as they talk, forefingers that wag. When they get animated, up pops a forefinger, always the right, and always rocking in a perfect sideways arc, back and forth, affirming or negating, as though they need a metronome to maintain the stream of conversation.

Now and then the metronome halts, and the forefinger points straight up in front of two gentle, but penetrating eyes. Then I know that what will follow is important:

"Your Dad got very hurt. He was only nineteen when he left East Africa. And he'd been like a king."

Dad hadn't been any kind of king when I knew him. Not in our house. So where was it he'd been king? In Zanzibar, in Dar Es Salaam or Nairobi? In Goa perhaps, or in England? Now that I think about it, I'm not really sure where he came from; whether it was from just *one* of these places, or *all* of them. But somewhere in the world, at some point in his life, he seems to have been strong; a king. Then, somewhere along the road, a king he ceased to be.

As I'm about to leave, Dad's youngest sister emerges from the bedroom carrying a black folder stuffed with old letters. I recognize the flimsy, blue air-mail paper from my childhood. It arouses memories of Dad sitting at the kitchen table reading.

"Your father wanted you to have these."

The folder holds all the letters he received from his parents and siblings during those difficult years when the family was scattered to the four winds, uncertain whether they'd ever see each other again. Dad wants to give the letters to my brothers and me, but since we're no longer on speaking terms, his sister has agreed to hand them over to me.

On my flight home to Norway I glance through one of the letters to Dad from his mother, Herminia:

Nairobi, March 19, 1965: "What passport have you got, Xavier?"

I open another, from the following year:

"We are in a desperate situation..."

Then another, also from my grandmother:

"Please, please, start talking to Baby in English, right away, do not talk to him in Norge [sic]..."

Suspended over the Atlantic Ocean I am grasping fragments of a world in my hands, a world and a history that I've started to realize is far greater than I'd ever imagined. Confusing glimpses into the thoughts and anxieties of a stranger – Herminia, the grandmother I never met. *Baby.* Is that me? A voice from a world about which I have a vague notion, but have never known because it is long-gone; a world that went under and disappeared years before he came to us. Dad's world. And perhaps mine?

THE EARLIEST PHOTOGRAPH I HAVE FOUND of Dad shows him sitting on a lawn. The year is 1939. I assume it was taken in Victoria Gardens, just outside the city of Zanzibar, where the family's African ayah often took my father and his siblings. It's unlikely the servant would have taken this picture. My guess is that Grandfather is the photographer. In which case the picture was probably taken on a Sunday, when he

was free. The rest of the week he sat in the office of the British District Commissioner shifting papers, while my grandmother, Herminia Sequeira took care of the housework at their home in Vuga Street. On second thought, the picture may have been taken on a weekday afternoon, since he finished work by one o'clock. The pace of life was slow in Zanzibar, even in the British Protectorate Administration. Dad sits there on the grass in the park. What is he looking at? He doesn't know. His gaze is open, as are his thoughts. He simply *is* who he *is* – Xavier Hugo Ian Peter de Figueiredo. Born in East Africa in an Arab sultanate under British rule, he has both English and Portuguese names, has been baptized into the Catholic faith, and has a complexion that bears witness to his Indian Subcontinent roots. When he learned to talk, it was in English, with some Swahili – just enough to communicate with the servants. He only understood scraps of my grandparents' mother tongue, Konkani – the language of the Goan people – and never learned Portuguese, which my grandmother spoke fluently.

This is Dad. A boy with a wide, open gaze and the whole world running through his young body. In this he resembles his birthplace Stone Town, the city of stone that occupies the natural peninsula in West Zanzibar. With the ocean on both sides, it looks across the island in one direction and the African mainland in the other. It is a city crammed with churches, with Hindu temples and mosques, yet its silhouette is not dominated by showy spires or minarets, but by the simple, whitewashed houses that lie cheek by jowl, forming a labyrinth of alleys and squares. The effect from a distance is of absolute unity and harmony, despite the fact that the architecture here is so diverse, influenced by the Swahilis, the Portuguese, the Arabs, the Indians and British in that order. Only upon entering the city can you see the contribution each ethnic group has made; from the elegantly carved doors, originally Swahili but elaborated upon later by Arab and Indian craftsmen, to the once unadorned outside walls, now graced with decorative balconies, a sure sign that a house belonged to an Indian merchant.

A unique place in the world, Zanzibar also is the whole world in one place, and this was even truer in Dad's time. The slaves were long gone, and European explorers no longer came here to prepare for their daring expeditions into the heart of Africa. But in and between these houses people of every shade of brown and black, and a few whites, lived out their lives. In the narrow alleyways, in the fruit market and the bazaars, there were coffee merchants who walked along clanking their bowls, women in black with their faces covered, majestic Ceylonese merchants in white robes and hair tied up in a knot, distinguished Arabs, and African porters who came running up from the harbor carrying cases and bags suspended from long bamboo canes. A few years earlier you might have encountered the sultan himself, reclining on soft cushions in an ornate sedan chair, surrounded by servants in livery, sedan carriers and runners, yelling, "Make way! Make way!" Nowadays the sultan sat in the back seat of a large, black car. When it appeared on one of the few roads wide enough to take such a vehicle, there was no choice but to stand respectfully aside.

And everywhere, the fragrance of cloves from the warehouses down by the harbor, newly arrived from Pemba, and from the *hamali*-carts carrying clove-balls through the streets; with the old women who walked behind them and swept up any cloves that fell onto the ground, sifting them and gathering them in canvas bags as they went.

One of the small boys who stood aside for the sultan was Dad. Yet despite his having described this to us, I've never really given it much thought, never fleshed out the image. Dad and the Sultan of Zanzibar. Sitting in school he could see the ocean through his classroom window. St. Joseph Convent School occupied a large building that was so close to the shore that in storms the waves crashed against its walls. Far beyond the horizon to the northwest, beyond the vast continent of Africa, lay Portugal, Great Britain, Europe. From his desk it was 7,712 km to our Swiss-style chalet in Langesund, Norway. In the opposite direction, a slightly shorter distance away of 4,513 km, lay Saligão in Goa, India, the little village that my great-grandfather Aleixo Mariano de Figueiredo had left in order to seek his fortune in East Africa at the close of the 19th century.

Dad's classroom did not face East, but West. Although this almost certainly meant nothing to him. He simply was where he was. After school he played in Victoria Gardens, or ran carefree in shorts and bare feet in the sand. Whenever Dad reminisced about his childhood in Zanzibar, it was this he'd choose to describe. Running in the sand, happy. Always happy.

I'd sometimes think: If he was so much happier there than he was with us, here at home, why didn't he just go back?

Occasionally, passenger boats would arrive in Zanzibar harbor packed with tourists. For Europeans, the island seemed plucked out of *A Thousand and One Nights*. To wander through Stone Town was for them like stepping into an exotic paradise of their own imagining. In reality, the town was neither as exotic nor as old as visitors might believe. The buildings might give the impression of being centuries old, but most were erected in the last half of the 19th century. It was its decay that gave the city its timeless aura. Several of the grander buildings were designed by the British architect, John Sinclair, based on his notions of oriental architecture. The Peace Memorial Museum in Victoria Gardens, Beit el Amani, for example, designed by Sinclair after World War I, has an undeniably oriental air, with its dome and arabesque windows, but it has little to do with the island's traditions. Sinclair took inspiration from the entire eastern world; a hint of the Arab, a dash of the Byzantine, according to whim. In that sense, Dad grew up like a film-extra in a European orientalist vision, a picturesque dark-skinned urchin running around the streets, the kind of kid whom travel writers described to spice up their books, and tourists were so keen to photograph.

When they fished out their cameras to snap a picture of Dad, or asked him to pose alongside his playmates, it was because they saw him as an exotic motif.

But was that how Dad saw himself? Did he see himself mirrored in these European camera lenses as the native? Or did he identify himself with the photographer – with the European? What went through his mind as he saw the tourists board the boat again, chattering away in his own mother tongue, about all the incredible things they'd seen? He would eventually realize what he was; that while the blood in his veins was Indian, many of the thoughts that whirled around in his head were European. And while his skin was dark, it was clad in western clothes. But wasn't his blood the same – pure and red – just like everybody else's? Wasn't he complete and whole? Just like Sinclair's buildings, an alloy of various cultures and beliefs, similar to everything on this island that had been fused together over the centuries?

The truth is that my father could feel as whole as he liked, but it was an entirely different matter what other people thought about him; from the farmers in the fields to the British in their offices, or the sultan in his palace. Or indeed, whether the grinding wheel of history – which has continually divided peoples and driven them from one land to the next in the hope of a better life or in flight from a worse fate – would even spare a place for someone like him.

Why didn't he go back?

Because his allotted place was repeatedly taken from him. The lawn in Victoria Gardens in Zanzibar where he'd sat with his open gaze. And later, the pink housing block in Dar es Salaam, Tanganyika, and later still the low modernist house in the Goan district of Pangani in Nairobi, Kenya, where he moved before his childhood was spent. Dad had so many homelands, but when the time came and he was living in the Norwegian countryside with my mother and my brothers and me, all these homelands had vanished, were wiped off the map. The only homeland he had left was the land of his forefathers, Goa, on the west coast of India, the village of Saligão, a place he had never seen and knew only in his dreams.

HE WAS ONCE MY WHOLE WORLD, my horizon, and it never occurred to me that his world was other than mine. I was from Langesund. I was Norwegian and so was Dad, even if he did speak rather oddly and called sausages "pilser" instead of "pølser" and occasionally broke into English. Sometimes he'd be gone for a few days and come home with a suitcase filled with spices and foods. The highlight being when he brought out a packet of papadums and dropped them one by one into a pan of sizzling oil. When they'd puffed up, big and crisp, he shared them out between us as we sat around a steaming pot of curry on the table – but just one half each, since he'd have to go all the way to London to get more.

Occasionally people would arrive at our house who were most definitely not Norwegian. They'd be standing there suddenly in the kitchen; exotic men with white teeth and beautiful women in soft silky clothes. Certainly not the kind of guests the locals were accustomed to seeing in the small coastal town of my childhood, despite it having been dependant on international shipping and shipbuilding from time immemorial.

In the photograph on the next page taken in the early seventies, two of my aunts can be seen standing in front of the shipyard in Langesund. Mum is behind the camera and the photograph is taken for a newspaper article in the *Telemark Arbeiderblad*, where she worked as a journalist. A pair of sari-clad beauties was newsworthy

in the area back then; something the local coffee-colored kid who had wandered into shot, was not. I don't recall this photo session, but my memory of the excitement that accompanied the arrival of these people is palpable. Especially my aunts, with their bright laughter and black sunglasses. To me they were like American film stars, whom fate had magically transported to Langesund. And I fell in love with each in turn as they appeared in our kitchen doorway. Occasionally Dad's youngest brother would arrive with a guitar and play "Jambalaya" and "Guantanamera" for us, and once Dad came home with an elderly man with chalk-white mane, a white mustache and dark eyes. This man stayed with us for a few months; Grandfather had done the rounds in the States, living with each of his children in turn, now it was our turn to take care of him. Grandfather made me feel on edge; it was as if he was used to being in command, despite that no longer being the case; he pottered about the house, smiled and patted us on the head, as though bestowing his approval upon us.

When I was a little older, a letter arrived from Grandfather to Mum, my brothers and me. In it, he gave us all advice on which line of study each of us ought to pursue. I seem to remember that I was to be an engineer and that my two brothers should be a doctor and lawyer respectively, while my mother should train to be a nurse. These were, I am sure, meant as instructions, not suggestions.

Like most youngsters, I never stopped to ask why the world was as it was. Nobody we knew ate curry, nobody went to London. Yet it never occurred to me that we were very different than anybody else. I knew that my skin made me stand out, but never felt it had bearing on who I was, or that this difference might have an actual name. But when my brothers and I heard that the townsfolk of Porsgrunn poked fun at the people from the rural hamlet of Bamble, calling them *Bamble-Indians*, it gave us pause. We knew Mum had been born in Bamble, so we reasoned that if anybody could be true Bamble-Indians, it must be us. What was the alternative? Half-Indian? Was there such a word?

And to add to the confusion, Dad had told us that we weren't actually Indian, we were Goan. And from Africa. And that we were British. And Portuguese. And Norwegian. It was all too much for us to grasp, so Bamble-Indian seemed as good as anything.

The truth was, I wasn't too bothered about my skin color as a child. Nor do I remember it bothering anyone else. The only exception being the time I got into a playground fight with Bønna. In the tense moment of silence when the last swearword had been spent and the fists were about to come out, he suddenly blurted out:

"Negro!"

Everybody froze. Looks darted across the circle that had gathered around us. Even Bønna looked shocked at his own flash of creativity. A split second later the first blow was struck. I believe it was mine.

Although the Norway in which I grew up was almost exclusively white, it wasn't my color that troubled me, nor was it my weird first name or even weirder surname. No, the cross I had to bear was my middle name, *Bjarne*, given to me in honor of my Norwegian grandfather. Sadly, you'd be wrong to think I took the least pride in this name. It was embarrassingly old-fashioned. Whenever the teacher took the register I waited in terror for the sniggers to rise from the desks around me the moment the B-word was uttered. People do not fear the unknown, as we imagine, they fear what they *think* they know. My exotic otherness must have effected my classmate's perception of me, but it was just that; vaguely exotic, indefinable. The name Bjarne, on the other hand, stood out like a sore thumb.

I can see all this now, but back then it hardly entered my mind. I was Norwegian. I was who I was. Why should there be any contradiction between my dark curls and the fact that I was called Bjarne?

What I understand now too, of course, is that even though Dad was Norwegian in my eyes, in his own eyes he was not. And thinking back now, I did have a sense of this even then. For example, when we went down to Steinvika for a swim. Dad didn't behave like the other grown-ups. He didn't walk calmly out to the water like Mum, he didn't dive in with quiet dignity. Instead, he'd charge through the kids standing at the water's edge, wade in and then plunge out onto his belly making the water splash over the shivering bodies all around him. I didn't know then, and still don't for sure, whether or not he could dive. He certainly hadn't learned to swim until he was an adult, nor indeed had his siblings. They came from a paradise with warm beaches and crystal clear water. But swimming wasn't something one did in Dad's family. Grandmother didn't allow it. She was determined to protect her kids from any danger.

The beach at Steinvika was just ten minutes away from our house in Langesund. It was generally only the four of us, Mum and we three boys, who would go there. Mum with a large, floral cool-bag containing her special ice-cold milk, made with a dash of vanilla essence and pink or green food coloring. Steinvika was our paradise, and the occasional times that Dad came with us were accompanied by a sense of embarrassment.

What is embarrassment? The painful feeling of something being exposed which ought to remain hidden. A tight knot that expands and unfurls as soon as it comes under other people's gaze. Like a Chinese paper flower in water. Like my father on the shore, taking off his shirt and revealing his hairy chest. I don't know how old I was when this sense of embarrassment was first triggered, but it must have been when I started to think that Dad wasn't quite like other dads. Partly, I think it came from my growing awareness of his visibility. I pitied him simply for being who he was, a handsome man with brown skin and black, curly hair, among all those pasty nineteen-seventies Norwegian bodies. But it came perhaps even more from my being troubled by, yes, ashamed of him. Because if Dad felt his own differentness, he wasn't the sort to hide away. On the contrary, it was as though he *had* to draw attention to himself; the way he took off his clothes, the way he turned the beach into his own personal stage, the path from the rug and cool-bag to the water's edge into a victory run. It was I who wanted to hide him away. Only when he was submerged under water, could I exhale.

Dad took up a great deal of space. At home he filled the rooms with his presence, with his loud voice. Yet I have remarkably few memories of him. When I try to picture Dad and I together, playing a game, or rolling a ball between us, or him pulling a duvet over me, I generally have to give up. There are several photographs in the family album of me sitting on his lap laughing, with his arms around me. I look relaxed and safe, but I have no memory of the moment. Rather my memories of Dad are like physical sensations, impressions left on my body. And what my body remembers is at odds with what these pictures say.

The strong hands never gave; they took. Grandma once told me something strange she'd observed when she watched Dad play-fighting with us. "He never let you win", she said. The game always ended with him pulling you down onto the floor, then going off to do grown-up things." I can't remember this, but as I try to picture the scene, the physical sensation of losing immediately hits me. Equally I relive the sense of unease that filled us whenever he entered a room; if he was happy, we had to be happy, if he was angry, we felt we'd done something wrong, although we rarely knew what.

"The weather's so beautiful today," he might suddenly declare at Sunday breakfast. "Let's go to the park, and take the guitar. Oh, I'm happy, so happy!"

When we refused or suggested we had other plans, his mood would turn. What was wrong with us? Why did we want to ruin his day? It was as though he continually wanted something from us that we couldn't quite grasp. And since we never got things right, and were never good enough, he was never satisfied. Whatever the case, his reproach and anger are what I remember most. The roars that issued from the living room; the fist slamming down on the table; the dancing milk glasses, the streams of milk running over the tablecloth. Why did he break things when he was crying?

Only as I got older did I consider that all Dad's sadness, his anger, might be related to his sense of being a foreigner, a stranger in his own home. "Why can't we be like a *real* family?" he would say, his voice filled with bitterness and reproach. "Why won't you answer me in English?"

And why didn't we want to sing together, or pray together? Like a real family. Was it his memory of the family of his own childhood that Dad was harping back to? The laughing uncles and beautiful sari-clad aunts certainly weren't like him. They were warm and gentle. Dad *demanded* that we speak English, *demanded* that we sing and sit in the park together, *demanded* we be a happy family. We never knew quite what to say, but defended ourselves as best we could. In Norwegian. In a childhood otherwise filled with sun-baked rocks on Steinvik beach, wild snowball fights, play-fighting on the living room floor, rambling in the forest alone with a sketchbook or with my mother, Dad became an increasing irrelevance in my life. He was against us, and we were against him. We made detours around him to get peace. Useless, of course, since he was still there with his over-sized emotions. Were we the cause of all this nastiness? Or was Mum? Eventually I realized it was something else. Something he carried within him from his own childhood. His own projection of the family we never were for him. That we didn't want to be. Or was there something he'd lost along the way, a loss that had left him with an insatiable desire, a restless anger that could descend on him at any time or place? At home, or in the car. Yes, especially in the car; the abrupt swerving, the roar of the accelerator, the aggression that transmitted itself through his arms to the steering wheel and into the heavy bodywork, the entire car becoming a vibrating metallic membrane for all the rage inside him. While I clung tightly to the driver's seat in front of me.

"Don't swerve so much, Dad, please don't swerve like that!"

The older I got, the more I questioned these things. Slowly but surely, I realized that my world was not the same as his, and that the answer to why Dad was who he was, lay somewhere far beyond my own horizon.

WHERE DOES DAD'S STORY BEGIN? Where does mine begin? The truth is that no story has an absolute beginning; all we can do is clutch randomly at the tangle of threads that lead from ourselves and back in time, generation upon generation, until they vanish into the vast darkness from which we all once issued. I scan the oldest photograph I've found in the family albums and open it on my Mac. The image is

Nascido em 6-2-1872

Falecido em 12-1-1940

Aleixo Mariano de Figueiredo

Sôbre a campa fria, volvido um ano, depõe esta prece a sua dedicada esposa

Elizena Etelvina de Souza e Figueiredo.

from the funeral card of my Dad's grandfather, my great grandfather, Aleixo Mariano de Figueiredo. He died in 1940 aged sixty-eight, but the portrait shows him in his prime; a slim, handsome man, with a moustache and wavy hair. Pinned proudly on his lapel is the medal he'd been awarded for his lifelong service as postmaster to the Sultan of Zanzibar. *Order of the Brilliant Star.* Those who remember him describe him as a stern man who rarely smiled, a strong, determined character with European manners. Apparently he had Dad's dark eyes, though it's impossible to tell from the image of the old crumpled photograph on my screen, in which his eyes melt into a haze of zigzag pixels. I zoom in, trying to capture his gaze. But the more the image fills the screen, the more the shadow over his eyes melts into the grey background.

It is as if Great Grandfather is struggling to emerge from a darkness that refuses to release him. All I know of his origins is that he was born in Goa in 1872, in the village of Saligão, close to Calangute beach. There he built a house for himself and his mother, Maria Santana, but I know even less about her, apart from the story of how she got her nickname. It's said that Maria had lent some money to a crook who never paid her back. Time after time she walked through the village to demand he repay her, and each time she returned empty-handed. Everyone in the village knew about it, and when her trips back and forth became a daily occurrence, they started to tease her:

"Where are you going today, Maria?" they asked.

Maria would simply answer "Zatã, Zatã", which in Konkani means, "It will happen." Which is how my great-great-grandmother got her name Maria Santana Zatã. To this day people in Saligão tell each other this story, laughing and slapping their thighs. Because the village never forgets anything; not Maria Zatã, nor the son who left, nor his descendants, nor even those of us who've never set foot in Saligão.

The house Aleixo built was on a hillside in the area of the village of Salmona. A traditional Portuguese-Goan house, whitewashed with tall, elongated windows, whose panes were made of translucent layers of oyster shell that let a soft glimmering light into the rooms. A wide set of steps led up to the front door and to a shaded porch which ran along the entire front of the house. It was a handsome house, even though many of the floors were made of stamped down cow dung.

The largest room however must have had tiled floor, since the family apparently held balls and other social events there for the village's *beau monde.*

Saligão was a typical Goan village, its houses clustered around a patchwork of paddy fields cut through by roads and rows of coconut palms. To the north of the paddy fields rose the neo-Gothic style church, Mãe de Deus, built in the year after Aleixo's birth. The entire village would have been visible from its gleaming white tower, were it not for the fact that most of the houses lay hidden in the shade of banana trees, jackfruit trees and other vegetation. It must have been a vision of tranquility; life in Saligão was allowed to unfold at its own pace, interrupted only by the Angelus bells calling the villagers to prayer at dawn, noon and lastly at sunset. It was then that families gathered after a long day in the paddy fields, and in the light of their kerosene lamps knelt down on the ground, turned toward the village church and recited the Angelus prayer. At eight in the evening they got out their rosaries, ate dinner and went to bed. Night followed, coal black, apart from the occasional dim light from a coconut lantern carried by a solitary night-wanderer.

Peace reigned over Saligão. As it had for centuries. Ever since the 20th of May in 1498 when Vasco da Gama dropped anchor outside Calicut. The first day in the creation of our clan.

Vasco da Gama had discovered the sea route from Europe to India by sailing around the southern tip of Africa. Since time immemorial the Arabs, Gujarati, Ottomans, Venetians, Chinese and others had sailed the Indian Ocean assisted by the monsoon winds, their ships loaded high with merchandise. But the Portuguese wanted the lucrative spice trade to themselves, and to strengthen their monopoly they levied taxes on their competitors, or simply blasted them to bits with their superior weapons and ships. In return the Portuguese shared Christianity's joyous message with the local heathens. The Portuguese wanted souls and sea routes, not land. But seas cannot be conquered without securing strategic ports and coastline fortifications. And it was Goa, the little enclave north of Calicut which had until then been under the sole rule of the sultan of Bijapur, which was chosen as the stronghold for the Portuguese. Which explains why Catholicism and spices would become the prime ingredients of my ancestors' existence.

In the decade following da Gama's discovery, Portugal's King Manuel I sent ship after ship to conquer Goa, managing eventually in 1510 to bring the territory between the Mandovi and Zuari rivers under Portuguese rule. These districts became the heart of the Portuguese colony of Goa, known as *Velhas Conquistas*, the Old Conquests. Over the next centuries the Portuguese took more surrounding districts, *Novas Conquistas*, the New Conquests, as well as the Diu and Daman enclaves.

The town of Goa, situated some distance up the Mandovi River, became the capital of the entire Portuguese Indian Empire. In just a few decades, the town grew in population and splendor, becoming a metropolis inhabited by Muslims, Christians and Hindus, and even a Jewish minority. Magnificent late renaissance and baroque churches and elegant Portuguese villas shot up between the river and the jungle. And the streets and bazaars streamed with soldiers, traders, prostitutes, the occasional wealthy Portuguese family beneath large parasols, surrounded by servants and African slaves. This isn't to forget the priests. After the arrival of various Catholic orders in town, you were likely to bump into an ecclesiastical habit at every other corner. The Franciscans and Jesuits christianized the town by the sword and threats, and before long Goa was transformed into the Rome of the East, the Asian center of Christianity. Not that all the natives were willing to give up their Hindu faith in favor of Catholicism, far from it, but those who did took the names of saints, and Portuguese heroes and nobles.

Many Goan families thus mirrored the ancient ancestral lines of Portugal. Names like Mendes, Almeida, De Souza, Paes and Constantino, later Noronha, Pinto and de Figueiredo, lived on among

Indians who cast aside their ancient faith and donned western clothes. These new converts, however, hung onto their old cooking pots and added their own ingredients to the Portuguese dishes they now adopted.

I look at the photograph of Aleixo; so stiff and formal in his white shirt and black waistcoat under his dark grey jacket. The medal, the bowtie, the high collar. And beneath it all, his brown body, which was markedly light, a feature much valued among the Goans. An Indian in a suit, Aleixo was a descendent of converts from the highest caste – the Brahmins, who, for generations, had adopted as much European culture as the Portuguese chose to share with them – a creole people, shaped not only by the meeting between Portugal and India, but also by what the Portuguese brought from their vast territories that stretched from Brazil to China. Aleixo's people, Dad's people, *my* ancestors, were a new, yet simultaneously ancient people.

And, one might add, an "unclean" people, in the view of others, at least. How else could you describe a Catholic Brahmin who drank alcohol and ate beef, and who not only adopted a European fondness for pork, but built a hatch behind his toilet where the pigs could feed, before being eaten by human beings – a lifecycle in its crudest form. The Portuguese and converted Goans were the only people who did not observe the laws of cleanliness that were otherwise prevalent in Indian culture; Catholics ate anything and everything. In the towns and villages around Goa, the Catholic Goans lived much as they always had, but now they lived in whitewashed houses with awnings over cool terraces, decorative oyster-shell windows, and azure or sea-green shutters; a sight that for any Western visitor must have conjured thoughts of the Mediterranean, rather than India. Where others saw an unclean people, the Goans donned their Sunday best each week – the men clean-shaven and in suits, the women in white dresses – and walked to church along the road between rice fields and coconut palms.

And the centuries ticked by.

Eventually as new powers took control in the Indian Ocean, the power of the Portuguese came under threat. The Dutch arrived first, then the mighty British Empire laid its milky-white hand over large parts of Asia and Africa. But with the exception of a short-lived British occupation in the early 1800s, the Portuguese maintained control, but their decline was already written on the wall. In 1775 malaria and cholera epidemics in the capital had forced the governing powers to evacuate their people to Panjim at the mouth of the Mandovi River. Once Asia's center of Christianity, the now abandoned city would become known as *Velha Goa*, Old Goa. The jungle threatened to invade its cathedrals and grand villas. A sweet slumber settled over the country. No significant modernization took place; any industry was modest. There was little for future generations to hope for. The better-off still managed to live a comfortable life in their spacious houses and secure government posts; they spoke Portuguese and sent their sons to the best university in Lisbon. Anyone else was left to wade ankle-deep in the paddy fields. The only alternative was to emigrate.

Some time at the end of the 19th century Aleixo must have made a decision. He'd recently married a village girl, Ermelinda Fernandez, and if they were going to forge a future together, they had to leave their homeland. They boarded the steamboat in Panjim that sailed along the coastline before heading north to Bombay. Great Grandfather must have been about twenty-five, Great Grandmother eight years younger.

Doubtless they weren't the only ones on that boat from their village. From their region alone, that of Bardez, nearly a quarter of the population would leave, most of them Catholics, and many of them Brahmins. They were among the village elite. And not only that, but the colonists had instilled them with the Portuguese culture and way of life, and tempted them with ambitions for a future that far exceeded anything that Goa might offer. What could be more natural than to emigrate, especially when the Portuguese were encouraging them to leave and administrate colonies elsewhere in the world.

They were not refugees. They were not escaping a disaster zone. They were leaving to improve their lives. To climb up, rather than to sink. To live, rather than to merely survive.

In Bombay, Aleixo and Ermelinda probably stayed in one of the Goan hostels that were found throughout the city at the time. Here they probably enjoyed a final moment of village camaraderie before their journey continued over the ocean. While some emigrants traveled to Portuguese Africa, Angola and Mozambique, others headed for the new imperial power, Britain, and its colonies and protectorates on the same continent. Like so many other emigrants, Aleixo and Ermelinda headed for Zanzibar. Unlike most others, however, they did not settle here, but continued on to the small, lush-green island of Pemba about ten miles north of the mother-island Zanzibar. The island had become a British protectorate some years earlier, so when Aleixo was made postmaster in the modest cluster of buildings that constituted Pemba's capital Chake Chake, he indirectly became a subject of the British Empire.

My family's fate was cast.

Aleixo and Ermelinda were the first in the family to break out of the cycle of rural life, leaving the only place to which they truly belonged, where their family had lived for so long in a harmonious pact with their forebears, the earth, the church and Portugal. Everything that had been woven together over centuries was about to be ripped apart. Aleixo left the sleepy Portuguese empire for a defeated Arab sultanate where he would serve the British Empire that would itself only survive him by a few years. Toward the end of his life Aleixo would return to Saligão – the ties of origin are not broken in the span of one man's life. But for those who followed, the circle had been broken, and homelessness was the inheritance they were left by Aleixo. He had been the first to leave his homeland, and he was the last to return. It is here, with Great Grandfather, that my family's journey through the era of dying empires begins.

EAST AFRICA

I'D HOPED TO TAKE THE FERRY from Zanzibar to Pemba, as Aleixo would have done. But sadly the ferry has been cancelled due to rough seas, and I have to travel the hundred kilometers by air. There are twelve of us tightly packed into the small propeller plane; a couple of tourists, the others residents of Pemba going back home, all of us fated to live or die together in the next half hour. We are soon juddering over Stone Town, yellow sands turn to blue, and then before I know it I see Pemba spread out below me, green and overgrown, indented with a myriad of twisting inlets that threaten to split the island up into a hundred tiny fragments.

I had decided to travel in Dad's footsteps in the summer of 2011, to learn as much as I could about his life. Visiting my aunts in Boston was the first stage in that process. Now I have set out on the second; exploring the world of Dad's childhood in East Africa. I've been constantly aware during this trip of the irony of my enterprise; surely it would be simpler to go to Spain, look up Dad's house and knock on his door? But I no longer know him. And scarcely did as a child. What feelings would seeing him arouse in me? I feel sure I'd see him through the eyes of my childhood, and I fear what these eyes would see. I need to observe him from a distance, to see him without him seeing me. Or, better still, search for him in another place and in another time. Which is why I am here on an island off the coast of Africa; there is no shorter route back to my father.

The terminal at Chake Chake Airport looks like an abandoned rural bus station. I sit on my rucksack under the canopy outside, scouring the surrounding hot landscape for life. Where have the pilot and my fellow passengers gone? All I can see around me are empty fields and a mass of vegetation swaying in a warm breeze. Slicing through the landscape is a red country road that winds its way down toward the forecourt in front of me. I follow it as far as the eye can see, without much hope. Half an hour passes, or perhaps an hour, and then a cloud of dust emerges on the horizon, only to disappear again behind a clump of forest. When it reappears, the cloud has transformed into a black car that turns abruptly onto the forecourt and stops two meters from my feet. A young man leaps out and opens the door for me, grinning from ear to ear. I smile back, put all questions aside and get in. Where are you going? he asks. Who knows, I think to myself, as I ask him to show me around the island.

I spend my first day in Pemba in the back seat of a car, that may or not be a taxi, driving between fields of carnations and banana trees, past simple huts made of cow dung, and carpets of sweet scented cloves spread out to dry. Driving up hills toward the sky and open vistas, and then back down into the thick vegetation of the valleys, as though diving into green cumulus clouds. It isn't for nothing the Arabs named this island Al Khudhra, the green island. Pemba has the dampest and most fertile climate in this part of Africa; you only have to spit over your shoulder and a mango tree will spring into life. It was just as much like this when Aleixo arrived here more than a hundred years ago as it is today. Just as then, the island is largely covered with jungle, plantations, and soil that is soft when it rains and rock hard in the drought. How can one find any trace of the dead here?

As evening falls, I check into a rather shabby hotel in Chake Chake, the dusty crossroads that purports to be the island's main town. My room has only one tiny, dirt-caked window high on the wall. The ceiling fan almost detaches itself from its fitting as it goes around. I pull the grubby sheet over me, switch off the light and disappear into the dark. Or so it feels. I'm disappearing from the world, floating into a hot, foreign night. But didn't I have this feeling the moment I set foot on African soil? This is no longer Great Grandfather's land, nor Grandfather's, nor Dad's. They came on a wave of hundreds of thousands, nay, millions of Asians keen to serve the British or build a future in the shelter of their empire. They settled in Uganda, Kenya and Tanganyika, the latter of which the Brits had taken from the Germans. And they came to the island of Zanzibar and the mainland Swahili coast, the ancient lands of the Arabs in Africa.

This is such a long time ago now. Wars and revolutions have been fought since; blood has flowed. Africans have reclaimed their country; the white colonists have gone their way, as have many of the Asians who worked for them. But surely nothing ever disappears entirely. We can fill suitcases, empty shelves, clean out the house, leave the key in the door and slip quietly into the night. But surely there'll always be something left behind? A trace, however faint, the words you said, the space your body once occupied, the image you've been in another's eyes. Nobody is completely eradicated, unless the memories of the person have been driven out by those who are left behind.

Early the next morning I look for the ancient Portuguese fort that now houses Pemba's Museum. Two friendly archivists lead me across the courtyard and into a windowless room where the walls are lined with shelves full of files and bundles of paper. Can they tell me something about my great-grandfather Aleixo, the postmaster? I am handed some useless, mildewy documents that almost fall apart in my hands. No register, only random payrolls and protocols. How about the post office, does it still exist? Nobody knows. I am told that there is one Goan man left in Chake Chake.

I find his house and knock on the door. No one answers.

That evening I sit in the only place in Chake Chake that even vaguely resembles a restaurant. The menu consists of the one thing that is presumably always available: chicken. A group of men in ankle length white kaftans are the only guests in this brightly lit room. They each sit clutching a Fanta, watching a football match on the television suspended high up in the corner. It feels like a men's pub night back at home. Sitting alone, under the TV, is a woman in a hijab. No doubt somebody's wife. I shovel the tasteless chicken down and force down the sugary Fanta. Over the last century the once religiously diverse Zanzibar islands have become almost entirely Muslim, especially here in Pemba. I think about the one lonely Goan they say lives in town. What does he do in the evening? Does he sit at home knocking back his whiskey behind closed curtains? Where does he get the pork he needs to make a vindaloo? Or has he too converted to Fanta and chicken?

I put my money on the table and walk toward the exit. The woman in the hijab averts her gaze as I pass by. Only when I turn off my light and arrange the mosquito net around my bed do I realize: there must be traces of my family on this island. True enough, Great Grandfather didn't have much when he arrived here, nor did he ever buy a house here. And when he returned to Saligão years later as a pensioner, all he took with him were a title and a medal.

But in return, he left his love.

During their years in Pemba, Aleixo and Ermelinda had four children. The first was born in 1900 and was given the name Michael Joseph. He would be my grandfather. Just as the two babies that followed, he was born at St. Joseph Hospital in Zanzibar, since, being so backward, Pemba lacked the necessary facilities for a safe birth. The fourth and last child, a girl who was given her mother's name, was, for some unknown reason, delivered here at Pemba. Ermelinda died here in childbirth aged thirty-three, her little girl surviving for a few years before she too passed away.

No photographs exist of Grandfather and his siblings from this time. Great Grandfather's face is only a collection of fuzzy dots on a photograph. Of Ermelinda there isn't a single picture. All I know about her is that she is my great grandmother, and the first in our family to be buried in foreign soil. It may, of course, have occurred to Aleixo to take his wife's body to Zanzibar. But the steam ferry only went between the two islands once a week, and it took the entire night. Instead Great Grandfather decided to take her coffin to the Catholic mission on Dongoni, a peninsula a few miles southeast of Chake Chake. This missionary post, founded by German missionaries who arrived in the 1870s, consisted of a church and school. After the abolishment of slavery, they took in freed slaves and offered them an education. They also made a cemetery for themselves and for the few Catholics who lived on the island, or rather, those who died here.

I decide to look for my great grandmother's grave. After all, stone survives longer than paper, and people in churchyards generally stay put. The only way for me to get to Dongoni is by the route that Aleixo once took. The two archivists at the museum offer to take me. As we rumble under the mango trees in an open jeep I imagine overtaking a cart carrying my great grandfather. I see him sitting with his head bowed and a hand resting on the coffin behind him. From Chake Chake he travels along the sound to the ferry port where the tall dhows are scattered like stranded swordfish on the wet sand. Then crossing the sound by boat, Great Grandfather sits grief-stricken behind the coffin, his face turned toward the thick mangrove forest on the other side. From the beach he goes up the hill, past the church and the school, into the clearing and sees the dark tombstones, and a hole in the red earth that waits to receive Great Grandmother's cold body.

Back in Saligão, the Mãe de Deus church rings out for her three times, but only on one of its two bells, as is the custom for those who die far away from the village.

I have four men with me, a local guide in a salmon-pink shirt, a scruffy looking boatman and the two archivists, all motivated by the prospect of a small fee. The boatman throws the anchor some distance from the shore, and we wade ankle-deep through a belt of ochre-colored mud, doing our best to avoid the sharp roots of the mangrove trees that poke up everywhere. The church and school were dismantled long ago, the stone taken away and put to other uses, while the jungle has claimed the graves for itself. Otherwise the landscape has hardly changed since Great Grandfather was here. We soon find the path that twists through the jungle, past the remains of the old church's foundations, before disappearing into the green overgrowth. For several hours we walk through thick vegetation, hacking our way onwards with machetes, step by step.

I have barely managed to accustom myself to the heat, or to Africa, before I am swallowed up by the jungle. Soon my arms and legs are torn on thorns and branches, on sticky leaves that grab at me and slice into my skin when I try to free myself. My guides are not only more appropriately dressed, in long trousers and shoes, compared to my T-shirt, shorts and sandals, but they are also very used to this. And not one of them considers giving up for fear of losing the fee offered by this modern-day Dr. Livingstone whose mood is worsening with each trickle of blood that flows down into his sandals.

I am seized by doubt. What kind of idiocy is this? What am I doing here in this jungle on an island in the middle of the Indian Ocean? I may be trying to follow Dad's story, but he never even mentioned Ermelinda. Aleixo died when he was barely a year old. His grandparents were mere stories to him, so what on earth would I want with them? The truth is that I haven't a clue; I am just clutching arbitrarily at the myriad threads that lead from me and Dad to the dead and long forgotten. In tearing at these threads, I tug at handfuls of stems and greenery, and hack at branches to penetrate the vegetation. Will I really get closer to Dad, closer to myself, by battling through this thorny jungle in search of a relative who rotted away and evaporated into the ether long ago? This jungle is too vast, our family tree like a giant tangle of branches that fills the horizon, that stretches across oceans and continents, across centuries, so large that it spans the rise and fall of empires, the birth and death of nations, the release of slaves, the displacement of peoples. And if Dad is one thread in this vast tangle, then I am dangling at the end of it, over an empty void.

That's what I'm doing. Hanging like a fly in a cobweb. The prickly leaves have twisted about my arms, my legs are caught in a cluster of thorns. Peevish and humiliated, I let my companions cut me free, before we continue our arduous task. We are soon separated from each other again; only the sound of swinging machetes tells me that I am not alone here in the jungle.

I'm about to call off the entire expedition when I glimpse a large, stone cross sticking crookedly out of the ground behind some bushes. And then another nearby. I shout out to the others:

"Gravestone! Over here!"

The others are hacking their way toward me; the scruffy boatman clears a little patch in front of the cross. Exhausted I fall onto my bare knees before the grave, run my hand over the rough surface of the grey stone. Not a letter, not a mark. Not even stone lasts on Pemba. It will take us twenty minutes to get to the next gravestone, and another twenty to the next. It's pointless. Any names are gone.

To my surprise, rather than feeling disappointed, I feel a strange sort of calm. I have no idea where Dad's story begins, or mine. But is it true that Dad never talked about my great grandparents? Might it be that I didn't listen? All those times he berated us for not caring about his background, for not writing letters to our aunts and uncles, for being so *Norwegian*. I realize now that there was something he desperately wanted to tell us. The fact that reproach was the only language he knew, and that all he gained was our rejection, does not make this any less true. Why did he save all the letters he'd received during his life, sorting them chronologically and filing them so neatly in ring binders? None of his siblings did this. Families who spend their lives moving, traveling over lifetimes, seldom save such things. There may be a few pictures, but for some reason letters are generally lost. But Dad saved everything. And didn't he, I thought, travel back to East Africa himself as an adult? He mentioned it once, long after the divorce, but I'd never asked where he went or what he found.

Did he come to Pemba too? Was he searching for the same thing?

The forgotten story, the threads that bind us.

Well, something's for sure, one of these threads ends right here. I know nothing about my great grandmother, she is just a name to me, and even that has been wiped away out here. And yet I feel close to you, Ermelinda Fernandez, because you lie in one of the graves in this overgrown cemetery, if not beneath this stone, then the next. Sweat pouring, blood trickling, I kneel in front of a nameless grave. I want to lie down, feel the warm ground against my face. Why do we imagine that people have their roots in the place where they were born? It is in the grave that we meet the earth, it is here that roots take hold. And doesn't some part of me belong in this place? And something of it belong to me? Something of this earth, this vegetation that has gashed at my body and pierced my skin? Aren't I sitting here on my great grandmother's crumbling bones? What is the warmth of this earth other than a caress from the hand of the dead?

Ermelinda is here. She came here once. And never left.

IN 1913, NOT LONG AFTER BEING WIDOWED, Aleixo returned to Saligão. With Ermelinda gone, he was responsible for four children; the oldest, my grandfather, Michael Joseph, was no more than thirteen years old. Aleixo needed a new wife, and he would find her back home in the village. That was the tradition among emigrants. No matter if you'd lived abroad all your life, you would still go back home to find a bride. Thus the community and village ties were maintained on the other side of the ocean. Within a surprisingly short time, probably only a few months, he found a suitable bride. Only twenty-five years old, Elizena Sequeira was, however, already a widow. She also had a seven-year-old daughter, Mariamorha Etalia Herman de Santa Rosa Sequeira, generally called Herminia.

This girl would be my grandmother.

My grandparents were step-siblings. However they saw little of each other in their childhoods. On returning to Pemba, Aleixo and his new wife Elizena left their two oldest children behind in the village, but with different families: Michael Joseph was left with his grandmother, Maria Santana Zatã in Aleixo's house, and Herminia with her aunt, Ana Flaviana. Known in the family as Ti Filu, she lived in her sisters' childhood home in another part of the village called Tabravvadó. Later, the two children would be sent off to different schools in Bombay and other Indian cities. When Herminia eventually completed her education and returned to Saligão, Michael Joseph had already left the village for Pemba to work for his father.

Grandfather and Grandmother had tasted exile long before they set out on the journey that would tear them away from their origins forever. That journey, at least, they would make together.

Of the family members who never traveled, and who stayed in the village of their birth, I must say a few words about Ti Filu. As the eldest of the two sisters, she had trained as a teacher to support herself and Elizena after their parents had died when they were still young. Just as the picture of Aleixo, the photographs of these sisters below are taken from their funeral cards. Why were these funeral cards so carefully preserved? So many letters and pictures were lost over the years, but these survived. Could it be that it is only after a funeral that we realize that death visits twice; once when the loved one breathes their last, and then a second time when the dead are slowly eradicated from the memory of those who live on?

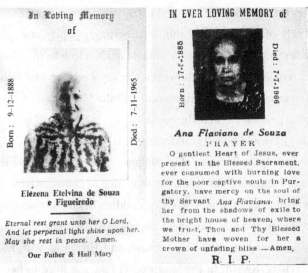

In Loving Memory of

Born : 9-12-1888   Died : 7-11-1965

Elézena Etelvina de Souza e Figueiredo

Eternal rest grant unto her O Lord,
And let perpetual light shine upon her.
May she rest in peace. Amen.

Our Father & Hail Mary

IN EVER LOVING MEMORY of

Born : 17-5-1885   Died : 7-7-1966

Ana Flaviana de Souza

PRAYER

O gentlest Heart of Jesus, ever present in the Blessed Sacrament, ever consumed with burning love for the poor captive souls in Purgatory, have mercy on the soul of thy Servant *Ana Flaviana,* bring her from the shadows of exile to the bright house of heaven; where we trust, Thou and Thy Blessed Mother have woven for her a crown of unfading bliss — Amen.

R. I. P.

What is fixed in a funeral card? Not life, but the first death; the memory of a shadow of someone who has lived. A funeral card postpones this slow second death, as do the stories we tell. For some reason, unknown to me, there are more stories about Ti Filu than Elizena. It seems that the older sister had the stronger character of the two. Yes, if I can trust my response to these photographs, Elizena has the gentle features of my own grandmother and aunts, almost over-sensitive to the feelings of others. I can't say the same of Ti Filu, and it seems right somehow that she should become the anchor for this exiled family, their *great-aunt* in the village back at home for two generations. Ti Filu remained single all her life, but she was like a mother to Herminia. It was she who took care of Herminia's education, and who encouraged her to continue her studies in Portuguese and English. She must have been bright, since there was apparently talk of her being allowed to study as a doctor.

When the time came, however, any such plans were dropped. Aleixo felt that Pemba was no place for a young, marriageable bachelor, and decided that the time had come for his son, Michael Joseph, to take a wife. And Herminia, it seems, was the obvious choice.

It was now the oldest son's turn to go back home to Saligão to get married. The wedding must have been a bit of a let down. The priest of the Church of Mãe de Deus got it into his head that Michael Joseph and Herminia were blood siblings and refused to marry them. No matter how much the couple assured him that they weren't related by blood and had barely lived in the same house. In the end the wedding was moved to Vengurla, five miles north. Instead of holding the reception in the village, it was decided that it would be officially celebrated in Pemba; after all, it had always been Aleixo's intention for his son and stepdaughter to live with him there.

And so it was.

One winter's day in the beginning of 1925, the newlyweds board the ferry in Goa's capital, Panjim. This is, for Herminia, her first journey away from home. All I know of this particular trip is that she discovers her wedding dress has not been packed. As I try to reconstruct my grandparents' journey, this is the most poignant picture that flashes in my mind: Herminia is standing in the cabin she will share with her new husband, staring disbelievingly into her open suitcase. It can't be long since the ship has left the harbor and has pointed its bow northwards; they've barely reached Calangute. But when she can't see the white fabric, she is immediately suspicious. Deep down she knows she is not mistaken, nonetheless she undoes the straps that hold everything firmly in place, removes her everyday dresses and blouses, and continues her search until she can run her fingers against the suitcase's hard outer-shell through silk fabric. Her heart sinks. But she repeats the entire operation, even more attentively this time, laying all her clothes systematically out on the bed. It's futile.

Nobody in Pemba would see her in her wedding finery. There was no escaping it, what awaited her now was the ordinary and everyday.

It's strange, but when I write about my forebears now, it is Herminia who I see. I met my paternal grandfather several times in my childhood, and despite his being an old man by then, I knew him. Not so with my grandmother. She is an unknown, yet she feels so close. Grandmother died shortly after I was born: hers was the lap I should have sat on, hers was the voice that should have sung me to sleep, hers was the

hand that once held the one who should in turn have held me. I have missed her without knowing it, unlike Herminia herself, who was so aware of the absence of those whom she had lost – the father who died, the mother and stepfather who abandoned her. In all the surviving photographs of her, she is a grownup woman, sitting amid a flock of children that expands with each picture taken. Her eyes are gentle, rather tired. She poses patiently for the photographer, yet her whole body seems weighed down with work. Her hands are always ready to attend to some task, to smooth a tablecloth or to cradle a child. Years later she would endure the disappearance of her own children from her life, one by one, with no possibility of her ever following them.

Longing for love is nothing compared to missing it: the dying empires, the interminable journey, nobody paid a greater price than Herminia.

But all this is still ahead of her. She is nineteen years old in 1925. She stands on the deck of a steam ferry on the way to the city of Bombay, where she and her new husband board a ship that will carry them over the wide, open ocean. Not until three weeks later do the white roofs of Stone Town rise from the horizon. The couple probably has to stay in Zanzibar for a few days to wait for the night ferry to Pemba. Electricity is scarce in Pemba, so they arrive at the harbor near Mkoani on the island's southern tip in the faint light of dawn. I don't know what Herminia thought, but I know what she saw – or rather, I know what Evelyn Waugh saw when he arrived here five years later: a green hillside scattered with bungalows, the water by the jetty so clear that every pebble on the bottom seemed drawn with unreal clarity. Along the tarmac roads across the island, everything was fecund and lush. After the teeming crowds of Bombay and Zanzibar city, coming to Pemba must have felt like a journey out of bright light and noise into darkness and silence. And darkness in more than one sense, since Pemba was the center of witchcraft and black magic along the Swahili coast. It was into this dark, green quiet that Michael Joseph traveled to work as assistant to his father, the postmaster in Chake Chake.

But what kind of life awaited Herminia here?

The answer lies in the two promises she'd made before leaving her homeland. The first, her marriage vow: to love and obey Michael Joseph to the end of their days. The other, a vow she'd made to her stepfather, Aleixo, the man who had replaced her father. To him she had promised to give each of her children names that began with the letters of his name. Herminia would keep both promises. Now she not only knew what her task was in life, but that her journey was far from over. Breaking from home was difficult for everyone, but nobody experienced this more than the women. In some families the women were left behind to give birth and bring up the children in the village, while their husbands only returned from East Africa at regular intervals to impregnate them again. In other families the women accompanied them, only returning home temporarily to give birth. And, since there were no suitable schools for Catholic Indians in Pemba, it wasn't unusual to leave the children behind so they could attend school in their homeland, just as Aleixo had done.

There is nothing to suggest that Herminia wants her children to go through what she went through. When she gets pregnant in her second year in Pemba, she returns to Ti Filu's house in Saligão to have her firstborn, A. – the first letter of her stepfather's name. But instead of leaving her baby boy behind she stays with him and her aunt. A year later Michael Joseph must have come to visit them, because in 1929 she gives birth to a second child, also a boy, who is duly named L.

Herminia stays with her sons for four years, before leaving for East Africa for good. And this time she does what she had been so reluctant to do; she leaves her eldest son behind with Ti Filu, taking only the youngest with her.

There's nothing sensational about that. Five-year-old little A. would brighten up his great aunt's life, and as a teacher she could educate him herself, just as she'd done with Herminia before him. This was common practice, and circumstances no doubt made it necessary. But does that mean that Herminia's heart didn't break when she said goodbye to her five-year-old little boy and boarded the steamship for the third time? Herminia was well accustomed to being abandoned, but not to abandoning others. But thus it had always been, and thus it would continue to be: in a culture and in a time when home and family meant everything, loss seems a never-ending way of life.

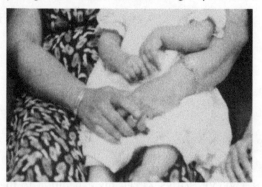

LESS THAN TWELVE HOURS AFTER my expedition to the cemetery I decided to leave Pemba. Michael Joseph and Herminia had not spent many years there either. In 1930 Grandfather resigned as the postmaster's assistant in Chake Chake, and was appointed as a government agent under the British District Officer in the port of Mkoani, southwest of Pemba. As such he was authorized to represent the government in all financial disputes where the sum did not exceed 300 rupees.

A couple of years later, Michael Joseph, Herminia and little *L.* moved from Pemba to Zanzibar, renting a house from an Arab in Vuga, in the center of Stone Town. For the next few years, he commuted back and forth between Zanzibar and Pemba, before finally being transferred to the District Office in Zanzibar, just a stone's throw away from their house in Vuga. Meanwhile Aleixo retired with a pension, and together with Elizena returned to Saligão to spend their last years in their homeland.

As far as my family was concerned, Pemba was now relegated to history. They had left nothing of themselves here, apart from Ermelinda's body in the red earth of Dongoni.

As I fly back to Zanzibar it strikes me how different life in Pemba and Stone Town must have been. They were, and continue to be, worlds apart. I am traveling now from the jungle to the city, from nature to culture. The Pemban landscape can't have changed much since my great grandparents' day. Nature seems to have a permanence, despite its continual flux. By contrast, the city strikes one as transitory, even if it remains much the same for generations. Perhaps because we think of nature in the abstract, not as the sum of individual plants or trees, whereas the city consists of *that* house, *that* corner, *that* bench on which you were sitting when she placed her hand in yours. Brick by brick the city is shaped by people's lives, and with this our lives leave their imprint upon it, in the grooves formed by a thousand passing feet, in the edges of the banisters worn smooth. In nature our surroundings are never quite the same from season to season, year to year, and our footsteps are washed away in the first rainfall. Cities, by contrast, store our memories, absorbing the sound of the laughter that has echoed between its walls, the urine that has trickled between its cobblestones.

"The city does not tell its past, it carries it within itself, like the lines on a hand," writes Italian author Italo Calvino. When the stones crumble, the memories crumble with them, only then is the life we lived here really gone.

I walk through Stone Town, along narrow passages of whitewashed houses barely wide enough to let people cross paths, twisting alleys that suddenly open onto small town squares, past men who sprawl idly on the front steps of their houses, while their womenfolk rattle the cooking pots inside, past kids running around in the golden hours between homework and bedtime. Watching these exuberant African boys in their bright white kanzus, I try to picture the Goan, Arab and Indian kids who ruled these streets in Dad's day. I may be walking in a city now, not a jungle, yet my experience is not so very different after all. This city is made of living stone, coral taken from the reefs that surround the island. Stone Town is a living entity. High above me the roofs are crowned with dazzling white sunlight. The light doesn't reach this far down, only the heat. Down here, the porous walls breathe in the dense humid air, their pores clogged with dark fungal spots. The city reaches deep into my lungs. And just as the paint is peeling from its ancient walls, the salt of my perspiration settles in a film on my skin. I drink as much water as I can as I wander around trying to find the house where Dad was born. The child in Victoria Gardens, the boy with the open face. The boy who was once King.

Is *this* his lost kingdom?

At first glance it's hard to believe, since neither Dad nor the people to whom he belonged were kings here in Zanzibar, they were the servants of others. Grandfather was a typical Goan official, and as an Asian his salary was based on the usual racial differentials, where an Indian earned more than an African but far less than a European. The hierarchy was firmly established in British East Africa from the start. According to a contemporary British diplomat the role of Europeans in the 1890s was to "direct, rule and instruct," while the Africans were put to physical labor. But since the Africans were regarded as unreliable and careless, mediators were needed between the blacks and whites. The Arabs were, according to this same British diplomat, too lazy for this task, while the Chinese were generally undesirable. By contrast, the "docile, kindly, thrifty, industrious, clever-fingered" Indians were perfectly suited to occupy the intermediate roles of functionaries, merchants, craftsmen and cooks who were required to keep the wheels of empire turning.

However ambitious Grandfather might have been, sooner or later he would have banged his head on the "race ceiling." The fact his passport stated he was a Portuguese citizen was of absolutely no practical use, except that the British would grant certain privileged officials permission to visit their homeland every five years. But while the British at least allowed Goans in their service to travel freely, the Portuguese consul had long demanded they buy expensive passports to leave the island – passports which in reality were no more than temporary travel passes. In the early 1920s the consul felt so compelled to mark his territory that he threatened to deprive Goans of their Portuguese citizenship altogether. The ensuing diplomatic crisis revealed to the Goans that they could not count on Portuguese support while in the employ of another state. It was equally uncertain that the British would take them under their wing if the Portuguese carried out their threat: "However altruistic we may be," writes one British official in 1922, "we are not, after all, a sort of international house for Waifs and Strays. Goans are without nationality, as Portugal no doubt intended that they should be, and they are entitled to receive no passports from anyone, presumably."

This was the general attitude of the British toward their Goan employees. Although some were rather more conciliatory and thought Britain should recognize its responsibility: "This is because we owe a duty to our clerical staff (many of whom have been for years in this service, and most of whom intend to devote their lives to it)."

This crisis passed and the Goans did not lose their Portuguese citizenship. Eventually the British would grant them the status of British Protected Persons, which represented a looser connection to Britain than full citizenship. What this conflict reveals, however, is the difficulty in placing the Goan people with any surety; in censuses they vanished into various categories including *Asian, Asian Christian, Indo-Portuguese, Portuguese, Indian* or even just *Christian*. They were dark-skinned, Catholic, Portuguese citizens in the service of the Brits. They looked like Indians, but insisted that they weren't. And even though they had Portuguese names, they grew increasingly British in mindset and language as the years passed.

So what and who exactly were they?

First and foremost they were loyal, and they prided themselves in being the most dutiful servants to whoever was in power at the time. In return, it seems these rulers often had a soft spot for them, be it the Portuguese, the British or the Sultan of Zanzibar. The Goans came to East Africa as officials, accountants, managers, station masters, postmasters, and those from the lower castes came as tailors, cooks and craftsmen. With their passion for food and music they were popular as cooks, butlers and musicians. From the 1860s on, the Sultans had their own Goan band, and as sailors they were frequently employed as musicians and cooks onboard British ships. The Goan bar was an institution in Zanzibar, and any eminent household would be sure to have a Goan chef. If we're to believe a British visitor to the island in 1905, the only problem was that they had a bad habit of getting drunk in the kitchen during dinner parties. Not difficult to believe; Catholic Goans love their alcohol as much as the Muslims shun it.

Most Goans in East Africa, however, were to be found in colonial administration; lured by a steady income, a predicable lifestyle and the prospect of a pension. Many a District Commissioner relied on a trusted Goan official. But where such bureaucratic posts were generally a mere step on the career-ladder for a European, for a Goan they were a lifelong calling.

Goans came to be viewed as a meek, conservative, and polite people with a passion for food and music. They were articulate, loyal and cautious. "Goans are a timid people," one of my uncles said once. While any attempt to summarize an entire people in a single clever phrase has limited validity, there can be little doubt that this description matches the Goan *colonial image*. No wonder the British loved them, especially when they were so cheap to employ. Of all their staff, the Goans were those they allowed closest into their lives, as nannies, physicians and butlers. And this is true across the entire colonial world. In French Indochina, for example, the setting for Grahams Greene's *The Quiet American* (1955), in which the cynical journalist Thomas Fowler tells us that his Goan assistant Dominguez is the only person he trusts in a world of inscrutable and deceitful Asians:

"I was fond of Dominguez: where other men carry their pride like a skin-disease on the surface, sensitive to the least touch, his pride was deeply hidden and reduced to the smallest proportion possible, I think, for any human being. All that you encountered in daily contact with him was gentleness and humility and absolute love of truth."

Fowler trusts the man who appears to have been created in his own image, the difference being that he was born to serve. It was a myth accepted by many Goans themselves, indeed they seemed to relish it. I have met retired officials who look back on their service in East Africa with nostalgia and pride: "The keys of East Africa were safe with the Goans," they say. Within this ruthless hierarchy based on race – with absolute power in the hands of the whites above them and absolute powerlessness for the blacks below them – the Goans embraced servility as a virtue and talent to be refined and perfected. They may have been servants, but of the highest order, the butlers of the colonial system.

My grandfather, Michael Joseph, was one of these butler-bureaucrats.

For a long time I had trouble connecting the idea of subservience with the authoritative man I recall from my childhood – the man about whom Dad and his siblings spoke with such deep respect. It's unlikely they would have associated this word with him either; all they knew about his professional life was that he "worked for the government" and occasionally took them to the British holiday resort in Chaka, where he was in charge of the holiday villas for British staff. Aside from these brief excursions, the worlds of the office and home, of the whites and the Goans, were strictly divided.

Michael Joseph was a serious and deeply religious man. He rose at 4:30 a.m. every morning, took out his prayer book and his carefully written list of those who should be prayed for that day. After an hour of prayer, followed by breakfast, he attended morning mass at 6:00 a.m., and then went to work. Despite this, and in contrast to the down-to-earth and self-effacing Herminia, Michael Joseph was prone to vanity. When he walked through Stone Town's narrow alleys, he sported a handsome black hat, shiny black shoes, and sometimes a cane for appearance's sake. An ambitious man, with an eye for the future, he was sure that the most important thing you could give your children was a university education, which, in turn, required perfect mastery of the English language.

And the children kept coming. Aleixo's name had not yet been fully spelled out, and through the 1930s the letters continued to roll into the world. First *E.*, then *I.* Then, some time in 1938, before the next came into the world, Herminia was forced to give up another child. It had been decided that *L.* should join his older brother, *A.*, who was still living with Aunt Ti Filu in the village back home in Goa.

L. was just nine years old and would spend the rest of his childhood in a foreign country, which he'd been told was his real homeland. The intention was that he, like his big brother, would be educated at home by Ti Filu. However *L.* proved so stubborn and difficult that his aunt saw no alternative but to send him to a school where the German nuns systematically beat the joy out of him.

Meanwhile, back in Zanzibar more children arrived. At the beginning of 1939, *X.* came along. The following year the final letter was in place, with little *O.* Herminia had now fulfilled her promise to her stepfather. But she wasn't done yet and before the decade was out she'd given birth to another three children: *T.*, *J.* and *M.* In total Herminia and Michael Joseph had nine children. *A.*, *L.*, *E.*, *I.*, *X.*, *O.*, *T.*, *J.* and *M.* As I was growing up in Langesund, eight of these siblings existed only as a vague, though important, presence in my consciousness. Or they would make a sudden appearance in our kitchen doorway, bringing with them the breeze of foreign climes. They had been born on two continents, over three decades and in three countries. And just as they were scattered when they first entered the world, they would be scattered throughout their lives.

Yet none would drift further from the others than *X.*, the boy who was to be my father.

HE RAN BAREFOOT IN THE SAND. What more? In the evenings, in our living room or when we lay tucked up in our bunk beds, Dad would sometimes sing what I believed to be a ballad in Swahili, but which was in reality a scout song in gobbledygook written by Robert Baden-Powell: *Ging gang goolie goolie goolie goolie watcha, ging gang goo, ging gang goo*. Among the few stories that Dad told us about his childhood was one about an old, poor-sighted man who walked down their street in Vuga at precisely the same time each day using a stick to guide him. When his stick struck their front door, the old man knew that he must turn left, and Dad that it was time to get up and get ready for school.

Once in a while Dad would put his arms behind his head, and with a dreamy look in his eyes would say something like: "Ah, Zanzibar! Beautiful beaches, nice and warm. Like Paradise!"

Nothing more. These were the only glimpses I had of my Father's childhood in Zanzibar: an orientalist scouting song, an anecdote, and a lyrical description that might have been written in a tourist brochure – white beaches, blue sea and swaying palms. That's not to say that Dad was a poor storyteller or lacked imagination. He lived in Zanzibar until he was eleven, and by the age of nineteen he had left East Africa for good. When Dad told us where he came from, he wasn't so much describing a place he had left, but a lost childhood. The landscape of a childhood paradise is simple, specific details are few; instead it leaves an impression on the body. Dad remembered the warmth of the sun on his skin, the cool breeze, the sand between his toes, the grinding sound of the huge stone pestle and mortar out in the kitchen, the aroma of roasted cumin seeds filling the room.

A picture of a childhood, fixed and unalterable.

In many ways Dad grew up in a land of bells jars. Zanzibar's inhabitants may have had an acute awareness of the world at large; nonetheless, its many communities lived lives that were turned inwards. The Africans, the Arabs and Indians: Hindus, Ismaelite Khojas, Bohras and Memons alike, all lived very separate lives. As did the Sunnis, the Zoroastrian Parsees with their own fire temple outside the city, the Christian Goans, the Comorians, the Chinese and Iranians. And finally, of course, the few but all-powerful British.

The bell jar analogy has, of course, its limitations; just as in Goa, communities had mixed for centuries in Zanzibar – the Shirazis, for example, were the product of the mingling of Africans and Arabs. Indeed, it was the British who were determined to divide Stone Town along clear racial and religious lines. Under their rule the Africans were expected to keep to the simple huts in the village of N'gambo on the other side of the strait, only entering Stone Town for work, while the Goans, the Parsees, the Indians and other large communities each had their own districts of town. But this was never wholly achievable in Zanzibar. Firstly, the island was always under Islamic law, and the divisions were based largely on religious rather than racial difference. Secondly, the society was too small and close knit for such clear divisions to be created. The education offered by the nuns of the Precious Blood Sisters at the St. Joseph Convent School, was, for instance, regarded so highly that educated Parsee and Arab families sent their children there. People greeted each other on the street, they met in the workplace, Catholics honored the festival of Id, and received gifts from their Muslim neighbors at Christmas.

But if the communities were never *physically* segregated in Stone Town, they still lived largely among their own kind. They saw other communities as if through a glass wall. Their identity, their sense of belonging, was shaped and cultivated in the mosque or church, in ethnically exclusive clubs and within the four walls of their houses. People socialized among their own and importantly, they got married and had children exclusively within their own groups. Thus a kind of indifferent tolerance reigned on this little island with its little town. Communities were obliged to live cheek by jowl, succeeding only because they lived parallel lives, and because arching over all of them was one giant glass dome – the British colonial power that protected all the little bell jars from the outside world.

Under one of these bell jars lived the Goans. They weren't numerous, a few hundred, and they were known for cherishing their exclusivity. Besides, it was commonly felt that the Goans considered themselves better than the Indians, the Arabs and, of course, the Africans. The private lives of the Goans were played out in St. Joseph's Cathedral, at the club and at the frequent festive gatherings and picnics. But this didn't mean that the Goans were totally unified among themselves; there were divisions even within the community. Marrying into a lower caste was unheard of. And at the club a separate Christmas party was held for the children of tailors and other low caste families. Additionally, light skin was prized more highly than dark, not least when it came to marriage. "When Goans marry, they ask for a photograph first," Dad told me once, clearly embarrassed on his people's behalf.

Within the castes too, there were further clear divisions based on sex and age: the youngest was always subordinate to the authority of his elders, not least within the family – the smallest bell jar in a land of bell jars.

This is Dad's homeland: he grew up in Zanzibar. He grew up among Goans. But more than anything he grew up within the family. Indeed, I can't help but think that my aunts and uncles, my grandfather and grandmother and their enormous flock of children were perhaps even more inward looking than most other Goans. The children never stayed overnight with friends, they found all they needed in each other's company, with their parents and with God. Even when they were running around in the narrow backstreets, they were watched over; if not by their parents, then by the neighbors. No one ever took part in any sport, nor did they swim in the balmy turquoise sea that surrounded Stone Town; Herminia wasn't willing to risk losing any of her precious offspring, and she was doubtless familiar with the ancient legend in which the ocean demanded one child from the town every year.

So who was Dad in all of this? Who did he become?

"He was a born leader," my father's younger brother replied when I asked. It was a loving family but based on a rigid hierarchy. Age was everything, a younger brother did not oppose his elder, and children never opposed their parents. Obedience was everything, although this was probably barely noticeable since the sense of unity in the family was so strong, and the parents' love for their children seemed so boundless. Yet this hierarchy was ever-present, and it applied to everyone. Except, it seems, to Dad:

"He was the one who broke the rules. He was the exception."

Exactly *what* set him apart from his siblings, my uncle found more difficult to put into words. "He was so aggressive that nobody ever questioned him. He had all this power inside him – physically too. He was tough."

And then I hear the story of how Dad once convinced his siblings that they should give him all their money; he was going to buy sweets and sell them and then they'd all share the profits. Time passed, and Dad's siblings asked what had happened to their business venture, only to find out that he'd eaten all the sweets himself. His explanation? He had none, he just shrugged his shoulders as if to say: That's life.

An innocent prank, perhaps, but I recognize Dad in it. When my uncle told me this story, it brought back a memory from my own childhood. A memory that had lain dormant for so long that when it surfaced it was with painful intensity. Dad, my brothers and I are walking through Porsgrunn on the way to his apartment. He suddenly starts to run. We know what he wants, this is a game he plays frequently; my brothers and I are supposed to try to catch him. He races down the street with his three sons panting after him, and as he runs he waves his arms in the air, shouting, "I'm free, I'm free." Disappointment fills us when we realize that he won't slow down as we somehow hoped; that this game of his will not end with his turning around, crouching down and welcoming us with open arms.

Indeed, he never did. We always fell increasingly behind, before we'd finally give up and stand there gasping for breath as we watched him disappear down the street. Free. Though I had no idea from what.

I AM SEARCHING FOR DAD'S HOUSE. But after wandering endlessly through Stone Town's labyrinthine alleyways, I realize I need help. A kind, elderly Goan couple show me the way. They don't actually remember my family, but they do remember a Mrs. Grabu who lived in the same house. We turn the corner onto a paved square, and suddenly I am standing before a large abandoned house with grey, flaking walls. The windows of what was once Mrs. Grabu's ground floor apartment are nailed shut. On the Figueiredo's floor above, iron grills lock the darkness inside, while the wooden shutters hang loose on their hinges. The frontage is wreathed in a tangle of electricity cables, carrying life to the next house. Dad's house meanwhile is utterly dead. The loft space is open to the world, allowing pigeons to fly in and out, and sitting above that again is a rickety tin plate roof.

Here is the house of Dad's paradise. The house in which he lived when he was a boy and not my father – when he looked up at the world and not down, when he still had a scrawny, hairless and fragile body, when his eyes didn't demand, but asked and inquired, and were filled with longing, not reproach. A little boy with a freshly ironed shirt and bare spindly legs between white shorts and white socks. I can see him now. Coming out of the front door. Walking, despite his body longing to break into a run. Down the street, around the corner, and across the little square and into the narrow backstreets, on a Sunday morning just as the early call to prayers from the mosques falls silent, and the bells of St. Joseph Cathedral fill the air.

The following Sunday, on just such a morning, I too venture into the labyrinth once more. Again I am unsure of the way, but the heavy church bells act as my guide through the narrow alleyways. The bells know something, they want to tell me who I am and where I belong – and it is not among the Arab women with their bright eyes, or the African kids who whiz past me in a cloud of dust, or even their fathers who are busily taking down the shutters and setting out their stalls with light cotton clothes and ebony figurines, with no thought for the Catholic day of rest. It's strange how indifferent I feel toward these people. As the liberal Norwegian that I am, I ought to show more interest and respect for Zanzibar's diverse communities. I was so eager to absorb everything when I traveled around Asia in my youth as a humanities student. As a Norwegian traveler now I ought to be *creeping* around Stone Town, smiling shyly to reassure everyone that even if I don't buy their wares (despite clearly having the money), I have the greatest respect for their culture and way of life. Instead, they seem irrelevant to me, just as the white-clad, Fanta drinking Muslims did in Pemba.

Perhaps that's how it is here in Zanzibar. Doubtless it was like this when my family lived here. In turning toward our own people, we turn our back on others.

But what has any of this to do with me? When on earth did the Goans become "*my* people"? The church bells are so alluring; they feel so safe. But something tells me to hold back now, to listen to the voice of reason that warns me not to lull myself into a false notion of self. I think of my brothers, of my friends back at home, and how they'd shake their heads if they saw me now. They know who I am. Ivo Bjarne from Langesund. The Bamble-Indian. The Norwegian. But I am spellbound by the sound of the bells in the air. And walking on, I think of Dad. I search for him in every child I pass, those, at least, that have the correct skin tone and are wearing the right clothes.

This is Dad's world. So it must also be mine? Surely? Whatever the case, I can't help feeling that wherever I go in this city, someone has forged the path before me. That there is something here in this stone labyrinth that is mine. That has always been mine.

Before I know it, I turn a corner and see the stately, sand-colored cathedral rising in front of me with its two towers. Gathered in front of its doors is a group of people whom I instantly recognize as my people, if for no other reason than that they are all wearing the traditional dress of my tribe: the women in blouses and skirts, the men in neatly pressed trousers and light-colored shirts with long or short sleeves. Among them I recognize some I have visited and had tea with. Now they meet my eyes by way of greeting, but say nothing. We wait for the bells to fade. Then the cathedral doors open and an African nun in a blue and white habit waves us in. Cautiously I greet everybody and nobody as I walk up the stone steps and enter Dad's church.

Inside the entrance I dip my right index finger into the bowl of holy water. I do it automatically, just as I did so frequently as a child. I raise my hand slowly and place my wetted finger on the center of my brow. Lowering my hand, I feel the trace of a cool memory on my skin. I bring my hand to my stomach, close to the solar plexus, and from there, diagonally up to my left shoulder. Have I made this gesture since abandoning the church as a thirteen year old? That awkward telephone call, the priest's worried voice at the other end. His questions. Was I aware of the gravity of this decision? Had I given it proper thought? Dad's despair at my rejection of the faith. Of his world. I pass my hand over my chest, before bringing my finger to a fourth point on my right shoulder. I fix my eyes on the Christ figure over the altar at the end of the aisle, just as I did as a child whenever I entered the old wooden church in Porsgrunn. It's all coming back to me now. The waft of incense, the acrid smell of tar from the timber walls, the gentle glow of polished wood, the deep shadows at the back of the church behind the columns that separated the pews from the walkway where the stations of the cross were depicted. And there at the altar, Father Rommelse dressed in his alba, turning to face the rows of bowed heads in the pews below, with his arms raised, like a saint stepping out from one of the stained glass windows.

Dad is somewhere in this church. I am the child, he the adult. I search for him in my memory, finally finding him sitting next to me in the pew. We kneel, but unlike Dad I reach for the cushion that hangs from the brass hook before me, and put it under my knees; one of the flat, brown cushions for those incapable of forgetting the world for the little time that God demands of them. Just one brief hour. That's all. But I am flagging. My little body is aching to run down the aisle before the nuns have time to blink, to shove the heavy wooden door open and to race down the gravel path into freedom, where I can spin beneath the chestnut trees.

That was what I wanted to do, but instead I replaced the cushion on its brass hook, and peered up at Dad as I registered the pain of the wooden kneeler against my knees. He had a solemn expression on his face. His eyes were closed; the furrow in his brow bore witness to a concentration I never saw with him otherwise. Was he just putting it on? It was as though his face said: this is how a Catholic prays. Or, this is how the son of a Catholic prays. The unsaid demand in Dad's face made me rebellious. I looked at him, at this virtuous mask, and realized that I was losing my faith. Not in God, but in my father.

There is little in Stone Town's cathedral to remind me of my childhood church in Porsgrunn. Yet, so much is the same. The nave is spacious and airy. The side doors stand wide open, just as they must have done when Dad was a child. Now, however, large electric fans stand along the rows of pews, driving the warm air through the building. Above the pink columns with their sky blue capitals, fluorescent strip lights cast a white and somewhat redundant light over yellow-limed walls. Apart from crossing myself at the entrance I can barely remember the rituals of mass. But I do my best. I rise and kneel in tandem with everybody else. The kneelers are hard; I imagine Dad on his little bony knees, next to his father. High up along the church wall, above the obligatory row of paintings depicting the stations of the cross, are the stained glass windows of the saints. I recognize St. Francis of Assisi, St. Sebastian and St. Ignatius of Loyola, the legendary founder of the Jesuits.

And there in a window to my left, I see Dad's name saint: St. Francisco Xavier. He is the only saint whose name is displayed on a plaque below. I imagine Dad lifting his head during prayers, careful not to arouse his father's attention, looking up to inspect his namesake's grief-stricken face encircled by a blood-red halo.

Was Dad as restless as I was as a boy? And was it some comfort to him to rest his eyes on his patron saint's tireless gaze toward heaven? Or did Dad grow disenchanted, as I did? It was easy for the saintly Xavier to maintain that eternally prayerful pose up there, without the burden of a physical body, without knees that ached, just a translucent spirit suspended between leaded strips.

But Francisco Xavier also had a body once, now lying in Bom Gesù in Velha Goa. The story of his body says everything about the kind of home the Catholic Church was for a family doomed to wander. On the night of December 3, 1552, Xavier died of a fever on the island of Sao João, just south of Macao. He was forty-six. Thus ended the temporal life of this missionary. But the moment life had left his body, the "Apostle of the Indies" started out on a new journey; the journey into the eternal world of the spirit and of legend. Not that his body was forgotten. Almost three months after his coffin had been placed in the ground, it was disinterred and transferred to a more fitting burial place in Malacca, Portugal's foothold in Malaysia. Great was the surprise however, when the coffin was opened and the body was found to be uncorrupted. There was no sign of decay; instead a pleasant scent rose from the dead man. And when the ship's captain, responsible for transporting the coffin, ordered a piece to be cut from the corpse's left knee, fresh blood flowed. This was just the first of many miracles that would follow Francisco Xavier's body. When it reached Malacca, his body was again laid to rest, but the list of miracles that had happened on the journey could not be ignored: the storm that had been mysteriously stilled during the crossing, the sick who had been healed from touching his body.

So the coffin was dug up again, and this time it was shipped to Goa, which, as the Rome of the East, was a fitting place for a possible miracle-corpse, or more delicately put, a candidate for sainthood. Here, in a side chapel of the imposing Bom Gesù Cathedral, one can still see the contours of this sacred body lying in a silver casket with glass sides displayed on a magnificent catafalque several meters above the floor.

But the story of Francisco Xavier's mortal remains does not stop there. According to several of Xavier's biographers a woman by the name of Doña Isabel de Carom, who wasn't content with just kissing the corpse's foot like any other pilgrim, decided to take one of its little toes. Trying to leave the cathedral unnoticed with the toe hidden in her mouth, Isabel was betrayed when fresh blood flowed once again from Xavier's body (or body-part), and was seen coming from her mouth. This event is said to have taken place in the late 1500s, and while the story is likely to be a myth, there is nonetheless a little glass box in the sacristy of Bom Gesù that supposedly contains one of Xavier's toes. One might think that after all this the missionary could finally be allowed to rest in peace on his elevated couch. Not a bit of it. On the night of November 3, 1615, four Jesuits opened the casket and cut off Xavier's right arm just below the elbow. The order to do so had come from Pope Paul V himself, and the arm was duly sent to Rome in what was the final stage in the elaborate and lengthy process of canonization. And, if we are to believe yet another legend, this arm incident is a rather curious apropos to a vow Francisco Xavier made in his earthly life: "If ever I forget thee, O Society of Jesus," he swore, "may my right hand be given to oblivion!"

He never did forget his order. In return, the brothers did not forget his right arm. The church in Rome was convinced; whether it was because blood continued to stream from his dismembered arm, or because, as another legend has it, the hand at the end of this arm grabbed a pen, dipped it ink and wrote "Xavier" in full view of the clergy, I don't know. But one way or another he was canonized, and his right arm remains to this day in Chiesa del Gesù in Rome; it is in the right transept, standing in a box of glass and gold, its palm open toward the chapel opposite, dedicated to his friend and superior Ignatius of Loyola, as though in eternal greeting and reassurance: Mission accomplished.

Four years later the remainder of Xavier's right arm was chopped off, including the shoulder blade. It was divided up, and the bits sent as relics to various Jesuit faculties across the whole of Asia – Japan, Malacca, Cochin and Macao. According to some sources, the list of body parts that were removed, including his intestines, far exceeds this, and an impressive number of churches around the globe claim to have a relic from Xavier's corpse. I know little about the fate of these relics, although a persistent Goan journalist purports to have traced the elbow, which, according to him, was sent to Macau where it was placed in St. Paul's church. When the church was burned down in 1835, the relic was moved several times before ending up in St. Joseph's faculty in Macao. In 1978 it was transferred to the St. Francis Xavier chapel in a procession led by a Chinese jazz band playing "When the Saints Go Marching In"; never mind there was only the *one* saint being paraded, and a rather small segment of him at that. The elbow made its final journey, when it was returned to the St. Joseph faculty in 1995, where, as far as we know, it still is today.

I don't know if Dad knew the story of his name-saint's corpse in any detail, but the legend of the opening of the coffin is certainly familiar to all Goans. But if he knew the story in full, he must have been impressed by the huge span of this Catholic Heaven under which his childhood city lay. Just like St. Francisco Xavier's body, the Catholic Church was spread across the entire globe. Divided and split, but nonetheless whole. Like the saint's body, the church itself was an empty, lifeless shell, yet it was alive. Didn't the bread and wine turn into Christ's flesh and blood during Holy Communion? At every mass, in every church, wherever it might be. The Catholic Church was a living entity, and it was everywhere.

Which was why, when the time came, Dad could leave his childhood paradise island for the unknown with confidence, first with his parents, later on his own. Wherever he went – to London or Manchester, or even to Porsgrunn – St. Francisco Xavier and the host of saints would be there to welcome him home. Just as they welcomed me in St. Joseph's Cathedral here in Stone Town.

FOR THOSE WHO HAVE NEVER lived in a paradise, it may be difficult to understand how easy it can be to leave it behind. The truth is that for every description of Zanzibar as a paradise, including in many travel books of the time, there are others who are ready to give another perspective.

When my literary companion Evelyn Waugh first arrived on the island he commented laconically: "It's pretty, but quite unremarkable." It would, of course, take a lot to impress a globetrotter like Waugh. And, in his defense, he did come at the hottest time of year and practically died in the heat. Poor Waugh! He seems to have spent most of his time under a mosquito net in bed, or in a bathtub of cold water, or at the English club where he was served with his chosen tipple and mango juice by Goan waiters. To get into the club, of course, a gentleman had to wear full attire; long trousers, shirt and jacket, bow tie, socks and leather shoes were obligatory. He had to get dressed very slowly if he was to avoid his clothes being instantly drenched in perspiration. Lunch over, he'd plunge straight into his bath, and then return to his bed.

Other Brits were even more disdainful than Waugh in their descriptions of Zanzibar. Among them the explorer Richard F. Burton, who used the island as a base during his search for the Nile's source in 1857 and criticized Stone Town's famed brothels, saying the whores looked like "skinned apes." When Livingstone arrived here some twenty years later, he named the island "Stinkibar" because of the stench that rose from the open sewers in the streets. The city regularly suffered epidemics, but by the time Waugh arrived, British building and sanitation projects had improved Stone Town to the extent that Waugh found the streets "absurdly clean," particularly in the European Quarter. Only now was the island about to become the exotic paradise described in the travel books.

But Waugh had another reason for disliking it here apart from the heat, and that was the stultifying boredom he felt there. Zanzibar was partly a paradise because so little happened. There were no political disputes and scarcely any intellectual life; even economically the island was stagnant, although the production of cloves and coconuts did at least keep the wheels turning. The young, soap-happy British, with their innocent pink faces and public school blazers, as Waugh described them, had few duties. They strolled into work at seven o'clock each morning and were finished by one. After lunch and an afternoon nap they played golf, tennis or cricket in Victoria Gardens. Later they changed their clothes – the men into stiff suits, the women into long dresses – and drank cocktails in the sunset.

Boredom, however, was a luxury Michael Joseph and Herminia could not afford with their ever-growing family. In 1946, when their youngest children *T.* and *J.* were still only babies, the two eldest boys *A.* and *L.* returned from Goa. They arrived on the doorstep of the family home in Stone Town one day, young men now of seventeen and nineteen, and looked into the faces of the parents they had seen so little, and at six wide-eyed little siblings about whom they knew barely anything; other than that, they sucked all the nourishment of parental love of which they had been deprived for so many years. Language also divided the family; although *A.* and *L.* spoke a basic English, their first languages were Portuguese and Konkani; the younger children, by contrast, spoke English as though it were their mother tongue. The power struggle between the two European empires had created a split even among the siblings.

Grandfather, and in particular Grandmother, must have been happy to have all their children under one roof at last. However, the situation could not last. Two years later *A.* and *L.* found work on the mainland; they had come back home at the age when it was time to fly from the nest. In December 1949, when Herminia fell pregnant again, Michael Joseph decided it was time for the rest of the family to head for the mainland too. There was no compelling reason to pull up sticks at this point, he *could* have stayed; what Zanzibar lacked in development or progress, it made up for in comfortable living standards. And Goan officials enjoyed much the same calm and pleasant lifestyle as their white bosses.

Grandfather's decision points to his having the same aspirations as his own father when he left Saligão in the 1890s. He simply wanted to improve his prospects and those of his family. Michael Joseph was a man of drive and ambition, and he must have decided early on that the only real way up was through his children. This, as evidenced by the letters he sent Dad when he was already well established, in which he continually handed out guidance, often inappropriate, not only planning careers for everyone, but even advising him in 1970 to have three suits tailored for different social occasions. Seen in this light, it is unsurprising that he should quit his job at the Zanzibar District Office and seek his fortune on the mainland, in Dar es Salaam. The colonial administration in the British Protectorate of Tanganyika, as it was then known, was far more developed and offered greater job opportunities, as well as better prospects for the children's further education.

Grandfather was keen to make this journey. But what about Herminia? When I ask my aunts and uncles, who made the decisions in the family, their answers vary. One says they agreed on everything, another that Grandfather's authority was absolute. Others insist that Grandmother ultimately made the decisions, merely letting her husband take the credit. In 1949 she was forty-four years old, a mother of eight with a ninth child on the way. Doubtless she shared

Grandfather's desire for a better life for them all. But again and again she expressed what this homelessness cost her.

"On January 11th we will complete 40 years of marriage, but so far we have not settled," she writes to Dad later in the mid-sixties. "It's my bad luck. I have no place anywhere in the world, I have been wandering all through my life."

But what did it mean for Dad to leave his childhood island at age eleven? In many ways this must have been the hardest journey for him, perhaps for them all. For the kids, Zanzibar represented safety, for Grandfather it was the place in which he'd spent most of his adult life. But did that make the island their *home*? When I sat with my aunts in Boston, the first question I asked them was: Where do you come from? The question proved less than easy to answer.

"East Africa ..." they said.

Then there was a pause.

"... but we identify ourselves with Goa. We are Catholics..."

Only after much toing-and-froing, did they came up with the following:

"We *come* from East Africa, but we *are* Goans."

Some historians are careful to emphasize that East Africa was also home to the Indians and Goans. And they have a valid point; seeds of discrimination lie in the notion that people who have lived somewhere for generations, do not *actually* belong there. Perhaps the question is not whether Zanzibar was home to my family, so much as – what is a home? Arguably there was little room for a true sense of belonging for a Goan family; whether it was under an Arab Sultanate or Portuguese rule or the British Protectorate, they only ever participated as subordinates. Doubtless they felt at home, but they existed wholly within their own community. A community that was ultimately transferable – Goans were to be found throughout East Africa.

The family was the primary unit, and you took that with you, together with your memories, faith and cuisine. A homeland can fit neatly into a couple of suitcases and a shoulder bag. The exception here being the enormous, heavy stone pestle and mortar, indispensable in any Goan kitchen, and which Herminia packed carefully in hessian sacks and sent ahead to Dar es Salaam. When the family followed, Michael Joseph went straight into the British administration, this time with the Department of Public Works. Just as in Zanzibar, there was a Goan community waiting to welcome them, with a Goan club, a St. Joseph's school and a St. Joseph's church. This might be a different town, but life here was much the same as before. It was here, in the two-room apartment in a pink modernist building on Kishwele Street near the town center, that the youngest and last child, a girl named *M.*, was born before the year was out.

But the journey still wasn't over. After barely four years in Dar es Salaam Grandfather was gripped by the need to travel again. The move from Zanzibar seems to have kicked something into motion; the exile's pulse was awakened. The children were growing up; everything was now focused on the future. One of his younger brothers had secured a good job in the tax department in Nairobi, the capital of neighboring Kenya, and he could arrange a decent job for Grandfather too. So the pestle and mortar was secured in its hessian sacks once more. Although this time it was loaded into the car that the family had acquired in Dar es Salaam.

The year was 1954, and the family was embarking on the last leg of its journey in Africa. Between Aleixo's arrival here and the eventual journey Dad and his siblings would take to the West, the family had moved step by step from the outskirts of British East Africa to its epicenter. From the darkness of Pemba to the white heart of the empire, Nairobi. And with each year that passed, with each move, each child that had been born, the family's ties to Portuguese India had grown weaker and their integration into the British Empire stronger.

Except perhaps for Herminia. After all, she had grown up in Goa, she spoke fluent Portuguese and had never worked for a British employer. For her, it probably didn't really matter to which state she belonged; all she wanted was to unpack her mortar once and for all, throw away the hessian sacks and make a permanent home for herself and her family.

I DON'T LIKE IT HERE. My hotel is a concrete block in which the rooms, the corridors and the foyer are constantly in shadow. What's worse, they're having building work done on the top floor, so there's a constant hammering of drills all day, and the air is thick with dust. When I come down to reception in the morning, the young Indian behind the desk tells me to stay indoors after sundown. Apparently it isn't safe for tourists to be out in Nairobi after dark, not if you're European or Asian. I am both and will do as I'm told.

I leave the hotel and walk under the January sun, pleasantly warm rather than scorching. I can at least breathe freely out here on the street. Nairobi is 1,800 meters above sea level, and at this time of year it feels like Norway in summer. The city gleams with late-modern optimism, with wide avenues and smart office buildings. There are people everywhere, yet the city strikes me as strangely soulless. I feel as though I'm walking around in a three-dimensional architectural model from the 1960s, into which a gigantic hand might reach down at any moment and move a building or two. Only when I get into the back streets do I find the organic chaos I'd expected of an African city; row upon row of little shops and stalls selling clothes with instantly forgettable brands, mobile phones, hair bleach and treatments for baldness, as well as an impressive number of chicken places with names like Chick King and The Funley Chicken. At sundown, I scurry back to the concrete colossus like a solitary man in a city of vampires seeking safety before darkness falls. I spend the rest of the evening in my room, lying in bed ruminating once more over the surprising level of hostility I feel for a place I don't even know. But at least I understand more now, I know why I'm here; I am searching for something that has gone, that no longer exists. I look out of the window. The night is pitch black except for the flashing brake lights in the endless lines of traffic. Progress, I muse, has certainly come to this African city, as evidenced by the increasing amounts of time its inhabitants spend going nowhere. And with this thought I drift into a restless sleep filled with colors and distant noises.

The next morning my Goan hosts are waiting for me outside. My aunts in Boston have put me in contact with a woman who knew my family when she was a child. Sylvia is a prim suburban woman in her fifties, with back-combed hair, childlike, and an almost coquettish way about her. She is as talkative as her husband Richard is quiet and reserved. Some years younger than my aunts, she thinks nonetheless that she can find the houses in which they lived.

Dad was fifteen when he came to Kenya. He would spend the last years of his youth in this country that was the epitome of a British colony; a land of the sun, where white settlers had created a little utopia for themselves in the fertile highlands. On their huge farms, built on the ancient territories of the Kikuyu, the British created the myth of a happy colonial life, with gin slings and smiling, obedient African subjects. Under the surface there was another reality, a culture of decadence, alcoholism, sexual excess and the exploitation of servants.

As a capital, they chose Nairobi, the city that had started out as a depot during the development of the Uganda Railway at the turn of the century. And since they were building the city from the ground up, the British were able to create what they'd never managed in Stone Town: a thoroughly racially segregated society. Almost everything was organized according to color in Nairobi; schools, hospitals, even toilets were allotted to whites, browns and blacks respectively. And the city plans were carefully marked out. While the Europeans lived in spacious, garden towns to the north, the Indians inhabited the areas in the west and around the railway station in the city center. Meanwhile, the native Africans had to make do with the dry, desolate areas outside the city to the south and east. To travel between zones, even to get to and from work, they had to show a valid permit.

Black. Brown. White. The British did their utmost to keep the colors apart in Dad's last city on the African continent. But these racial divisions were so successful as to be rendered almost invisible – that is, if you were young and hadn't yet looked beyond your horizon, or worked for a white boss. In retrospect it seems almost astonishing. Dad and his brothers and sisters lived in a society steeped in racism, yet it rarely touched their daily lives since they generally stayed within their own group. Particularly after the family moved into the little modernist house in Muthaiga Road, Pangani, where they were surrounded not only by Goans, but by Catholic Brahmins like themselves.

Naturally, when the children went into the city center they saw Europeans, and in church they looked at their backs – the front pews being reserved for whites only. And they had African servants and Ayahs, although there's no evidence that they reflected on the power they wielded over them. Africans were just servants, that's how it was. Besides we don't see the structure of oppression when it's a part of our daily lives; the black hand that rocks the cradle, or fills our bowl at dinner. We see what we want to see; the face of the person that resembles ourselves across the table.

"We retained our culture, our circle was tight," Aunt T. told me. "Even if we'd met other Indians who weren't Goan, we wouldn't have had much in common."

And, as before, the Figueiredos in particular kept themselves to themselves. They occasionally attended parties and dances in the city's three Goan clubs, but they never took out membership. Nor was it easy to penetrate this family circle, as any suitor of the beautiful

Figueiredo sisters would soon discover. If the prospective boyfriend were unfortunate enough to be invited home, the brothers would be so scathing about him after he'd gone that their sister would promptly dump him. One of the grainy films that still exists from this time shows Grandfather, Grandmother and the remaining children in one of the city's parks. Most of them are in their teens, the youngest still rather gawky. The girls are in pretty dresses with large white polkadots. The boys are joking and play fighting without the least sign of aggression. Surely they're too big to carry on like this, I think to myself, too old to mess around? But Grandfather clearly doesn't think so; he gathers the kids around him and gets them to form a circle. They've got to do something for the camera, so they dance to imaginary music in the middle of the park. Laughing, eager to please, only their bodies betraying some resistance. My family is a tight-knit circle. A ring of innocent frolicking dancers in the dying ashes of an empire.

But as the children grew up, the true nature of the colonial world they inhabited slowly began to impinge on their consciousness. As when T. accidentally brushed the arm of a young white soldier on a packed bus, and he immediately pulled away, not because she had touched him, but because her arm was the wrong color. Or the time she decided to visit her father at work. The man who received her at the offices of Nairobi District Commissioner had led her up the stairs and into a corridor where he opened a door for her. T. assumed it would lead into a small private office, where she'd find her father intent on his uniquely important government work. She was wrong. What she saw was an enormous room like a classroom, with row upon row of Goan officials, heads bowed, tapping away at their typewriters. Sitting at one end was a white man watching over them like a schoolmaster. Suddenly her father noticed her. He must have, since he turned to the door as she was led in.

But something was wrong. He saw her, yet didn't. His face was hard, with no trace of a smile or even recognition. Something sank inside her. She watched her father approach the white inspector, words were exchanged, the white man nodded and only now did her father turn to her with the smile she knew so well.

Everything is still in place; the bell jars and the colonial power that shields them are still intact. Admiration for the British remains; the kids love their music and listen to the BBC as often as they can, but they have begun to have their own thoughts, especially the youngest. It grates on them when their parents frantically tidy up the living room on the rare occasions they're expecting a visit from one of the older siblings' white bosses. Is it something about the British sense of entitlement, which no longer seems appropriate?

From what I hear about Dad as a youngster, he seems to have been the only one to remain untouched by this frustration. He was sovereign. A king everywhere he went – whether he was entertaining his siblings and parents at the dinner table or inviting the girls to dance. I too remember this side of Dad, especially when we had company; sitting on the sofa with his legs astride and shirt unbuttoned revealing his hairy chest, joking with the guests: "Everybody happy? Nobody crying?" I remember how he preferred to hold forth to the entire company; my memory may be distorted, but I can't picture him in conversation with any one person. People found him charming. They gravitated toward him as he took center stage. I know Mum didn't like it, and neither did I, because the more space he took the less there was for the rest of us. When our guests had left, he'd look at us despairingly:

"Why are you all so uptight? So Norwegian? Why can't you be easy going like me?"

And it's true; we sat there like puddings not quite knowing what to say. I can't remember exactly what went through my mind when I saw Dad's extravagant behavior, but I know what I felt – a deep unease, the same mix of pity and embarrassment as when he threw himself into the waves at Steinvika, the same nagging doubt as when I observed him praying in church. The same sense of conflict that fills me when I think back on these things today. Would I have had the same reaction if I'd seen him as a young man in Nairobi? Within the family circle that he saw as his natural habitat? For some reason I don't think so. I like to think it would have been different back then; that there'd have been a freshness about him when he made his parents and his brothers and sisters double up with laughter, or when he entered a party venue with the natural, innocent confidence of youth.

Increasingly Dad began to show qualities that singled him out from his siblings. In Dar es Salaam the family bought a car, a Ford Prefect, and Dad became the household mechanic. As a teenager he made his mother a wooden bowl and a stool to sit on when she ground spices in the big mortar in the kitchen. He was practical and technically gifted in a family of soft clerks' hands.

A Brahmin Goan in a boiler suit and with oil-covered hands. An oxymoron if ever there was one. Yet it describes him perfectly.

"Your father was strong enough to break the barriers," Uncle *J.* said, when describing their youth in Nairobi.

But what barriers did he break exactly? If Dad was a king, his fiefdom was strictly limited to his own little circle. The barriers of racial divide and imperialist oppression were far beyond his reach. Besides, there's little to suggest that he'd even noticed them – despite their being there for anyone to see, particularly now that the cracks were starting to show in the British colonial idyll. Immediately after WWI few people in Britain would believe the empire was under threat, even if some form of independence for India was already in the cards. But, the truth was that the *entire* colonial enterprise was teetering on the edge of collapse. Within a decade, one territory after another across the globe would fall; from Malaysia in the East to Jamaica in the West. But the idea that even the Africans would tear themselves free seemed unthinkable to many Europeans. Would the black man be capable of self-governance? Unlikely. Then it happened – in some places peacefully; in others like Kenya, blood was spilled. Here the Kikuyu set their feared Mau Mau warriors against the colonialists as early as the beginning of the 1950s. In some places entire settler families were massacred, spreading fear among the whites. The British cracked down heavily, and in 1952 they declared a State of Emergency that would last more than seven years.

The Mau Mau's anger was primarily aimed at the British, not the Indians. But almost everyone who served the colonial power was fearful of the insurgency, and though Dad and his family never experienced any violence themselves, they heard stories of Indian families who were killed. "We were scared," Dad once told me. "If you had a servant from the Kikuyu tribe, you felt uneasy. They might come in the night and kill everyone."

The British maintained an iron grip on Kenya throughout the '50s. But something fundamental had changed. The obedient servants were no longer so obedient; the African farm was ablaze. Naturally everyone was anxious, including Dad. But he was already looking toward the outside world. While the younger siblings went to Dr. Ribeiro's Goan school, Dad asked to take his final years at the Technical High School in Eastleigh. The fact that this was an Indian rather than Goan high school was of no concern to him. He wanted to be an engineer; and what Dad wanted he got. When he passed his senior Cambridge exam in 1958, it was decided that a grant awarded to his older brother should go to him. He would leave his family, and the Goans and bloodthirsty Mau Mau, to follow his star in Great Britain. He must have believed everything was possible, that his self-confidence would carry him far from the toppling world he was leaving and through challenges that awaited him on the other side the ocean.

Today, the population of Pangani, to the Northeast of Nairobi, is largely African. Sylvia has promised to show me the way to the family's old house if it's still standing. The problem is that Muthaiga Road lies at the poorer end of town, an area that the suburban Goans prefer not to venture in their shiny cars. Although, if I'm to believe Sylvia, it's even more dangerous in Eastleigh where our other family house is. When I ask if we might go there her abrupt response takes me aback:

"Impossible. No way!" After the outbreak of the civil war in neighboring Somalia in the 1990s, hundreds of thousands of Somalis sought refuge in Kenya, many of them ending up in Eastleigh. "You must never go there. You hear me? Never!"

We are crawling along the motorway, heading north out of the city center. I'm sitting in the front passenger seat. Behind me Sylvia chats away. Beside me her husband drives on in silence, alternating between neutral and first gear. Unsure whether to engage him in conversation or leave him in peace, I find myself contemplating the crash barriers along the roadside, hardly a tourist attraction. After an eternity stuck in this traffic we finally turn off and immediately find ourselves in a rundown residential area, where the trash spills out onto the dirt sidewalks, and on either side of the road, grass and bushes are left to grow wild between the low-lying brick houses with pealing paintwork, and shacks selling bottled water, fruit and vegetables, and other goods. With a sigh Sylvia recalls better times when Pangani belonged to the Goans: "Everything was well ordered then," she says. "All the houses were nicely painted and the gardens were beautiful, everything was clean, even the dirt roads were better."

It's strange. None of the Goans I meet in East Africa regret the liberation of Africans, yet many seem to be nostalgic about the days of the British, "when it was safe for a girl to go window shopping in Nairobi's city center on a Sunday evening." This fear of moving around in one's own city startles me. And Sylvia and Richard certainly aren't alone in feeling it; all the Goans I meet in Kenya look over their shoulders constantly. Like other Asians, the Goans generally belong to an affluent middle class, and they're wise to lock their car doors when they're sitting in a traffic jam. High crime rates clearly contribute to this fear, but so too does the knowledge that the land of their birth is no longer theirs; that they have lost the privilege they once had, and that the Africans are fully aware of this.

Sylvia gazes around her uneasily. We need to ask the way. She and her husband slip out of the car and into a corner shop, while I wait in the front passenger seat. The instant I'm left alone, the car is surrounded by children and old women. These are the ordinary people, the poor who stretch out their hands whenever opportunity presents. I notice, with some irritation, that the nervousness of my hosts is contagious. I instinctively check that the doors are locked, then shrugging my shoulders I make an apologetic gesture.

Soon Sylvia and Richard reappear in the shop doorway and push through the crowd with tense smiles on their faces. I give up my helpless pantomime and let them in. Richard swings the car around and takes a right turn down the hill toward Muthaiga Road. I recognize the modernist house from photographs, with its cream-colored walls, the iron trellises at the windows and concrete column at

the entrance. This is Michael Joseph and Herminia's last home in East Africa. I stand at the gate with Sylvia and Richard. Moments later two African children appear in the doorway and approach us cautiously. They are seven or eight years old, the boy in a green tunic, the girl in a white hijab. Soon afterwards the parents turn up. I try to explain what we're doing here, talk about the family that once lived here, about how special this house is to me. The husband and wife stand inside the gate, surveying me with indifference, nodding politely, before hurrying the kids back inside and disappearing after them.

Deflated, I get back into the car. I had come in the hope of getting something from this house, something I thought was mine. The family's reaction leaves me in no doubt; nothing here is mine. Nothing, whatsoever.

In Dad's day the divisions in Nairobi were clear, today they are unclear and therefore all the more noticeable. In theory a racially divided society has been replaced by one divided by class, yet these two dividing lines continue to overlap. While the center of town is predominantly black, the fenced-in shopping malls in Parkland and Karen are teaming with Europeans; white families with small children and flocks of fashionable teenage girls out shopping – (and some Asians and Africans too, from the upper classes). The lives of the wealthy are played out in these gleaming shopping malls, in smartly furnished clubs, and immaculate homes, behind high walls, equipped with barbed wire and the latest alarm systems. To travel between these fortified islands, they must drive in locked cars in traffic jams along severely neglected public roads.

Sylvia and Richard have strayed far outside their zone for my sake. But I have one more request. Just as in Pemba, my family has left one of its loved ones here in Nairobi. This time I know the exact location of the grave. But when I ask my hosts if they will take me to Langata Cemetery, they dig their heels in again. They don't dare for fear of being mugged. Langata has been the cemetery for the Goans since the late 1950s, and just like everywhere else in this country, divisions between people are clear here too. Graves at one end of the cemetery come under the policy of "bury and go," and are left untouched for five years at most. The more expensive and permanent graves are at the other end. The grave I want to visit is at the exclusive end; I know this from photographs I've seen of Dad's visit here in the 1990s.

Back then the grave was very overgrown and gradually sinking into the dark red earth. Dad had scraped away the earth, washed the pink marble and hung a rosary over the cross at its head. Then he had posed behind the cross and allowed one of the cemetery attendants to operate his camera.

Perhaps I should have been more insistent with my hosts, or gone to the cemetery on my own. But good manners and caution held me back; I'm probably more Goan than I realize. But I regret my cowardice now and wish I had gone. Not because I believe my presence at an old grave would be of any comfort to the woman who was left behind here, but rather for myself. I needed to lay my hand on the cold gravestone, like a doubting Thomas. This gravestone is all that remains of my family's life in this country. This coffin beneath the earth is the only space that is in some way still theirs. I know so much about the life she lived here from letters, pictures and photographs. I am familiar with her thoughts in the years and months before her death, and I share her longing for intimacy and closeness greater than words and pictures can offer.

When the stones crumble, memories crumble with them, only then is the life we have lived truly gone. And right now, I need something solid to hold onto, and in the absence of anything else, this grave would allow me to feel closer to Herminia. The woman who was destined never to leave this land.

THE CITY'S RAILWAY MUSEUM IS HIDDEN behind a tall fence that divides the train station from a motorway. Behind the brick building that houses the museum itself, is a neglected patch of pale-yellow grassland that holds a large display of locomotives and wagons. I come across a white and rust-colored carriage that must be like the one that carried Dad out of Nairobi in 1958. I jump up onto the running board. The door is locked. There was no formal segregation in buses and trains in Kenya; there was no need, economic differences dictated who traveled in which carriages: First Class for Europeans, Second Class for Indians and Third Class for Africans. Walking on, I find a locomotive of precisely the type in use at the time, an EAR 59 Class Garratt, the world's heaviest and most powerful steam locomotive, manufactured in Manchester by Beyer, Peacock & Co; the last steam train to run on The Uganda Railway before the introduction of diesel.

Once again, I am in a kind of cemetery. Not thick with vegetation as in Pemba, but barren and sun scorched. Perhaps because I'm completely alone here, with only these abandoned iron monsters for company, empty hulks from a world nobody cares about anymore, the past seems palpably close. I have the thought that I may be touching the actual boiler that once held the water, which turned into the steam, that drove the pistons, which turned the wheels, which carried the carriage in which Dad traveled through the Kenyan highlands and down to the coast, heading for England in time to meet Mum. As long as these carriages haven't rusted away, then Dad's journey from home still exists. History is contained in objects; but what releases it and brings it to life, is impossible to say. Nor do I have any intention of ruminating on that, as I stand here in this Nairobi railroad-cemetery. It's enough to run my hands over this old EAR locomotive, over its sun-baked surface, rough with rust and blistered paint, and to feel the weight of its carcass, 184 tons under my fingers. Remembering that in motion a locomotive can reach a mass of 252 tons.

A little more, if we add my father.

Later that afternoon I stand on the platform of Nairobi Railway Station observing my own train pull in. Why am I not surprised? I laugh out loud at my epiphany earlier that day. The carriages are exactly the same as those at the railway museum, but less rusty and painted a dirty-white and green instead of white and brown, with the addition of red and yellow stripes down the sides. Beyond that, there's little to distinguish my train carriage from Dad's. Kenyans may want to forget the colonial era, but scrapping a British-produced set of rail carriages would amount to carelessness.

Whatever the case, it was in just such a carriage, on a summer's day in 1958, that Dad was seen hanging out of an open window, while Michael Joseph and Herminia and all their remaining children stood in a group on the platform below. The train chugged into action in a cloud of steam from the great locomotive, everyone waving, everyone shedding a tear. All except the man who's departing. He saw an audience standing there on the platform, an unmissable opportunity to take center stage. Shocked, his family watched him dance and fool around as only he could.

Had he no idea of the gravity of this moment? Didn't he realize that years would pass before they'd see each other again?

The train is moving. The world is moving. As we roll through the slums of Eastleigh, it occurs to me that it was probably about now that Dad took his seat. It is already dark outside, but I know what's beyond the mosquito net that covers the windows. A shifting landscape of maize fields, dense scrubland, soon replaced by the pale yellow steppes and open savanna where solitary trees stand like sentinels. Herds of antelope, zebras, giraffes and lions here and there. And above everything a vast sky.

The train makes a stop at Simba. A spot recommended by Winston Churchill, who suggested that people taking The Uganda Railway bring a rifle with them, and ride back and forth a rail tricycle. The wild game animals were so used to this sight, they were scarcely bothered by it. Shooting them was almost too easy, he suggested, so a hunter with a little sporting spirit should dismount and hunt on foot instead. Churchill was traveling in the opposite direction, from Mombasa to Nairobi, shortly after the railway had opened in 1901. As he saw it, the purpose of the Uganda Railway was so that "the white man and all that he brings with him, for good or ill, may penetrate the heart of Africa as easily and safely as he may travel from London to Vienna." How many lions were shot by British hunters along this stretch of rail? How many Indian koolies were killed by lions?

And the British? The lions got their claws into a few at least. Like the poor policeman, whose gravestone still stands in Nairobi South Cemetery:

In loving memory of
Charles Henry Ryall A.D.S.
Punjab Police
Born July 13th 1875
Died June 6th 1900
He was attacked whilst sleeping and killed by
a man-eating lion at Kima.

I too am drifting off to sleep now. From the lower bunk in my compartment, I can feel the cool breeze through the netting at the window and hear the steady thudding of the rails. Soon we will begin the descent toward Mombasa, leaving the gentle landscape of umber and ochre to enter the tropical heat of the dark green and blue Swahili Coast. We are on our way. Out of Africa. I to return home to all that is familiar. Dad to start a new life on a foreign continent.

If the gravity of this venture had not yet dawned on him, then surely it must have as he boarded the ship that waited in Mombasa harbor? There was no going back now. He was alone.

A South African ship, it initially followed the coast of East Africa, down past Tanganyika, through the Mozambique Channel and to the city of Durban, before it finally turned its bow north toward the Red Sea, the Suez Canal and then headed for Europe. Half a century after Aleixo had broken out of the circle of rural life in Goa to take his family to a new continent, his grandson was now crossing another ocean. A pioneer for what would be the family's second exodus. Two oceans and three continents in three generations, and still the journey was not over.

When the ship came into Durban the European passengers were allowed to go ashore, while the Asians had to stay aboard. Among those left standing at the ship's rails was a nineteen-year-old Goan from Nairobi who, for the first time, glimpsed the world as it really was. A door is not shut before you try to open it, a border is not a border before you try to cross it. A ship is not a prison before you want to go ashore, and a white man points at your face and bars your way.

But they were soon on the open sea again. Africa's coast slowly dwindled into a narrow strip on the horizon. He was on his way to something new. But right now, the ship became his world, as it once had for his parents and grandparents before him. We imagine that emigrants have two lives, the one they leave behind, and the one to which they travel. But the interim journey is also a place. Here too a life is lived. Or it was once; when people traveled the world more slowly, before sails were replaced by coal, and coal by diesel. Aleixo and Ermelinda took three weeks to travel from India to East Africa. In Michael Joseph and Herminia's lifetime, this journey had been shortened to a fortnight. But it was with the introduction of long haul flights that a journey was transformed from place into a temporary state of being; a forgettable, dreamless sleep, from which you wake with the taste of yesterday still in your mouth.

"The airplane is faster than the heart," says one of V.S. Naipaul's fictional characters. This was not, however, the case for Aleixo and Michael Joseph, nor even for my father. Dad belonged to the last generation of slow travelers; his heart was in sync with him every minute, every hour and every day that he was on that boat.

But if a ship is a world unto itself, it is a world with shifting borders, a world between worlds, with memories of the old as well as promises of the new. There's a photograph in the album of Dad standing on a ship's deck with a group of young people, the men in white shirts and ties and two women in floral summer dresses. Dad stands between the women, his arms around their shoulders. Yet it seems he is holding back from touching their bare skin; he may, of course, be about to lower his arms, but I get the sense that he is careful not to. I've never given much thought to this picture before; it was just one of many Mum stuck in the family albums, in her quirky collages of photographs,

magazine cuttings and little comments. Only upon looking at it now, do I realize this picture must have been taken on Dad's first trip to Europe. And then a story he once told me about this boat trip comes to mind.

There are two white people in the photo, whom I assume to be the Belgium couple he got to know on board. In the restaurant the couple had to sit with the other European passengers, while any Asians, including Dad, had to sit elsewhere. While there wasn't any racial segregation on deck, there certainly was at meal times. One evening, however, something remarkable happened. The white South African pianist, who played for the guests during dinner, had finished his set and was about to leave, when a young Goan man suddenly jumped up and began to play "In the Mood." Dad and the others at his table were shocked and somewhat unnerved at this. They were no less shocked, however, when the South African turned in the doorway, and with a broad smile on his face returned to sit on the piano stool beside the young man. Together the two pianists entertained the company with a short impromptu four-handed concert.

Unthinkable in the world Dad came from, but clearly possible here on the open ocean. How would it be in the world he was going to?

EUROPE

I'VE OFTEN THOUGHT THERE MUST be a moment in everybody's life when they discover themselves for the first time. I'm not sure this is absolutely true, and if it is, this moment is probably generally forgotten. But I can remember exactly when I saw myself for the first time. Or I should say, when I saw myself as a uniquely individual "self."

The reason I remember it so clearly is that I decided, there and then, never to forget it. It was during the summer of 1974. We were on a family holiday in a big house somewhere in Wales. My brothers and I had been racing up and down the corridors, from room to room, before I finally dashed up the stairs. Suddenly I found myself completely alone in a large bedroom. The windows stood open onto a courtyard below, white net curtains billowing gently in the breeze. In the center of the room was a huge free-standing mirror.

I stopped still and stood there, waiting for my heart to cease thumping and my breathing to slow. I could hear Mum and Dad's voices from the kitchen downstairs, the laughter of my brothers. I was eight years old, and it was the first time I had ever seen myself full-length. The sight of myself as a whole person seemed inexplicably momentous. In a flash I decided to memorize every detail. I let my eyes follow the unbroken contour of my body, examining it minutely. My bare feet with their skinny toes; the long bandy legs; the gangly arms, darker where the sun caught them, lighter where my skin met my torso; the narrow chest under a yellow polo-neck; big, brown eyes;

curls that went in all directions, but which I hid beneath a yellow and black cap. All apart from the hair on either side – I thought it was cool to brush my hair so it stood out like two fans over my ears.

There's no greater slave to vanity than an eight-year-old boy, and I was determined to fix this image of myself for all time.

Why? I didn't know. But as I stood there studying the figure in the mirror, I remember thinking: *This is me*. And then a moment later, I was struck by second thought. I realized that I wouldn't always look like this. I was going to change. Someday I'd be a different person, and yet the same person. In a single moment I had perceived both my mutability and immutability. It was too big a thought to grasp, but despite that, or perhaps because of it, the situation felt very solemn. So overwhelming was the mood that had descended on me, that it wasn't enough just to stand there. The moment demanded I say something. That I make some kind of declaration. And in a voice that sounded alien in this empty room, I said:

"I am Ivo. I am standing here now."

Looking back on this event, I'm struck by the limitations of my child-perspective. Despite the enormity of this thought, my sense of self was entirely confined to my body. My surroundings, my mother and father, my brothers, my language, my skin color, the fact that I was a Norwegian boy on holiday in Britain; these were things I took for granted.

I realize now, of course, that who I am is also dependent on how others perceive me. For example, I know today that the eight-year-old boy who stood in front of that mirror had only been a Norwegian citizen for about three years.

It was Mum who told me, almost in passing. We were sitting, one afternoon, at the kitchen table in the large white house in Langesund where I grew up. Mum in the chair nearest the sink, I in Dad's old place opposite her. Mum with her flame-red hair and a body that bristles with activity, even when she's at rest. The same as she ever was, just older. When I think of my childhood, my memory of Mum is as a bodily presence behind me, her scent and warmth enveloping me. Dad is always elsewhere in the room. Either coming toward me or moving away.

Mum and I have always talked a lot about my childhood; since starting my search for Dad's story, I'd grown increasingly demanding. I wanted to know every little detail, everything she remembered and didn't remember.

"I don't think you were Norwegian when you were born," she said one day, as we sat at the kitchen table.

I looked at her questioningly.

"No, something in the rules back then, meant that children were given their father's nationality. I don't remember exactly ..."

I was determined to find out more. On the Norwegian Immigration Department website I found a link labeled: *Are you a Norwegian citizen?* I clicked on it and answered the requisite questions. *When were you born?* I ticked the box for those born between January 1, 1951, and January 1, 1979. *Were your parents Norwegian citizens when you were born?* My mother was Norwegian, my father was foreign. *Were your parents married when you were born?* Yes.

The answer that flashed up on the screen after my completing the final question came as no real surprise, I was prepared for it. Nevertheless my scalp crept from the nape of my neck to my forehead, as I read the words:

No. You are not a Norwegian citizen.

I stared at the screen in disbelief. Wasn't I Norwegian? There had to be a mistake. This website was meant for immigrants and asylum seekers, not for someone like me. A phone call to the Immigration Department clarified matters. A kind woman explained that before a change in the law in 1979, children with a Norwegian mother and foreign father automatically received their father's citizenship, unless the mother registered the child as Norwegian with the local authorities. Since Mum hadn't done this, my brothers and I did not become Norwegian citizens until Dad received his Norwegian passport. I was born on April 30, 1966. Dad got his passport on June 16, 1971. Whatever he was in the interim, precisely five years and forty-seven days, I was the same.

A Norwegian with a British Protected Person's Pass, which had in all likelihood expired. Not quite Norwegian, not quite British, but a bit of both. Stateless, if not in practice, then in principle.

That holiday in Wales was my first trip abroad. A dream that lives on in the home movies of my childhood that I found in Mum's house. Like Dad, she has kept everything: school books, sketch books filled with drawings and stories, photographs, letters, articles she wrote for the *Telemark Arbeiderblad*, Grandpa's diaries, diagrams of the family tree, home movies, audio tapes and cassettes on which Grandpa interviewed Great Grandma, and I interviewed Grandma. It's all there, in the bureau, in the blue chest in the living room and in the bedroom cupboards upstairs.

We continually document our lives. Over and over again my family tells its story. I'm not sure any of us really knows why.

The home movies were housed in black tins with yellow lids, each of them three minutes long. My brother had them all digitized recently. The images are flickering before me right now across my screen. Dad, Mum, my brothers, Dad's father, who'd been staying with us in Norway for a few months and was going back to the States. My guitar-strumming Uncle *J.* who was living in London. He and Dad, with their big hair, flared trousers and dark glasses. Me, running up to the camera and making faces. Full of mischief, never still. A red double-decker bus driving past in the background. We're in London, some time in the seventies.

It occurs to me how well we fit in; an Indian family in this world city. Being the only Norwegian, Mum is the foreigner here. The scene switches to a country road. Dad's dark blue '54 Mercedes-Benz W 180, with its star glinting on the front bonnet, driving through a Welsh

landscape of stone walls, pastureland, wheat fields, shades of green and yellow, divided by woodland and hedges. Damp mist rolling gently down the hillsides.

Suddenly everything goes white, red letters tumble down the screen. A new clip. High mountains, snow covered peeks, log barns and round pole fences. One of the films must have ended up in the wrong order when they were digitized. The camera moves slowly across a Norwegian landscape. And there comes Grandma, sledding down a bank of snow, wearing nothing but short ski pants and a chunky '70s bra. Laughing like a little girl. Then Grandpa appears, a canvas rucksack on his back and wearing shorts that reveal a pair of very pale, but sturdy walking legs. Summer in Telemark. In the next clip we are suddenly back in the green valleys of Wales with my Indian-Anglo-Scandi family. It is strange how both landscapes seem equally familiar and exotic to me. Presumably I inherited my love of Britain from Mum and from the countless episodes of *Emmerdale Farm* I watched, and the Agatha Christie books on our shelves, not to mention the HP sauce on our table. But equally, or perhaps more, I could sense back then that this was Dad's world. Particularly since everyone spoke his language here. And it was always Dad who, together with Uncle J., knew the way. He seemed to belong here, to feel at home.

And so, in a sense, did I.

I was who I was. And yet not. I was eight years old and stood in front of a mirror in a house in Wales. The year was 1974. I was in the process of discovering myself, but did not yet suspect that I was far more than any mirror could capture. In the chest in Mum's house, I also found the letters Dad sent when he was living in England, his letters to Mum and to the family in Nairobi. Only when I read these now, do I realize that his encounter with Britain sixteen years earlier must have had much in common with my experience in front of the mirror.

The question is: what did he see in his mirror? Did he find himself or lose himself in this country? Where he both did, and did not, belong.

I LOOK AT THE PHOTOGRAPH OF DAD on the ship, with his new Indian and European friends. *In the mood*. Was he equally light-hearted just two weeks later, when Dover's white cliffs appeared on the horizon? Or did he stand alone at the bow of the ship looking uneasy?

Whatever he felt, millions of emigrants had experienced the same thing before him; refugees, fortune hunters, the poor and the optimistic. They had all left the world they knew behind them, and spent weeks and months on the open sea. They too had been greeted by screaming seagulls, embraced by breakwaters, and then when the ship's whistle had blown, the powerful propellers had been set in reverse and the boarding bridges lowered, they set foot on a new shore. From here the story of each emigrant parted ways. Those who streamed to America sought a new life with opportunities that the old Europe could not offer. Not so, the illegitimate sons of the British Empire. Unlike those bound for America they were not heading for a new and promising country. They were like irksome boarding school boys, conceived outside marriage, disowned by their parents, sent home because their school had gone bankrupt. Now they came knocking on the door of the home that had never been theirs, and they were not altogether welcome.

In Britain, any colonial subject was in principle a citizen. From 1948 onward, these rights were extended to those from independent Commonwealth countries. That millions of people from around the world could now immigrate to Britain if they chose did not seem to awaken any immediate concern. For decades Britain had been proud of its empire, but no one had dreamed it would follow them home. But this was about to happen. As early as 1948 a former German cruise boat, *Windrush*, brought 492 West Indians from Jamaica to London. Others soon followed; Indians, Pakistanis and Africans.

These immigrants were coming to a country that had barely recovered from the bombings of WWII. There were high levels of poverty and homelessness. The inevitable happened in the summer of 1958 in the district of St. Ann's in Nottingham, when there were clashes between West Indian immigrants and the local young working class men – among them the Teddy Boys. Unrest spread rapidly, and during the late summer carloads of armed Teddy Boys were observed looking for trouble in London. Here, in the capital, a social pressure cooker was about to explode. In Notting Hill, where poor Londoners and immigrants lived cheek by jowl – West Indians, Gypsies, Irish – there were dark pubs, gambling dens, prostitution, poor street-lighting and a small core of racist activists who stood on the backs of lorries shouting the slogan of the time: "Keep Britain White!"

The country's leading fascist of the interwar years, Sir Oswald Mosley, found that he had an eager audience once more. Around the time of Dad's arrival in Britain, riots broke out in Notting Hill. For three days in the last week of August hundreds of white thugs rampaged through the city on the hunt for victims:

"Come on, let's get the blacks and the coppers!"

"Kill the niggers!"

A woman called out of a window to the passing mob:

"Go on, boys, get yourself some blacks!"

Hatred of immigrants was not isolated to the yobs on the streets. As Mosley was keen to point out, he was only voicing what many politicians thought. In 1954 the then-Conservative Prime Minister Winston Churchill asked: "Are we to saddle ourselves with color problems in U.K.?" The following year a cabinet member, Harold

Macmillan, noted that the "P.M. thinks Keep England White [is] a good slogan."

But Labor politicians had also started to worry about the levels of immigration from former colonies. In the late '50s a tightening of the immigration laws was expected, leading initially to a rush of those wanting to beat the deadline. 1959 saw the arrival of approximately 3,000 Indians and Pakistanis, and two years later the figure reached 48,000. This increase fueled further tensions between the British-born population and new arrivals. Rumors were coming out of Kenya about the cruel Mau Mau warriors and the white settlers' fight against them. Considering that Britain a few years earlier had spearheaded Europe's fight against Nazism, it's striking how racial hatred and the feeling of white supremacy came to the surface in the 1950s, both at home and in the colonies which were under pressure from the movements for independence.

This was the witch's cauldron into which my nineteen-year-old father now stepped. Alone. Outside the bell jar for the first time. He was used to living in a country steeped with racial division, but in Nairobi everyone had known their place. Not so in London.

He must have assumed he'd meet other people like himself. That he'd find friends among other lonely young men from Colonies. But what would be the value of friendships based only on loneliness and homesickness? In East Africa he would never have formed a relationship with an Indian Hindu or Muslim, far less an African or an Arab. Should this change now?

According to the dominant postcolonial narrative, the meeting between these young men and the U.K., and especially the metropolis of London, represented a return. The Indian, Willie Chandran, in V.S. Naipaul's novel *Half a Life* (2001) imagines a "wonderland of splendor and glitter" but is disappointed as soon as he comes off the boat, followed by a sense of shame at his own naivety. The East African Indian, Salim, in *A Bend in the River* (1979) by the same author, feels bitterness about his own ignorance of the world. Life in Africa had been easy, but he had in reality lived in a jail. He was trained to accept how "civilization" functioned and to appreciate its developments in science, philosophy, and law. But that was all: "It never occurs to us that we might contribute to it ourselves." In London therefore, Salim has only one strategy: to avoid appearing stupid, to hide his ignorance and hope for the best. Things were certainly simpler for the white South African J.M. Coetzee. When he arrives in London in his autobiographical novel *Youth* (2002), the question he asks himself first is what does he need to do to become an Englishman? And next, which class will he identify with in Britain: the middle class or the working class?

For Dad there was no question of becoming an Englishman, far less choosing a class. Like all dark-skinned immigrants he stood outside British society. No doubt he belonged somewhere between Coetzee and Naipaul's Salim, although his skin color inescapably placed him closest to the latter. Unlike Salim, however, Dad hadn't come from some little backwater in Africa. He had grown up in the bustling cities of East Africa. He was not Muslim or Hindi. He was Catholic. And he came from a family where education and self-advancement meant everything.

But even if he had ambitions, they must have been limited, just as they were in Salim. Dad was Goan. He came from a family of bureaucrats. He was raised to carry out orders, not to give them. The U.K. must have been less of a culture shock for him than for many others; nonetheless it was perhaps harder, since he felt so distanced to the other colonial subjects, and simultaneously so close to a European culture that would need to let him in anyway. He was, in the words of the Indian scholar Homi Bhabha, "almost the same, but not quite." Or, as Naipaul described it, living "a half-and-half existence"; colored colonial subjects who focused all their ambitions on the colonial motherland, while knowing deep down that they were second rank and would never be anything more. Half-people who lived a half-life.

However, the biggest difference between Dad and the fictional

Salim in Naipaul's novel was that my father didn't have an author to put his feelings into words. Dad wasn't an intellectual, and possessed no real political awareness. Had he been different, he could have sought out London's more bohemian circles, as described by Naipaul, where immigrants and liberal whites (yes, they existed) hung out together. He could have embraced sexual freedom, thrown off the yoke of tradition, and sought the company of British girls as rootless as himself (they too existed). Or he could have found his way to the little clique of young Goan students who had formed the Goa League two years earlier to fight for a free and independent Goa, in close alliance with the Indians, who had already succeeded in their struggle for independence. Together with these young activists he could have stood up against European colonialism, whether it be Portuguese or British; he could have rebelled against the system of racial discrimination he had lived under all his life.

He did none of these things. When Dad walked off the boat in London in the late summer of 1958, he was not gripped by "colonial rage." Instead he politely greeted the British Council representative who was waiting for him at Tilbury. Together they went to the station and took the train to Kingston upon Thames, which was then a small, quiet, leafy town, not yet swallowed up by London. The representative had brought an overcoat for the new arrival, predicting, quite rightly, that he wouldn't be adequately dressed for the weather. Like others coming from Asia and Africa, Dad's impressions of this new country were inseparably linked to the weather; the fog and the constantly shifting light, the twilight hours of dawn and dusk, the colors in the sky. But more than anything the cold that came with the autumn, particularly when it bit your ears. He'd never *felt* his ears before, not like this, frozen, painful. Somebody had told him that he mustn't touch them when they were cold, or they'd fall off.

In Kingston on Thames, the British Council man showed him the way to a tall, narrow brick house, the home of a friendly British family with lots of children, whose loft room would be his new home.

The house was close to his future place of study, the Engineering Department of Kingston Technical College.

He was at a safe distance here from Notting Hill. He must have heard about the race riots in the city, and doubtless he attracted the odd suspicious glance. But on the whole he seems to have enjoyed a pretty good life as student. His ingrained centuries-old suspicion of other groups, including Muslims and Hindus, must have evaporated pretty quickly. In the few photographs I have from his first year in Kingston, he can be seen sitting alongside Arabs and Persians; curls clipped short, black horn-rimmed glasses and a carefully groomed beard. It seems, after all, that the fear of feeling lost and alone was more unifying than fear of others was divisive. In the international college environment he entered a new bell jar, safe from the harsher realities beyond its walls. He began to frequent the International Club in Kingston upon Thames, and to save his grant and the small amounts he received from home, he made Goan curries and served them to his fellow students in his lodgings for a small payment.

He continued to enjoy a sheltered life for a while more, until this bell jar would eventually be shattered too. It was then that the rage came.

WHILE DAD SAT LATE INTO THE NIGHT battling with mathematics, chemistry and electronics, someone else was using her nights to dream. Marit Walle hailed from exotic Nordic climes, and nothing could have predicted that she and Dad would ever cross paths. She had grown up among dark, heavy spruce trees, on the distant Telemark coast. Here, in a place with no name, sometime during the interwar years, her parents had cleared the forest. They had pulled roots out of the ground with their bare hands, built a house, a chicken coop and pig stalls, and planted fruit trees and laid potatoes. And behind the little hill in the middle of their land, Grandpa had found a spot for his beehives. Finally, they had named their little farmstead *Lyngheim*, "Heather Home," after the purple heather that grew in such abundance there.

My grandparents were modest people. They were teetotalers and members of the local prayer house. Fiercely independent smallholders, who turned their hand to various other work to pay for anything they couldn't grow or make themselves. They belonged to that section of society that was essentially outside any class system, but were also determined to better themselves. Grandpa, in particular, lived and breathed for art and literature. Since his youth he had carved wooden figures. And in the evenings he wrote serials for the local papers; stories set in the 18th and 19th century Norwegian countryside that were later published as novels. He'd built all the bookshelves in the living room himself, carving them with motifs from Norwegian folktales. Books by Mikkjel Fønhus and Jacob Breda Bull, filled with depictions of Norwegian rural life, lined the shelves, and on the wall hung a small, pencil sketch by the national romantic artist I.C. Dahl.

As their four children grew bigger, Grandpa extended the house, first with one room, then another. As the house expanded in all directions, its clean functionalist lines were soon lost in quirky angles and varying floor heights. Today, years after Grandma and Grandpa have died, the house stands like a mausoleum to the life they lived, and to the world that was once theirs. A world that spanned just a few square kilometers between three houses – the old family farmstead, Great Grandma's modest house, and Mum's childhood home in Lyngheim – yet it was big enough to sustain a vast array of lives, of births and burials. A world big enough to contain rivers of tears, of prayer-house coffee, of sweat from bodies digging the potato fields, a symphony of rocking chairs and creaky oarlocks, hymn singing from a thousand throats, to contain books, art and dreams. But only just big enough to hold Grandpa's artistic ambitions and was certainly too small for Mum.

I think it was the silence that got to her. The silence and heavy presence of the spruce trees and mountains behind the house. Some of us are born restless, some of us will always seek a way out. Mum's first escape was through the books she found in the small library, kept by the local grocery store owner, Sigrid, in the hallway of her apartment. Here Mum discovered Steinbeck, Hemingway and Remarque; she devoured novels about the English upper classes and all of P.G. Wodehouse's books. And when she had exhausted Sigrid's collection, she took out books about art and architecture from the Telemark Agricultural Library that were delivered on the Valle bus every week.

Aged only fourteen, she moved out into her own little studio flat in Langesund to attend the high school, followed by six months in at the boarding school for domestic science in Seljord, where girls were taught cooking, nutrition, childcare and traditional crafts. Her second escape.

Her third escape began with a letter that landed in her mailbox one day in July 1960, a month or so before her nineteenth birthday. The letter came from S. Nielsen, who was writing on behalf of a certain Mrs. Gerda Trimble, director of *Continental Help*, an au pair agency in London. Frøken Nielsen was writing to inform my mother that she'd been offered a job with a family in Esher, not far from Kingston upon Thames, and close to where three of her girlfriends had also gotten jobs. Her responsibilities would include housework and looking after Mr. and Mrs. Wyllie's two children. Frøken Nielsen informed her that she'd have one whole day and one evening free every week, and went on to report that Mrs. Trimble was sure Mum would thoroughly enjoy working for the Wyllies, as they seemed to be such a happy, Christian family.

Esher is 1055.9 kilometers precisely, as the crow flies from Grandpa's house at Lyngheim. Apart from the sailors and emigrants in the family, nobody, and certainly no women, had ever traveled so far from Norway. Mum had only been away for a few weeks when she began teaching her parents about international affairs.

"England is a world nation, you know," she writes to her father on October 11, 1960, "where all sorts of people live together. And the clubs I go to are for foreigners only. We often joke that all we miss here in England are some English people."

The word that made Grandpa pause must have been "club." Nobody went to clubs in Bamble; they went to the prayer house if they had a meeting or if a traveling pastor was passing through. But Mum, it seemed, went to a *club*.

On their evenings off, my nineteen-year old Mum and her best friend Gunhild backcomb their hair and put on their red lipstick. Then they take the bus to Kingston upon Thames and walk the short distance to the International Club held on the first floor of The Swan, a pub near Old Brick Station on the west bank of the River Thames. This is where they gather, the young Scandinavian au pairs, and the equally young students who have flocked to British colleges from across the globe. Up the narrow staircase they go, past the strange man with a bowl of two-shilling bits, past the clothes pegs piled high with coats, and straight into the ladies' washrooms to check their makeup. Not that it's necessary, everyone looks beautiful in the glow of the candles perched on the windowsills in Chianti bottles, and the red crepe-paper-covered ceiling light. The crowd of young men, still longing for their mother's lap, hope instead to take comfort in the dove-white necks of the Norwegian girls, who now sit in a huddle, giggling and scanning the room, while being careful not to catch any of the men's hungry eyes, keeping appetites sharp.

It is Mum's free evening. She is with her friend Gunhild. The air is laden with cigarette smoke and perspiration, oozing through the pores of these pale and dark bodies alike, releasing an intoxicating fragrance of textiles, spices and perfume. In the corner a record player tries to break through the laughter and broken English. Somewhere in this crowd is Dad. He will meet Mum soon, but not quite yet.

When I ask my mother about her England-adventure today, she just smiles and shakes her head. "I didn't *really* think," she muses. "I just wanted to experience the world. And take in as much as I could."

Not only did she achieve just that, but she took this world back home with her; more of it than she had bargained for. Among the bundles of letters in the blue chest in Langesund, most are from Dad. Only a small handful are from her, and most of these are to her parents back in Lyngheim. The story they tell is of a Norwegian village girl conquering the entire world at a stroke. In the early 1960's scarcely anybody in Bamble had ever seen an Indian or African, except in the pages of Aschehoug's Encyclopedia. But Mum had. And she wasn't shy of sharing the details of her thrilling life in Kingston upon Thames: "There are Chinese people, lots of Negroes and Indians and people from Iraq, Iran, Africa and the Continent too," she writes in one letter home.

Nor was she content to write letters only for private consumption. Before leaving for London she had suggested to the local paper

Telemark Arbeiderblad that she write a travel letter for them. Not only did they accept and publish her first offering, but they commissioned more. These too are stored away safely in Mum's chest, a little pile of Saturday articles, neatly cut out, and dated in ballpoint pen. In them I get glimpses of Mum's sizzling nightlife upstairs in The Swan – as did her parents, the local pastor, the entire church council, and the congregation of the chapel where Grandpa was a Sunday School teacher. Here, for example, is a snippet of conversation taken from an article published on May 13, 1961, in which Mum describes an evening dance where she was being chatted up by an African, and Gunhild by an Indian:

"Where are you from?" I hear the turbaned man ask Gunhild. "Norway," she says. "And where do you come from?" asks the negro. "Norway," I answer.

— The Indian: Nice to meet you Gonil.
— The Negro: Nice to meet you, Mary.
— The Indian: You speak very good English.
— Gunhild: Oh ...
— The Indian: Your English is amazing.
— Me: Oh...
— The Indian: So when are you free?
— Gunhild: Sunday evening and Tuesday.
— The Negro: What's your phone number?
— Me: I don't remember.
— The Indian: You are very lovely Gonil. Can I see you again?
— Gunhild: No!!
— The Negro: You are very romantic, Mary. Can I see you again?
— Me: No!!

Mum accompanied these articles with illustrations; this one with a drawing of young people dancing and flirting, jet-black Africans, busty señoritas, bohemians smoking; in short, a perfect den of iniquity. But in her letters home she also records walking along the Thames and Regent Street. She wears low heels, she tells them, because the high heels in Marks & Spencer cost almost 30 kroner; a reasonable price, but more than she can afford. On the positive side, she tells them, it's free to go up and down the escalators in the big department stores. I can see her walking under the giant illuminated Bovril and Coca Cola advertisements where Regent Street opens onto Piccadilly Circus, buzzing with traffic and people, with life and noise. And what was Grandpa's clock in Lyngheim, compared to Big Ben? Did she breathe more easily here, where there were no dark spruce trees, other than the one that stood in Trafalgar Square at Christmas, sent from Nordmarka forest to mark the friendship between Norway and Britain during the war. But doubtless she tolerated this tree; after all, wasn't she just a touch homesick? When the record players stopped and the young men weren't drowning out her thoughts, when she wasn't consumed by the city?

Not that she has much time during the day to be homesick or even to think. Most mornings she has to get up and make breakfast for the Wyllies and serve it to them in bed, before taking the oldest boy Bruce to school. After a day of cleaning she takes little Lilibeth with her to pick up Bruce from school. On their way home they walk under the birch trees, kick through the yellow autumn leaves, or collect the seeds of horse chestnuts in the park. Only in the evenings do her thoughts drift back home to Lyngheim. Have they dug up the potatoes yet? Have the water pipes frozen, and has Dad finished fixing up the bathroom? She hopes it will be done by the time she gets home; "just in case I come home with some squeaky-clean Englishman, HAHA, only joking, it's more likely to be a hottentot or somebody of that sort."

Mum continually goes out of her way to tease and goad her parents; punishing them for sins that are unclear to me, and to her perhaps.

"I simply followed my nose – and that is up-turned," she says when I ask her.

What does that mean?

Who knows? Mum was nineteen years old and wanted to have fun. To laugh herself silly with her girlfriends. To see the world, rather than just read about it in books. As a child she had filled sketchbooks with drawings and stories. Now she wanted to fill her senses instead. And, of course, her parents had to pay; for all the silence she'd suffered, for a childhood spent in the shadow of the spruces. And they took it all in good stride; Grandma because she was kind, Grandpa because he probably realized where his eldest daughter had gotten her dreams and sharp pen from. But one thing was certain, Mum was determined that her parents should know every little detail, not just the crazy things she did but the crazy things she might have done.

On the other hand, why shouldn't she prefer *hottentots* to Englishmen? One day, a Hindu by the name of Bob invites her on an unusual date to a farm-show in the heart of London. He tells her how he longs to milk a cow once again, to sit with his head against its warm belly. When they reach the first show stalls and hear the steady pumping sound of the milking machines, it is Mum who feels a rush of emotion. How many squeaky-clean Englishmen in this city have ever milked a cow? Mum has. And so too has her suitor, Hindu-Bob.

"He is the kindest, most steadfast Indian on earth," she tells her parents, before adding reassuringly, "he's terribly old, and I am NOT in love." Hindu-Bob had, on the other hand, threatened to get himself work in Norway.

"Whatever would Randi and Auntie Olga say? Sigrid's shop will be buzzing with gossip if Marit comes home with an Indian."

And her parents?

"Hand on heart, though, would you be cross? I mean, I hope you're not like those racists who look down on colored people? They do most certainly here in England, but I don't."

Nonetheless, Mum does her bit for Western civilization. One Sunday, Gunhild, Hildur and Mum persuade Bob to accompany them to the Norwegian Seaman's Church.

"I think he'll be a good protestant before I'm done with him," she writes, presumably in some sort of attempt to further reassure her parents. "I can't understand why he doesn't get baptized. He believes in God and says he prays to Him every night. But I tell him he can't go around being a Hindu all his life, so I must try to help him. In a way, I admire Catholicism, if only because they attend church every Sunday. At least, the other chap I have in Kingston does. It's part of their religion, and I think that's quite admirable."

Bob was clearly not the only man on Mum's radar. The *chap in Kingston* was the man who would become my father. But it's worth noting that this country prayer-house girl from Norway thought Catholicism almost as exotic as Hinduism. Although, to complicate matters, this particular Catholic, who looked every inch an Indian, insisted he was Goan, had been born and bred in East Africa, had a Portuguese name, and spoke perfect English. There must have been something both exotic and familiar about him; perhaps that was what gave him the edge over Hindu-Bob. Dad had successfully completed two years at Kingston Technical College now, and had just entered his third year and second from last year. He also frequented the International Club in Kingston, and it was there in the cramped room above The Swan that they first saw each other through the clouds of cigarette smoke.

Later they drink tea at Waterloo Station, on Platform 2, or perhaps 3. For Dad it's serious from the first moment. For Mum it's a game that gradually loses its attraction. Maybe the world is too big for her after all; she doesn't want to make a choice. As far as her parents are concerned, and probably to their despair, she is keeping her options very open:

"One day Hildur and I were asked out by two very handsome Indians with white turbans and beards, but we didn't accept. I can go out with lots of unusual chaps, but a pagan with plaits seems pretty way out."

What my grandparents didn't know, of course, was that it was more respectable to go out in the company of a man than alone. But what could they know about dating in 1960s Kingston upon Thames?

This couple who had sealed their love and future as they strolled back together one day in Bamble from the prayer house in the poverty-stricken 1930s? By December Mum's worried parents had read between the lines and realized that one of her suitors was gaining significance. They let their suspicions be known. But their globe-trotting daughter wasn't about to tolerate anyone poking about in her business.

"Can't I have even one secret in peace? There was I, pleased that I had at least *one* Indian that my mother and father wouldn't find out about, but what happens? Well, I hope you both take it 'like a man', I almost said. But you can rest in the knowledge that I shan't marry him. No, I intend to find a Norwegian artist with a beard and a house in Seljord, we shan't have any snuff-brown Indians in the family."

As one of Mum's three snuff-brown children, I ought perhaps to feel rather offended at this remark. Instead, my thoughts wander to the artist from Seljord, a big burly chap perhaps with a ginger beard: I picture him crossing the courtyard, followed by a kid with red curls and milky white skin. Not Ivo Bjarne, but plain, straight-forward, Bjarne. Plain Bjarne, the boy who could have been me if Mum's wishes had come to fruition. The boy I should have been. The people we should have been. An alternative reality emerges from between the lines of Mum's letter; the story of what did *not* happen. The bearded artist and I, little Bjarne, walk together toward the woodshed, where a solitary light bulb gives a warm glow that doesn't reach the corners. My artist father is going to chop some logs for my mother, and sets out the little wooden chopping block. He hands me the axe, handle first, and standing behind me, he gently wraps his big hands about mine, and helps me lift its weight and bring it down in a gentle curve. I feel the warmth of his breath, and his big beard at my neck. When we're done, he lifts me up in one arm and a pile of firewood in the other, and carries me inside to Mum for no other reason than he wants to.

I read these letters over and over again. I want to see beyond Mum's defiant laughter, to understand why she made the choice she did.

Why did she never find her Seljord artist? Why did she choose the unknown? The thing she'd *never* dreamed of? In an undated letter in the spring of 1961, she writes that she has decided to return to Norway that summer, when her job with the Wyllies is finished. And afterwards? Maybe she'll sail on the seven seas, roam the Mediterranean somewhere, before hitchhiking back to Norway.

All she knows is this: the instant she goes home, her adventure will be over. Mum belongs to the last generation of Norwegian women who were born to get married. She can't have known what freedom was before she'd made the bold decision to cross the sea between Lyngheim and London. And once there, she must soon have realized that this metropolis was nothing more than a gate to an even wider and exciting world of heathens and Catholics, hottentots and handsome Indian men. Was that it? Was Mum's choice to take Dad an attempt to compromise with her fate as a woman; to get married, and simultaneously carry a slice of her new found freedom back home with her?

If that was the case, it's a pity she didn't take a train up to the small industrial town of Burnley outside Manchester before going back home to Norway. For here, in a little house on the outskirts of town, lived someone to whom she could have gone for advice; the only woman in the world who knew exactly what it meant to import a Goan from the Figueiredo clan into Europe.

THERE ARE MANY ROADS INTO AFRICA. And the Africa you encounter depends on which is open to you – as the thousands of Indians who traveled west in the wake of colonialism found out. The boatloads of clerks and officials brought over to oil the machinery of imperialism on a continent to which neither they, nor their employers, belonged. Or the Goans, who were the most loyal and would always be servants to the colonial power, but who nonetheless occupied a more privileged place on the social ladder in Africa than they had in Goa, simply because they had so many people beneath them here; the black Africans, being the lowest in the imperial system.

Pam Cherry's Africa was different. She came from the land of the colonial rulers. But she did not feel like a part of the ruling class as she boarded a ship crossing the Atlantic in the late spring of 1960. Pam was twenty years old, a budding journalist and daughter of a paper mill manager from Burnley, Lancashire. Socially aware from an early age, she was involved in the local International Club, where she worked for the liberation of Nelson Mandela and the other ANC members who sat in South African jails. She certainly wasn't like any of the usual recruits for colonial service, who had no problem accepting that public toilets had separate areas for whites, Asians and blacks, the usual upper-class yobs sent overseas by their parents to improve their ways, or the bureaucrats, the military men and the businessmen, who were content to slip into the sleepy high-society life with its interminable gin slings. In short, Tanganyika was no place for Pam; a fact she should already have been alerted to at her job interview in London when she was asked, "How would you respond if an African asked you to dance?"

But Pam was desperate to escape her hometown, to get away from the rows of drab houses and acres of bleak farmland. For her the colonies represented a way out, nothing more, which was how she ended up working for the press in Dar es Salaam. She can hardly have imagined that her African adventure would last a mere eight months, nor that this adventure would follow her home in the person of Dad's brother L.

L. whose full name was Lionel, was Herman's second son and ten years older than Dad. It was Lionel who'd been sent, at the age of nine, to live with his aunt back in Saligão, who had then sent him to the international school run by the German nuns. When Pam met him in Dar es Salaam, he had been in East Africa for fourteen years, mostly alone. Tall and strikingly handsome, filling his carefully chosen suits perfectly, Lionel looked like an Indian film star. His porcelain-white smile was irresistible. What's more, he could dance, an invaluable talent in Goan circles.

He could have had anyone he wanted, and did.

They met just a week after Pam's arrival in Dar es Salaam. She'd already begun to regret this whole colonial enterprise; she despised the decadent lifestyle of the British ruling class and felt deeply uneasy at having to instruct servants in their duties. It was probably only natural she should be attracted to this decent young man. He took her to the Goan club as the only white woman. She adored it: the feeling of solidarity, the parties where young and old alike came together, the swing bands, the dancing, the women in their white dresses, the men in their white jackets, black trousers and bow ties, and the endless pots of curry and pilau, the stacks of chapati and enough cakes and sweets to start a diabetes epidemic. Herminia and Michael Joseph were clearly skeptical about this relationship, but they were nonetheless

married in January 1961 and soon afterwards traveled back together to her hometown of Burnley. Their haste was explained by Lionel himself in an interview in a local newspaper shortly after their arrival. Tanganyika was apparently, despite its beautiful beaches and swaying palms, not a good place for a romance between a white, British girl and a dark-skinned local.

"Beneath the surface," Lionel told the journalist, "it is a seething volcano of racial tension." The article's headline summed it up: "Tanganyika 'whites' frown on Burnley girl's marriage." Pam and Lionel, however, did nothing to hide their love, and Pam didn't wait to be dismissed from her job, instead she handed in her resignation before packing a suitcase and returning to Burnley. Just months later, Mum would leave London and *her* dark-skinned boyfriend – Lionel's little brother – to return alone to her home in Bamble, Norway.

Burnley and Bamble. Pam and Marit. Two Western women who wanted more. They were restless, thirsty for experience and knowledge. Mum would, just as Pam, become a journalist and feminist. They belonged to the generation of women born a little too early to share in the democratization of higher education, but late enough to demand more from life than their mothers. Born to marry, but not to stay in a marriage at any cost. The fact that their rebellion would start with their marrying these two patriarchal Catholics is of greater irony than we, their offspring, can even begin to fathom.

But these two women had not yet met each other. During the autumn and winter of 1960–61 Mum was busy living her new life, which, despite the interminable working days, must have seemed like a fiction, reminiscent of what she'd read in books or seen in films: a bohemian-style life, albeit in the most innocent form. Whenever possible, Mum, Xavier, Gunhild and their friend Rex would wander around Kingston upon Thames. "Bearded artists in raggedy clothes sit on the street corners, with their paintings spread out on the pavement. In the evenings we go to our bohemian club, dimly lit by candles in bottles."

When the money runs out, which is often, they meet in Xavier's bedsit to gather round the electric heater, drink coffee from big glasses because Xavier only has one cup, and slices of bread with a scraping of margarine; no luxuries, just the pure taste of freedom. Nonetheless, as the date for her return approaches, Mum mentions Norway in her letters increasingly often. Her relationship with the Wyllie family seems strained. She is sick of the kids and the housework. She longs for Norway, not so much for her childhood home Lyngheim as for Seljord, where she'd spent half a year at the boarding school. Writing to her father she declares that wearing a pair of dungarees and plimsoles, and sitting by the Seljord Lake with an old battered coffee pot on the campfire are twice as lovely as any silk dresses or parquet floors. "These are the kind of things," she says, "one longs for. An old grey fence in Øvre Bø, the snow on top of Skorve. The other things are all quite wonderful, but they're just the salt on the potatoes. And, by the way, I don't much care for salt on my potatoes."

She longed to be a bohemian; in London perhaps, but preferably in a side-road near Seljord Lake. Most importantly she wanted to be free.

That was how she felt at least, but not Dad. He'd had enough of a bohemian-style existence; of shirts with buttons falling off, leaky shoes, frayed trousers. For two and a half years he had lived in this foreign country, in the relative security of his student circle. Now he was coming to the end of his studies and could no longer ignore the big outside world. Should he leave Britain? Or stay? The raucous streets, the pubs, the parties with girls and boys from all over the world, with nobody to stop them, no fathers, no priests, no clear boundaries between enjoyment and sin: was there really a future for him here? Wasn't it time to return to the place he called home? And what about his girlfriend?

What worried him most was that his family didn't know about her. "Marita," as he calls her in his letters, was Dad's protestant secret, his little white lie. He had stepped outside his own circle, just as his big brother Lionel. Would his parents accept this relationship? They had to. Would Marit convert to Catholicism for his sake? She *had* to. And would she follow him wherever he ended up in the world? Did she love him enough to be true to him, especially with her imminent return to Norway? Filled with doubt, Dad cries himself to sleep at night.

And Mum? What does she do?

There is nothing to suggest that she is equally serious about their relationship. She may be with Xavier now, but Hindu-Bob is still hovering in the wings. He frequently proposes to her, she tells her parents in a letter in March 1961, adding that both Bob and Xavier may well visit her in Bamble – "then we can start the Help India Association!"

In May, she goes home. The night before her departure, Xavier and Rex go to the house where she's been working. She has asked Xavier to lend her a suitcase, but he can't bear to meet her face to face to say goodbye. Instead, he stays in the shadows, eyes filled with tears, watching as his friend hands over the suitcase. In the next few months they can only meet courtesy of the postman. Letter after letter arrives brimming with drunken tears, Dad's tears; it's as if he is documenting each torturous excess for her to see.

She must have wondered where all these tears came from, this violent passion. Had she known then how deep their source, she might have broken off contact there and then. As it was, the flood of saline fluid had its desired effect; it was Dad, not Bob, who received an invitation to Bamble. In the late evening of July 9, 1961, Dad got off the plane at Fornebu Airport. Mum met him and together they took the bus to the Students' Travel Office near Oslo's town center. They spent one night together in the capital before taking the train and then bus to Lyngheim. Mum had promised her parents that she wouldn't bring any Hottentots or Indians home. Instead, she brought a snuff-brown Goan, the likes of whom had never previously set foot in Bamble.

WHEN I THINK OF MY GRANDPARENTS in Lyngheim, I think of the birch trees in the courtyard, the little workshop with its window frames delicately carved with flowers, the wind in the tree tops, insects zig-zagging among the perennials. Every day Grandpa would sit on his stool in his workshop wearing his ankle-length leather apron, carving figures out of linden wood; timber that had been seasoned for two years in the shed, before being sawn into suitable lengths and roughly shaped with an axe, and then placed firmly in his lap to be carved into the charming figurines of gnarled old country folk, elks, bears, and trolls from folk tales. Most of Grandpa's adult life was spent here sitting in a shaft of daylight, a cup of coffee on his workbench and the radio playing quietly on the shelf.

What I liked best, when I visited Lyngheim as a child, was to sit beside him on my own little stool carving a troll figure or a relief into a plank of wood, carefully following his drawings. We could spend entire days like that. My little hands coming up in blisters, while his big fists dug his chisel into the wood as though it were butter. As the hours passed, the wood shavings would pile up around us until they covered the entire floor. And the aroma of coffee would mix with that of the fresh cut linden wood and timber-stain kept in the row of yellow Nesquik boxes lined up on the shelf. Then, when the clock struck four, the shavings were swept into a hatch in the floor, and we went inside to Grandma to have our supper.

Years later, as an adult, I inherited all Grandpa's singlets when he died. Each one had a rip in the front from when he'd forgotten to put on his leather apron and his chisel had slipped. He always lived dangerously, Grandpa, and, appropriately enough, he died of wounds suffered in a moped accident. I still miss him.

But on this summer's day in July 1961, Grandpa is as old as I am today. It is a Monday. He'll have taught at the Sunday School yesterday, and kept the rest of the Sabbath in the best way he knows: alone up in the hills, in the forest among the spruces. But today I imagine him sitting in his workshop, chisel in hand, and the beginnings of a wooden figure in his lap. I can hear Grandma rattling the cutlery through the open kitchen window. Two teenage girls and a little boy would usually be around, but it's the holidays so they may have gone swimming at Rakkestad Beach. 1961 is the year when the Norwegian Socialist People's Party is founded, when Norway ordains its first female pastor, when the Shah of Iran comes to the country, as does the new craze for the "twist," and a dark-skinned man with horn rimmed glasses and short-cut curls, who would be hopelessly lost now were it not for the girl who signals for the bus driver to stop outside her childhood home. Busman Nils is probably behind the wheel that day, as he always was in my childhood.

There are fewer than a hundred and fifty people from Asia and Africa in Norway at this time, mostly living in and around the capital, so I assume that Busman Nils and his passengers (if there were any on a Monday afternoon in July) watch Dad and Mum closely as they jump off the bus and stroll down the hill toward her childhood home. Grandpa lifts his gnarled hand to greet the newcomer. I don't know what was going through my grandparents' minds, but I do know Dad's reaction to his first Norwegian dinner. He laughs at the thick rice pudding sprinkled with cinnamon, followed by fish balls in a milky curry flavored sauce. Do they serve dessert before dinner in this country? Is *this* food? He isn't laughing later, however, when he tastes his own curry made from the seagull that bit on his hook when he tried to go fishing in the Langesund Fjord. Tough, tasting like cod liver oil, not a bit like his mother's delicious chicken curries. Or his own curries for that matter.

More than anything, he is struck by the silence; alien to anybody who has spent their entire life in the city. Scarcely a soul on the road, nothing but the whisper of the tall spruce trees.

In the middle of July, Dad got himself a summer job at Langesund Mechanical Workshop, rolling steel plates for the boats down at the shipyard. He was clearly over-qualified for the job, but grateful for whatever he could get. And he was made to feel welcome. Later he'd remember that first summer in his girlfriend's homeland as a happy time. But nothing suggests that he intended to live there forever.

"Remember," he told Mum emphatically. "I am not a European. I am not going to settle in Norway."

Dad had difficulty understanding Norwegians and their strange ways. So little passion. So indifferent to their faith. Nonetheless, he had tremendous respect for Grandpa, who was, in his eyes, everything a man should be. Practical and strong. No doubt he was surprised by Grandpa's free lifestyle; living with his family in a forest clearing, surviving on nothing but his woodcarvings and whatever the family managed to grow or collect from the chicken coop and beehives, as well as the occasional carpentry work. Didn't they need money in this country? Or neighbors and community? Stranger still, they didn't even seem to need each other. Where was the sense of family? The respect for a father's authority? Dad was astonished at Norwegian individualism. He couldn't understand why the whole family didn't contribute financially to the children's education, not least that of the daughters. In Nairobi it was taken for granted that the girls should have access to higher education. But that clearly wasn't the case here. And how could Marit's father be so acquiescent when it came to his daughter choosing a foreign suitor like him? Dad seemed almost angry: "No father," he said in a letter later, "would keep quiet, after all, you are his oldest daughter."

No. Dad wasn't at all convinced that he wanted to live among Norwegians. Nor that he could feel at home anywhere in the West.

Come mid-September, the long summer is over. Marit gets work as a proofreader with the *Telemark Arbeiderblad* and moves to Skien, while Xavier goes to Fornebu airport with a glowing reference from Langesund Mechanical Workshop in his suitcase and a woodcarving of a deer under his arm. As he walks from the departure hall to the awaiting plane, tears well up in his eyes. He has one year left of his studies, and his future is unclear. He has no idea whether he will ever return to the country he is about to leave. But he knows he wants her, and for that reason he has spent the summer learning Norwegian. In his first letter to her on his arrival back in Kingston upon Thames, Dad demonstrates the results of his labors:

"Jeg elske dai."

His spelling was not impressive, but his meaning was clear: "I love you."

NOTHING DISAPPEARS, WE CARRY OUR BURDENS for all time. A medieval legend tells of a giant of a man named Christopher who wanted to serve the greatest of all kings. After a long search Christopher found a hermit who convinced him that Jesus Christ was the greatest king. But how best to serve him? The hermit thought that the best way for this giant to serve the Lord was by carrying travelers across a rough and dangerous river. Christopher did as the hermit suggested. One day a little boy appeared on the shore. Christopher lifted him onto his back and waded through the swelling waters, but the boy was so heavy that the giant almost sank beneath his weight. It was only after a terrible struggle that they reached the other side. A somewhat astonished Christopher asked how a little child could be so incredibly heavy; as heavy, it seemed, as the entire world.

"You have not only carried the weight of the world," the boy told him, "but also the weight of He who created it. I am Christ, your king, whom you serve with your work."

For a fallen Catholic such as myself, destined forever to fear what I have abandoned, this legend has an irresistible fascination. Since if Christ bears all our sins, then we in turn bear the accumulative weight of our sins as well as the savior who carries them for us. Dad was no giant, but like many people he managed to carry a great deal, many times his own weight. He carried his parents, as we all do. As a practicing Catholic he had to carry both the cross and the church; as an emigrant he bore the longing for those he had left behind and the weight of gratitude for the sacrifices made on his behalf (especially by his brother *I.* who had relinquished his travel grant and continued to send him money). In Europe, Dad had to carry his brown skin, a far heavier burden for him than it ever was for me. Not least, perhaps, he bore the burden of uncertainty. He had very little money when he returned to Kingston upon Thames and moved into new lodgings with Rex; the future was an unknown, and though Dad had tasted love, he had no idea if it would last.

In addition to all of this, two empires rested on Dad's young shoulders. At the dawn of the 1960s the colonial cauldron was about to boil over in East Africa. In January 1961, the British had been pressured into introducing democratic elections in Zanzibar. In January 1960 the state of emergency following the Mau Mau rebellion in Kenya had been withdrawn, and the following year the freedom leader Jomo Kenyatta was released from captivity, after which he began negotiations for independence on behalf of the Kenya African Union. Meanwhile Julius Nyerere and the Tanganyika African National Union were leading the fight for independence in Tanganyika. One by one, Dad's many homelands were threatened with annihilation. Britain had already lost the jewel in its crown, India. Now the colonies and protectorates in Africa were about to fall.

These developments must have been worrying enough for Dad and the family in Nairobi, as they were for anyone who had attached their fate to the U.K.. But another empire was teetering on edge too, a far older empire, an empire of even greater significance to the Figueiredo family, although Dad's knowledge of it was limited to stories and vague childhood memories.

Dad had only been to Goa once. Before WWII the family had been able to travel back to Saligão every fifth year in accordance with British permit rules, but the war had put an end to this, and thereafter these trips were sporadic. It wasn't until four years after the war that Grandfather and Grandmother took their children back to Saligão.

Dad never talked about this trip, so I have no idea what impact it had on him, but throughout his childhood and early adulthood he felt deeply certain of where he came from.

Goa inspired longing. Goa was a dream. A dream that came, it should be said, with a duty. Now that Portuguese rule was threatened and Goa's future stood in the balance, this sense of duty seems to have grown in Dad's consciousness. And not just in his. In a letter from his father at about this time, it is clear that he saw a future for his son in Goa too, and not just the West. There is no indication that Dad wanted to go there – but who was he to go against his father's wishes? He was the chosen one, the first of the siblings to be sent to be educated in the West. He was bettering himself on behalf of the whole family, to help those siblings who came after him, and to secure his parents' old age. He owed them everything, and never forgot it. But he also shared his parents' conviction that there was something in the village of Saligão that could not be found in Africa or anywhere else in the world; a deeper meaning, connection to the earth from which he hailed. The news that the Portuguese might wish to remove St. Francisco Xavier's corpse from India would have shocked and worried him.

"Saint Francis Xavier is my Godfather and my Protector. So Mama has asked me to pray to him, and he shall help me."

But however close Dad felt to Goa, this sense of belonging did not depend on his actually being there. This was what separated his own and his father's generation. For Dad it was sufficient that Goa remain a golden possibility, a place of pilgrimage or a last refuge. But from the moment India gained its independence, he and his father must both have seen that Portugal's days as a colonial power were numbered; both on the Indian subcontinent and elsewhere in the world.

For India's Prime Minister Jawaharlal Nehru it was not a question of *whether*, but of *when* the country would throw the last colonial power out of the country. From 1960, the tension between India and Portugal escalated with each passing month. In December the Portuguese dictator António de Oliveira Salazar spoke on television expressing his shock and disbelief at the Indian authorities' failure to recognize Portugal's historical rights in the country. Goa was not a colony, Salazar declared, it was a piece of Portuguese land on the Indian continent.

But time was running out for such imperialist rhetoric. Less than a year later, on November 13, 1961, Portugal was defeated by an overwhelming majority in the U.N. General Assembly; the only governments who supported the Portuguese claim were fascist Spain and the apartheid regime of South Africa. In reality Salazar stood alone, which did not prevent him from racking up his military presence in the Indian territories of Goa, Diu and Daman. Soldiers were sent from Mozambique, shots were fired, a Goan fisherman was killed at sea on the 25th of November. Barely two weeks later two villages were attacked, landmines were laid on the roads along the border, people began to flee their villages. New and more blatant threats from the Indian authorities followed.

In October of that year Dad receives a letter from his parents. They are deeply concerned about the situation. The looming prospect of an independent Kenya means they don't want him to return home. Instead, Grandfather tries to get him a grant to go to America after all. If this fails, Dad is afraid that his father will send him to Goa. He is of two minds about this. In a few months he'll have finished his education. Where will he go after that? Where *can* he go? Will he even have a passport, any national identity at all, when that time comes? It states in his passport that he is a British Protected Person of Zanzibar. That sounds secure, but will the British really protect him when it comes to it? When the cauldron boils over in Zanzibar, in Tanganyika, in Kenya and Uganda? When the empire collapses entirely and the flocks of local servants, Indian bureaucrats, railway workers, pensioners, widows, the hundreds of thousands of Asians who have lived under the wings of the colonial empire in East Africa, the subjects and stooges of the imperial power, begin to move, will the

U.K. take care of them? India is a possible alternative for the Indians, but not for a Goan. And Goa may soon disappear too.

The empires are toppling, everything is in turmoil. But Dad knows of a world that's far away from racial hatred and poverty. A place where people live as though nothing really happens. Norway. Bamble. Lyngheim. Is this where his future lies, after all? But now Marit is living alone and free in the little town of Skien. Is she faithful? Will she wait? He can't be sure. He doesn't think so. He is falling apart. He is sinking.

"Marita, help me I am crying again. Everything is quiet and it is about 11:00 p.m. I cannot do anything except go through this torture myself!"

She does not answer. Weeks pass and still no reply. Surely her silence ought to have been answer enough. Nevertheless he writes to his parents telling them all about his Norwegian girlfriend. He knows that his parents will assume he has marriage in mind. It's a big step, a leap of faith, but his mind is made up, regardless of Marit's silence. He *will* marry her. But in marrying him, he says in yet another unanswered letter, she will also be marrying his parents, the Holy Catholic Church and the entire Goan community. And yes, it is possible that he will end up in Goa after all.

"That is the only place I can say I have some feelings for," he tells her. "It is a poor country, yes, we have a few fields in Goa which belong to us. We also have a small house. I am not fooling when I say this. I have within me a certain sense of responsibility so far as helping these poor people is concerned. If you think you will find it difficult for you to live in this backward country which is my motherland, please tell me now."

What should she say? Was she ready to exchange the forests of Bamble for a life in Saligão, in a house with floors made of flattened cow dung? Did she see herself as a dutiful wife, mother to a flock of well-scrubbed kids, good little Catholics? Was she willing to exchange the potato fields of Lyngheim for a patch of land in a Goan village to grow coconut trees and vegetables, sending the servants to sell them at market along with baskets made of woven palm leaves? Unlikely. But why doesn't she write and tell him? Instead, she lets him suffer. A young Norwegian girl, just twenty years old, with her own lodgings, independent and free. She doesn't want to make choices. But hope that is not snuffed out lives on, and Dad isn't about to give up. He sends her letter after letter. Will she give up her religion for him, marry him, rescue him?

"What to do, darling? Please come to England and love me and keep me warm."

In November Dad has received a verdict from his parents. "They do not say no to our friendship," he tells Marit, "but they have asked me to be careful and to pray to God." Herminia has enclosed the picture of a saint to whom he can pray and a lengthy list of questions. "She wants to know about your date of birth, year, month, and about your family and studies. How long our friendship has been going on?" She has also asked him about Mum's parents, and what they think about Dad.

Then comes the sting in the tail: "She also says that she hopes you are not a cheap girl – please forgive her for this, she does not understand."

"Can I write back," he asks Marit, "and say that you respect the Catholic Church and will become a Catholic if we marry?"

But he is plagued with doubt. Not only does he understand his mother's skepticism about European girls; he shares it. "I feel that all white girls are not faithful and good to their lovers. You get such girls all over Europe, but at home in my community such things are never heard of."

And he is also worried about what her family really thinks of him. "Do not be afraid to tell me if your parents do not like the idea of you marrying a colored boy."

One morning a few weeks previously he skips class and wanders around the streets of Kingston, troubled and unhappy; he writes to Mum afterwards detailing his every move, which is how I can now follow his steps along the road, into the train station and back into town. His thoughts that day emerge from the yellow letter paper and blue ink, in the tracks left by his pen, tracks that reflect the weight of his hand, and leave impressions of his mind on the page. What is a letter but thought and emotion solidified, an analogue imprint of living vibrations, like the grooves on an LP, or the lines in a face? Few sources provide truer access into the past than a letter. Not because it is impossible to lie in a letter, we can always lie (perhaps Dad exaggerated his melancholy to arouse her sympathy?). But unlike a diary our letters are addressed to another, to someone who knows things about both you and the world to which you both belong. You can lie, but not without limitation, the presence of the other person forces you to follow certain rules, and for the historian this is enough: where two people from the past agree on a set of rules, a door opens onto history.

It is a little past ten in the morning, a cold and foggy day. Dad has probably sent Mum another letter of proposal, but receives no answer. In the evening he goes to the Granada Cinema in Clarence Street to chase away his gloomy thoughts. The film being shown is *A Taste of Honey* (1961). It proves cold comfort to a young Indian man in love with a European girl. "The picture was about a girl whose mother was a prostitute somewhere in Manchester," he tells Marit. "And this girl was spoilt and got a child from a negro boy, and it was pitiful because she was afraid the child would be black."

The film that Dad sees that evening is based on the gritty social drama written by the young, working class Shelagh Delaney. Watching it now, as I do on YouTube, I can see why he would find it such disturbing stuff, although he has completely misjudged the character of Jo, the main character, who far from being "spoilt" has been abandoned at the tender age of seventeen by an alcoholic mother, who is herself trapped by grinding poverty. Jo finds solace with a black sailor, Jimmy. But when he has gone back to sea, she discovers she is pregnant. Rescue comes in the shape of Geoff, a gay design student, who promises to take care of her and the child.

> Geoff: You need someone to love you while you
> look for someone to love.

This unlikely couple move in together, two outcasts, each lonely and lost in their different ways. *A Taste of Honey* is a story about rootless youth, played out against a grey, rain-sodden working class district, in a northern industrial city in Britain. In one scene we see Jo and Geoff balancing on a rotten raft in the middle of a canal choked with rubbish, the dark silhouette of a factory looming in the background, and a gang of street kids singing and playing at the water's edge.

> Jo: Can you smell that canal? Filthy. And all
> those dirty children.
> Geoff: Well, you can't help [but] get dirty
> around here.

It is as they stand there, rocking on the dirty water, that Jo feels the child kick for the first time. Suddenly her face breaks into a smile, there's an unexpected glimpse of hope in her eyes, which is soon extinguished. How does one nurture a child in a dirty and evil world? Jo has never experienced anything but hopelessness. She doesn't want to be a mother, doesn't want to be...

Rita Tushingham gives an amazing debut performance, the defiance in her face, the innocence and directness of her gaze. She somehow reminds me of Mum as I imagine her at this age. And it is this young girl that my twenty-two year old father, wallowing in his own misery, condemns in the darkness of the cinema. And the worst is to come. Geoff and Jo are in a cemetery one rainy day when Geoff gives Jo a doll so she can practice handling the baby. She looks at the white baby-doll in horror:

> Jo: The color's wrong, the color's wrong!
> *She strikes its head against the flat gravestone,*
> *and throws it away from her.*
> Jo: I'll bash its brains out! I'LL KILL IT!

Did Dad fully absorb this scene through his tears? Did he really, really see the film, or did he just see immorality and ugliness: an intensified, distorted and magnified reflection of his own situation? The black sailor certainly resembles him. Paul Danquah was a British-born actor, son of a Ghanaian freedom fighter, of a similar light complexion so that Dad might well have seen himself in him. And why not, Danquah plays the only sympathetic character in the film aside from Jo. Jimmy

is handsome and exotic, but also kind and thoughtful. When he disappears from view, sitting on deck peeling potatoes, any hope for a better future disappears for Jo. If he had known she was pregnant, I feel sure he would have come back to her and to the child. He'd have come to take care of them, to take care of all of us. But Jimmy disappears over the horizon, leaving a young Goan with horn rimmed spectacles and short-cropped curls sitting there somewhere in time, in 1961, somewhere in the world, in a cinema in a London suburb, with tears rolling down his face, shattered by the thought of the shame it would incur to conceive a half-caste child like me.

It is perhaps here, in this cinema, where my own story begins in a desperate thought:

Xavier: I feel so very afraid of our future. What society are we going to be in? Life is sure a struggle. Everything I see around me seems so dirty and horrible. Every picture I see is full of crime and dirty sex, which the whole audience seems to enjoy very much except me. Sometimes I try so hard, so very hard to be like some of the European boys. Never show their feelings, always in a good happy mood even if deep down in them they know they are sinning and like it – yes accept it as normal living. But I know I can't never [sic] make it.

The next evening, on Saturday October 14, 1961, Rex invites Dad to a party. An all-nighter with girls and alcohol. Dad spends most of the evening sitting in a chair, his only interest is the bottle in his hand, he finds the girls who talk to him repulsive. He drinks on, falls asleep in his chair and doesn't wake up until it's light outside. Sunday is filled with gloomy thoughts; the only solution is to go into town and hide in the cinema again.

The film being shown that day is *East of Eden*. Dad has already seen it previously and leaves the cinema before the lights come up. I follow him down the street. Initially, I think he'll wander around aimlessly again, but he is soon heading for the Kenya Coffee House, which from previous letters I understand to be one his regular haunts. He is so young; to my middle-aged eyes he's still just a child. There's a vulnerability about his body, the bowed head, the contours of his shoulder blades as he pulls his coat around him to keep the autumn chill at bay. I know he is crying as he walks. I am so close I can put my hand on his arm. Was I ever this close to him in reality? Or do I see him clearer through the words he wrote in his youth, when he was someone else and I did not exist? I don't know. But I can't let go of him now. He reaches the cafe, orders a coffee, lights a cigarette, and enveloped in a cloud of smoke leans over the table and writes the letter I now hold in my hand. He momentarily disappears from me. I run my fingers over the even, blue handwriting, and when I find him again he is walking up the stairs to his lodgings, and into his bedroom, where he takes his rosary from the bedside table, falls to his knees and locks himself in prayer.

I WATCH HIM FROM ABOVE NOW, like a dot moving between rows of rooftops, along London's arteries, among streams of black cabs and red buses, weaving between the millions of other human dots. Over everything is the steady buzz of the city, which only the loudest and sharpest horns penetrate. Or are they screams? I think I know what triggered his despair; his disgust for the glitzy stores, the raucous pubs and cinemas with darkened auditoriums, the faceless people, parks with empty benches, all those lithe girls' bodies: it was the fear of freedom. He was a city person, but things had never been so chaotic in Dar es Salaam and Nairobi. He had grown up in a tight-knit Goan community, within a cathedral with closed doors. Among his own people he was counted a rebel, but it's easy to be a rebel in a cathedral, where every little sound is echoed a thousand times. In London's open and cacophonous landscape, he could scream as loud as he wanted, but nobody would hear him. There were no parents or teachers or nuns here to give him reprimanding looks, nobody to cuff his ears, nobody to keep him in check.

If he wanted to hear God's voice here, he had to do as the protestants and listen to his inner voice, whose only resonance chamber was his own heart.

Here, in London, his heart had to suffice as his cathedral.

One day before the close of 1961, one of his sisters arrived at his door. Working for an American oil company in Nairobi, she had been offered the same permit to travel to Goa as Grandfather but had negotiated a trip to Europe instead, to visit her brothers. Dad took her to a hotel, then out to a restaurant. His sister quickly noticed a change in her brother. He wasn't the young man she remembered; he was moody and aggressive. Bitter.

"You don't know what I'm going through," he told her repeatedly.

"What *are* you going through?" she asked.

She didn't get an answer. It was as though he had no words to describe what was going on inside him. Or, more likely, he was keeping it to himself. After all, he had nothing to say that his sister could report back to their parents.

He'd have to carry the burden of freedom alone.

But couldn't he have relished this freedom? Wasn't he relieved to have escaped the stifling love of his family? As I remember Dad, he was made for freedom; he certainly seemed to snatch at it greedily in my childhood. But by then he was an adult, strong and able to carry his sins with ease. After reading his letters and traveling with him through his life, I find to my own surprise that my perspective on him has changed. I can see now how heavy freedom once was for him. I can understand why he clung to his rosary, as though to a rope that would prevent the weight of his sins dragging him down. Protestants think that Catholics take their sins lightly, that they merely enter the confessional box, kneel in the dark, confess their sins to God's clerk at the counter, and then receive a bill of forgiveness in exchange; rather like going to the bank to pay their invoices, except that the fee consists of reciting a given number of Our Fathers or Hail Marys.

In reality, the Catholic's relationship to sin is anything but easy. Nothing illustrates this better than Evelyn Waugh's novel *Brideshead Revisited* (1945), which tells the story of the fall of the Catholic aristocratic Marchmain family and the British aristocracy at large in the 20th century. In one scene the daughter of the house, Julia, is overcome by guilt at having lived in sin with her lover, the novel's narrator, Charles Ryder. He witnesses her unexpected outburst:

"Living in sin; not just doing wrong, as I did when I went to America; doing wrong, knowing it's wrong, stopping doing it, forgetting. That's not what they mean."

Julia sobs in Charles' lap as they sit on a bench by the fountain on the Marchmain estate. But what weighs heaviest on her is not the sinful act itself, for which one can beg forgiveness and then return to work as the Protestant, pragmatic and ever efficient. The Protestant God is pure spirit, accessible to humankind through His grace and mercy. The Catholic God has a far greater physical presence in the world, immanent in the church building, the holy Eucharist, the portraits of saints, and not least in the pictorial representations of Jesus' pierced and bleeding body. For Julia it is not so much the wrong she has committed, as the *corporeal* and *constant* image of a suffering Christ that keeps her sins alive.

It is perhaps when she talks about her mother that we see Julia's most vivid description of the power of Christ's ever-present image: "nailed hand and foot; hanging over the bed in the night-nursery; hanging year after year in the dark little study at Farm Street with the shining oilcloth; hanging in the dark church where only the old charwoman raises the dust and one candle burns; hanging at noon, high among the crowds and the soldiers; no comfort except a sponge of vinegar and the kind words of a thief; hanging forever."

I too remember the Christ of my childhood that hung above the altar in the Church of Our Lady in Porsgrunn; an ever-bleeding, ever-suffering carved wooden figure of faded-gold, lit from below to accentuate the ribs and taut sinews of his emaciated body. His face hidden in shadow. The image of a Christ dying eternally, in perfect grace, with the weight of my sins on his broken body; my sins, Dad's sins, and Julia's sins, the guilt of all mankind.

I was ten when I first took confession. We sat in a row waiting our turn outside the confessional box. One of the nuns walked back and forth casting a controlling eye over us. Quite superfluous, since we were all deep in thought. As my turn approached, I began to panic. Not because of the severity of the sins I was about to confess to the priest hidden in there behind the grill. On the contrary, the problem was that I couldn't think of anything impressive to tell him – after all, what sins did I have to report? I was ten years old, what could I confess? That I'd quarreled with my brother? Forgotten to do my homework?

And for this I'd be deserving of the sacrament of forgiveness, this solemn ritual, the priest's valuable time? It simply wasn't good enough. And I knew it. *I had nothing.*

Later my sins would be of more respectable magnitude, but by then I had abandoned the church long ago. Now I have to carry them alone. If that makes any difference, since if Christ bears our sins, we in turn bear Him. But now Dad is alone in his Kingston lodgings, rosary in hand, unsure whether he can manage the weight of his sins, or whether the inner voice in the chamber of his heart is strong enough to rise above the clamor of the traffic and people outside. He knows he has just three alternatives. The first is to return home to East Africa after his graduation that spring, and find a nice Catholic girl with a ponytail and a prayer book tucked under her arm. The second, if he even contemplates it seriously, is to return to his actual homeland – Goa. The third is to try to create a pure Catholic space in this godless West. In other words, he must start his own family and found a new cathedral for this wandering Goan clan.

If he chooses the latter, he must not only win the heart of this Norwegian woman, but decide whether she passes for a God-fearing girl and whether it is right and proper to have a child (or indeed three) with her:

"I pray every time that you will someday become a Catholic, and sit by my side in church with a nice white dress and a black veil and holding a rosary in your hand and praying to Our Blessed Virgin Mary for purity and love." Dad's big brother, Lionel, had shown this was possible; Pam had recently converted. If Marit was prepared to do the same, there was hope that he too could find happiness in the West. If not, he'd have to gamble on returning to Goa or to one of his homelands in East Africa. In which case, he was dependent on just one thing: that his homelands were still there.

By the end of 1961 two of these options were already ruled out. On the 9th of December 1961, Tanganyika tears itself free from British supremacy and declares itself an independent state, with freedom-activist Julius Nyerere as Prime Minister. Nine days later, after months of provocation and diplomatic horse-trading with Portugal, Nehru lets his troops stream across the borders of Goa and the other Portuguese enclaves, Diu and Daman. Early on the morning of December 18th the first warships appear on the coast, and soon leaflets are raining down from the skies, exhorting people to stay calm while the Indians neutralize "the foreigners"; that is, the Portuguese. The invasion is, the leaflets explain, a cause for celebration for Goans, Hindus and Christians alike: "Be calm and brave. Rejoice in your freedom, and help to safeguard it."

Within twenty-four hours the Indians had surrounded Panjim. They'd moved in so quickly that the Portuguese barely had time to collect themselves, despite this invasion being far from unexpected. Portugal's only warship, the frigate *Afonso de Albuquerque*, was destroyed and grounded in Mormugão Harbor, bridges were blown up and sporadic shooting could be heard. But only sixteen Portuguese soldiers and sailors and twenty-two Indian soldiers lost their lives that day. Before 11:00 a.m. on December 19, the Portuguese surrendered. Portuguese India was history, after having existed for over four hundred and fifty years. Now the Indian flag was raised in every house, Hindus and Catholics celebrated together in the streets, while a bronze bust of Salazar was dragged through Panjim to be hung from a tree with a noose around its neck.

That, at least, is how Indian historians have presented the liberation of Goa from Portugal. But what did the Catholic Goans think? Those who shared their faith and names with their European masters? What did Grandfather think? And Dad?

In the week between Christmas and New Year, Dad traveled to Burnley to visit Pam and Lionel, and their new baby. He spent five or six days there with his older brother, who it seemed to him had achieved everything he hoped for himself. If I am to believe Dad's reports to Mum, there was some excitement in Burnley that Christmas.

The recent events in Goa had turned the brothers' world upside down, as they had for their siblings and parents back in Nairobi. Years later my Goan aunts and uncles – indeed, just about any Catholic Goan I meet – describe India's intervention in Goa as an invasion. They look upon the Indians as foreigners, and while they don't exactly embrace the Portuguese, they generally wax lyrical about Portuguese Goa and the good old days when nobody locked their doors at night. If the Portuguese were a dominant ruling class, they were also guarantors for the Goan culture and way of life.

This is the perception now. But it was not always so. Nehru had intimated earlier that he would give the Goans some form of "special status." Many Catholic Goans therefore saw India's intervention as one of liberation. And it was this sense of freedom and future that explained the mood in the little house in Burnley that winter. Even Pam, the anti-imperialist factory manager's daughter, was fired up at the thought of the Goan people's new-won freedom.

On New Year's Eve the three of them sit together and celebrate the end of the old and the beginning of the new. I watch the evening unfold in Dad's lengthy letter to Mum, written just fifteen minutes into the new year, after his brother and sister-in-law have gone to bed. He seems a little tipsy, but whatever the case he is bursting with a unique sense of joy, at being here, in this place, at this time. His description of the evening he has just spent with Lionel and Pam is so vivid, so alive, that I can see myself pulling out a fourth chair and joining them around the table. I am the invisible guest who is allowed to listen and watch, but not speak. In the background is the Christmas tree that Pam has decorated. Lionel is thirty-two years old, Dad will be twenty-two in ten days; he is filled with an enthusiasm I've never witnessed before, as indeed they all are. Together they have made a decision:

They have decided to sell all their possessions and settle in the two brothers' ancient homeland. Like modern-day settlers they will help build the new Goa.

Freedom. Future.

In silence I observe them, sitting there looking at each other, exhausted but happy, united in their pact, intoxicated more by the solemnity of the moment than the wine. The idea of leaving everything behind and living a simple life in the country their grandfather had once left in pursuit of work in another century. For Pam perhaps this represents an adventure, the chance to rid herself of the burden of colonialism and repay a little of the white man's debt. A big decision, made by young people around a table late at night. Fire in their eyes; the same fire, I imagine, that lit up the eyes of hundreds of thousands of young Jews across the world when news about the creation of the State of Israel was announced in May 1948. The joy of having a goal, a homeland to fight for, a future to shape.

It is a night for great thoughts and words. But the more Pam and the two brothers talk, the more uneasy their invisible guest becomes. Steady guys! It's not as though the plans you make now won't affect me! Am I to be born in Goa? Am I to grow up among palm trees and cashew trees? Will German nuns warm my backside, as they once did Uncle Lionel's? Later, when the dream of building a new Goa is laid to rest (which of course it soon is), Dad suggests yet more future homes in his letters to Marit. How about Manchester? Would she come to live with him there? This industrial city offers good opportunities for a graduate engineer. Or Nairobi, will she follow him there? But what about me? And my brothers? Are we to be little Mancunians in school blazers and caps? Or am I to be my Goan Grandmother's little helper, grinding spices for her in a Nairobi kitchen; a squeaky-clean

Catholic boy whose only prospects are as a clerk and father of eight? I'm sitting opposite Dad now; I am a middle aged man of forty-seven, he is twenty-two, bursting with that feeling I recognize so well, but lost long ago; the feeling that anything is possible. But it isn't! *Stick to the plan, Dad!* Any deviation now, however small, will have dramatic consequences on my life. I am itching to interject, but, of course, I have no right. All I can do is to watch and learn. Besides, on reflection I realize that if any of the various scenarios Dad conjured up in those last months in England had happened, my parents' love-making would probably have fallen at another time, on another day, and it would not have been me, but one of my millions of competitors in the race to the egg, who would have had to endure life under those foreign skies.

Some days into the New Year Dad gets a letter from his father in Nairobi. As Dad suspected, his father also saw a possible future for him in the newly liberated Goa. He suggests that with his training as an engineer, Dad should open a workshop in Saligão where he can repair cars and radios, while Marit can train as a nurse and midwife. Grandfather clearly has little understanding of an engineer's work, nor indeed, of the likelihood of a Norwegian girl taking instructions from a prospective Goan father-in-law. But Grandfather had dedicated most of his adult life to planning his children's future, and he wasn't about to stop now.

It's hard, however, to imagine that Mum could be seduced by the idea of this Goan adventure, which Dad clearly intended when he wrote to her on New Year's Eve. Mum was from Bamble. She had no imperialist past to atone for, nor any strong desire to rebuild a rural community on the Indian west coast. To be honest, she didn't even seem overly interested in building up the rather forlorn Goan she'd met in Kingston upon Thames. But his letters confirm that she *still* hadn't managed to crush his hopes entirely. So, in the spring of 1962, as he entered his final term as a student in London, he had one potential wife and a vision of building a new life in his ancient homeland. The only problem was that his prospective bride and his homeland were on separate continents.

In reality, Goa was a lost dream. There were never any serious talks of a "special status" for Goa, and it wasn't long before the Catholic Goans realized this. When Graham Greene visited the region the following Christmas, he noticed a bitterness and resignation among the Catholic residents. The invasion had disturbed the centuries-old balance between the local Catholic and Hindu Goans. And Hindus were pouring in from elsewhere; foreign Indians with no understanding of the Goan lifestyle. Greene observed the old men shaking their heads wistfully over the increased price of wine, when and if they were lucky enough to get hold of any alcohol at all. On his way to midnight mass at Bom Gesù in Velha Goa, Greene walked among the ruins and the deserted memorials of Goa's golden years. There was barely anybody around, apart from a pig that crossed the square, now an outcast, demoted from delicacy to unclean meat under the new Hindu rules.

Greene must have passed Se Cathedral, one of the best-preserved churches in Velha Goa. Here, in a chapel, were the remains of the wooden cross that had miraculously grown on a hillside. And in a chapel of the nearby Santa Monica Convent was the Christ figure that had opened its eyes on a February day in 1636 and started to cry, while fresh blood poured from its wounds. On the holiest night of the Catholic calendar, in the Bom Gesù Basilica itself, only about a dozen or so people turned up for mass. In a side chapel, Dad's patron saint, St. Francisco Xavier, lay slowly shrinking. Attending this mass Greene felt as though he was witnessing one of the very last Christian ceremonies: the traditions in this ancient town had always been so strong, it was hard to imagine how Christianity could survive when this place was reclaimed by the jungle.

Later, when Greene came down for breakfast at his hotel, he was met by a despondent waiter:

"'No bacon' he said sadly, when I tried to order an English breakfast.

'No one asks for bacon now.'"

Times had changed. Goa was now part of India, the Hindus were the masters. History's machinery had been set in motion once again; people were about to wake up from the Portuguese sleep, the hundred-year slumber when the cathedrals and palaces had been quietly decaying, while the Catholic residents mumbled on about Goa's past greatness. The era of industry, traffic, hotels, hippies and waves of tourists had arrived. St. Francisco Xavier's body would remain more or less intact, but the time for miracles was over in Goa.

DAD'S LIFE AS A SETTLER IN A NEW GOA is over before it begins. In just a few months' time he will be sitting for his final exams. Throughout the spring he applies for jobs in Norway, but receives only rejections. He is worried that if he returns to Nairobi, he'll be forced to stay and work for the authorities because of a small state grant he said he'd received. In the beginning of April he passes his finals. He can now officially call himself a Mechanical Engineer, the first in his family with a higher education. With his newly won self-confidence he overrides any concerns and goes to Nairobi after all.

But first he wants to visit his girlfriend in Norway. On Saturday April 14 the plane takes off that will carry him to Oslo. He has scraped just enough money together for the ticket, but is broke; unable even to contribute to a gift for his teachers before his departure. He can no longer expect any money from home. Michael Joseph has retired in May of the previous year, and the whole family is now living on his pension and the salaries of the oldest children.

He stays for less than a fortnight in Lyngheim and Skien, where Marit now is living. There'd been an ever-increasing gap between her letters, and their meeting is fraught. She is cold and dismissive. Nothing seems to be as it was last summer. But he needs her now more than ever. By the second day of his stay he has a meltdown, his emotions run wild. He is still in an appalling state when he seeks reconciliation two weeks later in his first letter after his departure: "I cried and asked you to love me and not to leave me... I would have gone mad if you did anything... I'm sorry... I would kill you if you did anything to me... I have tears in my eyes."

Did he even notice the growing violence in his own words? How could he? After all, they came with a flood of tears, and Dad was a man seduced by his own tears; the more he cried, the more justified he felt. I love you. I am so sorry. I'll kill you. The destruction starts from within, then works its way imperceptibly to the surface.

But Mum still fails to see this, and once again his tears hit target. She gives in, and by the time he is on the final lap of his journey to Nairobi, he is more certain than ever before, almost euphoric: He will have her, no matter where in the world they end up.

Dad was on his way to the only place he could still call home. But it was a long way to Nairobi. With the family so short of money, the route had to be arranged accordingly. First he crossed the channel to Dover, then took a train to Luxembourg. Here, on May 6 he boarded a cargo plane to take him to Juba, Sudan. Dad's brother had booked this flight with an Indian who organized "chartered tours" from Europe to Africa. Dad and a handful of other passengers sat huddled between wooden crates in a dark cargo hold. Nobody talked; the roar of the powerful engine drowned everything out. The little party was largely made up of Indians, apart from two women wine merchants from Luxembourg who, tempted by the cheap offer, now sat huddled in a corner, terrified. In the middle of the night the plane stopped off in Benghazi, Libya. The hatch opened and fresh air flowed in from the darkness outside. Some makeshift steps were lowered, and while the plane was reloaded and refueled, the passengers spent the night in the middle of nowhere, in a hotel with no electricity. The next morning they flew to Juba, where they were transferred onto a bus that would take them to Kenya. Dad's route home says much about the vagaries of life for a Goan. Four years earlier, a young man of nineteen had gotten off a boat in London with empty hands but a scholarship in his back pocket; now a twenty-three year-old graduate engineer was being flown back as freight to a colonial Africa in a state of total collapse.

Due to the flooding of the Nile they were forced to drive via the Congo and Uganda. While Sudan had gained its independence in the wake of Egypt's taking of the Suez Canal in 1956, chaos now reigned in the Congo after the Belgians had suddenly pulled out four years later, with no proper transition plan in place. The group was stopped at the border by armed guards, and since it was unsafe to travel along Congolese roads at night, they were ordered to spend the night at the border post. Several of the guards spoke Swahili, and Dad sat with them through the night. Was he afraid? I think so. The guards had taken their cigarettes, and drank and danced around the fire with loaded guns. In the morning the group drove on until they reached Uganda. The British were still in control here, as they were in Kenya.

For now, at least.

On May 11, 1962, Dad set foot on Kenyan soil for first time in four years. For a few brief summer months he found a certain calm in the family home in Muthaiga Road. Having grown unaccustomed to the heat, he felt lazy, but tried to make himself useful. In the mornings he'd repair things around the house and do a bit of gardening, in the afternoons he'd cook European specialties like goulash and french fries for the family. In the evenings he'd sit on the terrace, smoking and listening to the crickets singing in the dark, or go to one of the Goan clubs, where his friends treated him to drinks, and the girls flirted. He was twenty-three years old and back in the colony.

Things were much as they'd ever been, although a new obsession had gripped the family: Norway. While the children of the house brushed up on important Norwegian phrases like "Yay mor paw doo" (I need the toilet) and "du are en flink sex bomb" (you're a smart sex bomb), Herminia lay in bed browsing through a book about Telemark that Dad had given her. Grandmother was ill with diabetes and a heart condition, but she did not forget her maternal duties. From her bed she cross-examined her son about his girlfriend. "Has she got blue eyes?" And, importantly, "Is she a nice girl?" She had asked this in her letters, but now she had the chance to read the answer in his eyes. Finally Dad got what he wanted: her blessing and his parents' permission to marry this Norwegian girl.

The only thing missing now was the bride's acceptance.

Dad writes to Mum again. Won't she come and stay with him in Africa for a couple of years *before* they go back to England? His joy at being at home, of being on his own territory, in control of his life once more, had overshadowed any other plans. He wasn't wholly serious about his promise of returning to England. Goa was forgotten; Nairobi was everything to him now.

But did he really believe this either? The African dream wasn't for him. The days of empire were numbered, and he already had one foot in the West; he had no real choice but to go back to England and get work while he could. The problem was that the British government had recently made it more difficult than ever. The Commonwealth Immigration Act which came into force in July 1962, finally made the expected tightening of British immigration policy a reality. In short, a quota system was introduced that, without the removal of citizenship, made the entitlement of colonial subjects to enter Britain dependent on their qualifications and job prospects.

The Figueiredo family was near the back of the line. While Goans born in the British colony of Kenya were in principle given the right to British citizenship, Dad's family were Portuguese citizens born in a British protectorate. He had traveled to Kingston upon Thames on a British Protected Person of Zanzibar pass. This didn't necessarily preclude him becoming a full British citizen, but the new law undoubtedly made it more difficult. If he had taken the chance and traveled back to the U.K., dug his heels in and worked hard for a few years, he would probably have been granted permanent leave to stay. But everything suggests that the new immigration act took the wind out of his sails. Besides, did he *really* want to return to that godless country?

He puts increasing pressure on Mum to come to Nairobi and join him in his familiar world. But, he reminds her again, that if she chooses to do so, she *must* convert and improve her English. And, of course, they *must* get married as quickly as possible. And above all, she *must* distance herself from the immoral life of the West. "Girls go out there and get spoiled," he says, "and I'm so glad I met you before you got spoiled. You haven't got a strong will, Marit, you are mixing with the wrong crowd of people." But from now on, rest assured, he will take care of her: "The minute I get a job here then you're coming down here and I'm going to marry you, and take you to church 6–7 times a week."

But what about Marit? What did she think?

I ask Mum one evening as we sit at the kitchen table in Langesund. We talk into the late hours about my childhood and her life before me. Not for the first time, but things have moved on now. I have learned more, and not from her, but from the young woman she was back then; the woman I was never meant to know. The shame of having read my parents' love letters, the intimate revelations, about her, and about him, feels like an assault on my innocence.

But there is no way back from knowledge, all I can do now is ask more questions. Did she never read these letters? Didn't she understand their content?

"I read them as I read a novel," she answers. "It was unreal."

Then she starts to tell me things that seem to have little place in this story: about a childhood in a postwar Norway; a little boring perhaps, but safe. About growing up in a family where people were free to do whatever they wanted, and be whoever they wanted. But also of how a young woman in early 1960s could have an indefinable sense of having no way back, that marriage lay ahead of her as certainly as confirmation had just a few years earlier.

"Were you in love?"

"He was so intense. So fierce. It was as though I didn't have the option of rejecting him. I felt as though I belonged to him."

"Did you talk to anyone about it?"

"No, nobody. We didn't talk back then. Not with friends. Not with our parents."

He overwhelmed her, but the pressure also came from within. She *had* to care for this poor lost lover in Nairobi. That was just how it was. To the extent she even thought about him. What she wanted most was to go out with her friends, to laugh and have fun.

"I didn't really think," she says repeatedly.

I don't know what to believe. Mum may have been young and thoughtless, but she wasn't weak, as Dad supposed. She was strong, much stronger than him. It just took time for her to realize it; much longer, it proved, than he could give her.

So, what was your answer, Mum?

She can't, for a moment, have thought that a better life awaited them in Kenya. And I don't know what possesses her when she finally picks up her pen and writes to suggest that she come to Nairobi and get a job as a maid. Precisely how misjudged this suggestion is, she learns with full force on opening Dad's next letter: "I would beat you up if you came to my home and take up a job as a servant (that's what it really is) for an English family. You don't know what trouble there is between the different races."

He now does a complete U-turn: she must *not* come over under any circumstance. She is too naive. Too white. She will put them both in danger: "I believe," he tells her, "some of the young ex-Mau Mau negroes in Kenya have a secret society and they plan to have so and so with white women. They tell the Indians that if they want to stay in Kenya, they must give them their daughters."

His tone is increasingly violent. He does not see it himself, nor does she. For her the words are just words; he is so distant from her everyday reality. The changes that are happening in him in these months are happening on another continent, in another world – *his* world, which is slowly sinking as he seeks an escape. I have underlined the most brutal words in Dad's letters, and she ought to have done the same. But the letters that dropped so regularly into her mailbox in Skien, the desperate, pleading, threatening words, didn't really sink in, or perhaps she simply didn't want them to sink in.

But Dad was right about one thing. Mum did not know the global value of her skin color. It was perfectly acceptable for her as a white girl to work in Britain as an au pair, but such a thing would be totally unthinkable to anyone in Kenya. To Herminia, for example, who was very excited about meeting Mum but worried what a European girl would think about her family and their modest home. The only whites she knew of lived in smart houses, with an entourage of servants. But Dad knew better. He had visited Mum's childhood home and seen the outside toilet at her grandparents' house in Lyngheim. He came from a metropolitan family, urbanites who were, in many ways, more sophisticated than the average inhabitants of Bamble:

"We have our own bands, we dance everything, cha cha cha, twist, waltz, etc. We are ahead of the Norwegians in this respect."

A pertinent observation. Social events in Bamble were generally limited to prayer meetings or held over afternoon coffee. Or occasionally over an Asina orangeade, as in this picture taken at

one of Grandma's girls' evenings. It's difficult to imagine Herminia among these ladies, with their Asina and pea soup, or whatever it is in those bowls. I don't remember much about these women, Grandma's friends, except their powerful arms, hands that might grab my curls without warning and ruffle them vigorously, hands that lifted me into their bosomy laps, where I'd sit limp with embarrassment and lack of oxygen, until they were done rocking me. They were filled with life, laughter and gossip. Dad probably never understood the social mores of these people, let alone their culture, literature, or earthy sense of humor. Had he witnessed my grandfather, the respectable Sunday School teacher, shock his fellow residents dressed as the Phantom (blue swimming trunks over his all-in-one thermals) on Independence Day some years before, he might have thought differently. But still – the cha-cha-cha? Hardly. Dad knew this. He had tasted rural life in Norway, and drawn his own conclusions. He had seen Marit working in the fields and carrying water from the well. They had running water in Nairobi, and a car and servants. In Dad's head this devalued Mum's skin color. He and Mum were, he decided, more or less the same socially:

"We come from the same class, darling."

Early in July 1962, Dad kisses his parents goodbye. Choking back tears, his father gives him his solemn blessing: "God bless you, my son, and may He bless you two and your life together."

Previously Dad had taken the train to the coast, and gone from there by ship through the Suez Canal and over the Mediterranean. This time he takes a plane from Nairobi to London. The world is shrinking. He is returning to the land of boundless freedom, but this time he avoids staying in the city of sin, and travels directly to Burnley. He intends to stay here with Lionel and his sister-in-law, while he looks for a job in Manchester and waits for Marit's arrival.

This may have seemed like a good plan, but it proves to be anything but. While he is living in his brother's house, everything is fine. He makes dinner, teaches a heavily pregnant Pam how to make spaghetti bolognese, takes his little nephew for walks. He fools around and tells jokes as usual. But Pam notices that he's troubled. Whenever they talk he always returns to the subject of Nairobi and his life there. Beyond these four walls he is seeing another world, one he was barely aware of when he lived in Kingston on Thames. Back then he was a student at an international college in a relatively privileged area. Now he is encountering the gritty side of the U.K.. Where he previously mixed with fellow students and teachers, he now meets laborers who hang around in public houses, kids on the streets, wives who peek out from behind their net curtains, bedsit landladies, and the foremen of Manchester's factories and industrial companies. And what he discovers here, or to be more precise *experiences*, more strongly than in all his twenty-three years, is this:

He is brown.

His skin, his body, is brown. Not dark-brown like a Tamil, but definitely brown, an indeterminate Asian shade. And sprouting from the pores of his brown skin are jet-black wiry hairs, which curl over his chest, his legs, arms and back. His eyes almost black.

He is not alone. In the 1950s and '60s thousands of Caribbeans, Indians and Pakistanis flocked to industrial cities in the Midlands and North of England. Many headed for the old factory workers' areas in Manchester, but some found their way to smaller towns, like Burnley. Dad is far from impressed by these fellow immigrants, the Indians and Pakistanis he sees around him here. "They are a big disgrace, they don't dress properly, and have funny characters," he writes. "Honestly, Marit, I just cannot understand them. They are poor, illiterate people."

What did he have in common with them? Nothing. While the Asian immigrants who had arrived prior to 1960 were often educated and able to speak English, increasing numbers were now coming from rural India and Pakistan, old fashioned, uneducated, and with poor language skills. Dad was a Christian, a Brahmin, well educated and smartly dressed – as long as he had the money to buy clothes. But these people? Simple folk with strange habits. He wasn't like them, he was their superior. The problem was that only he knew this. In other people's eyes he was just brown. A darkie. A paki, like any other paki. It was only when he opened his mouth to speak that the British might understand there was more to him. But his skin had already spoken for him, before he even opened his mouth, and he read only rejection in their faces.

He was brown. Manchester was grey, the people, the streets, the houses were grey, even the moon looked a dirty yellow as it peered through the smog. The soot issuing from the factory chimneys and coal-fires coated the windowsills and was churned up by passing cars, it got under your fingernails, and turned your hair grey within the space of a day. Kids without socks or stockings, sheets of newspaper up at the windows just as in the film that had made him cry a year earlier, *A Taste of Honey*. This film was now his reality, with one difference – unlike Jimmy, he couldn't slip away on a ship. He had to stay and to try to make a life for himself in this grey world, while he waited for his white girlfriend.

For a while he lived on National Assistance payments, and starting mid-August, he traveled into Manchester regularly to look for a job and accommodation. This was easier said than done. In the early sixties the U.K. labor market was struggling to absorb the stream of job seekers from the colonies. Unemployment lines grew, employment offices were full of men with furrowed brows and trousers that sagged at the knees. For immigrants who had come in the hope of improving themselves, the employment office was a bleak introduction to the reality of Britain: "a kind of place where hate and disgust and avarice and malice and sympathy and sorrow and pity all mix up," wrote the West Indian author Sam Selvon in *Lonely Londoners*, "a place where everyone is your enemy and your friend."

Dad trudges through Manchester's streets, going from door to door, day after day, with no luck. He saw it in the eyes of the landladies as they opened their doors with security chains stretched taut, and in the faces of the foremen; he watched the thought form in their minds as he reached out his hand – No work for pakis. No room for darkies.

"I cannot fight this lonesome world on my own," he complains to Marit in Norway. "Please understand what I have to face because I am a foreigner in this land, besides being a colored foreigner. And who are not very much liked in this area. Marit, come soon, borrow money, do anything, but come soon!"

Come to me. Rescue me. Carry me. I can see in Dad's letters how his confidence is dwindling that autumn. Practically all of them concern race, and there's a painful clarity in his descriptions of the changes happening inside him. "My mind is almost going mad," he says. "There is too much of a color-bar in this area, and I have developed a complex."

At other times he seems to test Mum's resolve: "Do you know, Marit, you may or at least we may have a few more troubles because I am a colored person. Does this worry you – ANSWER!" He wants her to come, but is worried that she'll be ashamed to be seen with him. Yet, this does not stop him dictating the terms to his female rescuer: "About being the boss, I have talked to you about it, you know my views – you either accept them or not." There is a total mismatch here: he is weak but wants to be strong, needs rescuing but wants to be in command. More than anything he just wants to go back to his old life in Nairobi.

"Oh, darling, we have to leave this horrible Western world."

Between his humiliating rounds of the city, Dad gets cheap meals and plays table tennis at the Manchester International Center. And here something remarkable, but inevitable, happens; he finds friends among people he'd never have mixed with before. Jamaicans, Africans, Pakistanis, Hindus and Muslims. He'd met people from all over the world in Kingston upon Thames, of course, but they were always students, privileged and from a similar social class. All these people have in common is that they cannot get past the white man's door.

One day a young Pakistani invites him back home to his dirty bedsit. Dad accepts, and from that day on he has a travel-companion with whom to share his cheerless wanderings. "We went to thousands of places looking for a job, but people look at us and see we are colored and say 'sorry, no job'. This is true, Marit. There are thousands of colored people without jobs. They couldn't care less whether you are an engineer or not. I am terribly depressed, and do not know what to do."

He is nervous and restless. He chain-smokes. Finally he can contain himself no longer:

"Last night when I came back I was so ANGRY, I could kill every Englishman in England, spit in their faces."

Then one evening Dad hears a story at the International Center. A man from Thailand tells him about an area called Moss Side. There are thousands of colored people living there, and some white girls go out with them quite openly. But this is rare, Dad explains to Mum, because "once an English girl is seen going out with a colored one, then no other white man will ever go out with her again." Lately, however, a number of the local girls are thumbing their noses at the rules and choosing to go out with colored boys in preference to white boys – "they say they want to produce a NEW RACE of people, the half-castes."

Perhaps it is the prospect of a new world in which dark boys and white girls might come together to create a new race which gives Dad the confidence he needs to keep on. That September he gets himself a job with an electronics firm; Harmsworth Townley & Co. Soon afterwards he finds lodgings in Cheetham Hill, another working class area that attracts immigrants. His new accommodation comprises a tiny bedsit, which he shares with a very large Scotsman who works in a bakery. Not that they often cross paths; when Dad gets home after a long working day, the Scotsman has left for the bakery where he works until dawn. In fact the only regular evidence of his roommate's existence is a dent in the empty neighboring bed when he dives into his own bed at night. They share the kitchen and toilet with their Yugoslav landlords. It's a cheerless existence; a sixty-hour working week, pitiful wages and dismal lodgings. But at least he has a job and a roof over his head. The only thing missing now is Marit.

AT THE END OF AUGUST 1962, Mum had received the application form from an employment agency, *May I Help You*. She fills in her answers on the dotted lines:

"Do you speak English?"

"Yes."

"Can you cook?"

"Yes."

"Can you sew and darn?"

"Yes."

"Do you like children?"

"No."

This last is at least an honest answer. Clearly life as an au pair with the Wyllies and their charming children was not an experience to be repeated. Her preference now is to be a *chambermaid/waitress*. She lists everything she has achieved in her twenty-one years: high school exams, a year working in a book shop, six months at the house-craft school, summer jobs as a home-help and carer in a nursing home, nine months as an au pair in England, currently employed by a newspaper manning the switchboard, proofreading and doing general office work.

For reasons unknown to me *May I Help You* does not sign her up and she fails to get any job offers. She will have to manage on her own. In mid-November she leaves Skien and her job with *Telemark Arbeiderblad*, she says goodbye to her severely tested parents and leaves for Manchester with neither a job or work permit.

She has finally gone to him. He needs her, and she has indeed come. She also believes, at this point, that he has returned to England just for her sake; any other reasons that might have contributed to his making the trip – the imminent collapse of Kenya, his search for a homeland – seem not to have occurred to her.

Whatever the case, the adventure is on again. But this time things are rather more serious. Gone are the security and the relatively carefree life she'd enjoyed as an au pair in Kingston upon Thames. Unemployed in Manchester she trudges from place to place asking for work, unable even to afford the bus fare. In the evenings she goes to basement cafés with round tables, candles, and wine bottles in straw baskets hanging from the ceiling; a touch of Paris. This is where the would-be bohemians hang out with their shabby clothes, beards, polo-necked sweaters, and world-weary eyes (yes, she's back writing travel letters for the *Telemark Arbeiderblad* – she needs some sort of income). Eventually, after a couple of weeks, she finds work as a live-in canteen assistant in a nursing home in Salford, just outside Manchester. It doesn't seem too bad. The hospital looks like an old castle with a tower and spiral staircase. She starts work at the crack of dawn and has to be back before 11 p.m. But on the positive side, she has a fair amount of free time, and gets eggs and bacon for breakfast every day. Xavier lives in Manchester town center, just a bus ride away.

I don't know how their reunion goes. Now that they are together again, the only extant letters are the few that Mum writes home. Her first from that Christmas, opening a window onto the past once more. She spends Christmas Eve at the Norwegian Seaman's Church in Liverpool. Xavier has no place in a protestant church and stays in his lodgings for the evening. But Mum is there, having been given special permission from the nursing home manager, with the understanding she gets back on time.

The Seaman's Church was a grand old Neo-Gothic building on the River Mersey. The harbor had once been filled with Norwegian tankers, but those days were coming to an end; now sailors sat alongside home-helps and au-pairs, all dreaming of Norwegian Christmas dinner and home baking. No doubt Mum did too, but she was about to embark on a life that promised more spice than her mother's ginger cookies or cardamom wafers contained. She had come to the young man who had, for months on end, sent her letters, pleading, begging, raging, crying out to her in pain.

But did she want to stay? Here she was, sitting in the Norwegian Seaman's Church, singing her favorite childhood hymns. Among her own people. It wasn't too late to change her mind. No bridges had been burned.

It is exceptionally cold that Christmas Eve, light snowflakes dance in the air. A few days earlier a cold front had gathered over Scandinavia, bringing freezing winds from Siberia across the British Isles and causing the coldest winter in memory. The Big Freeze. Mum's last winter in this country. When her train arrives in Manchester late that night, she stands outside in the station courtyard and feels the icy chill biting into her. The streets are deserted, there's not a cab in sight.

She looks at the clock. It's already past one o'clock. Whatever she does now, the manager of the nursing home will give her an earful in the morning. So she starts walking. In her thin shoes through empty streets. An hour later she is standing in front of Xavier's lodgings, he opens the door. It is Christmas Eve, she is freezing cold and has snowflakes in her hair. He closes the door behind her, wraps her in his arms, and takes her to bed to warm her.

I can't follow them in there. I have read Dad's letters, and know more about who he is now. I also know what will happen, what *must* happen, if this story is to take its course. Perhaps this is why I have such a burning need for something momentous to happen on this night, for the future to be conceived, for a moment of belief that when the cold is driven out and the warmth penetrates, all will be well. Outside, everything is quiet, Manchester's landladies are fast asleep under their quilts, the factory wheels are still down by the canal at

Trafford Park. Everything is calm, the British Empire grows neither bigger nor smaller tonight, nobody will be hired, nobody will be turned away because they are of the wrong color or wrong faith. It is Christmas 1962. There are still three and a half years until I'm born. I know nothing about this night beyond the bare facts in Mum's letters, her description of the trip from Liverpool, the late hour, the weather, the empty streets, the walk from the station to Dad's house. That is all. And yet, I feel certain. There must be a point in time, a moment of hope, in which all that follows has meaning. When *she* chooses. When *she* wants. And I choose this moment.

The next morning they take the bus to Burnley to celebrate Christmas with Lionel and Pam in the little house they've borrowed from Pam's parents. Mum is well wrapped up, scarf warmly tied under her chin. They drive through a December-grey Burnley, get off the bus and walk along rows of drab houses, and out of the city. Here rolling fields disappear into a veil of dawn mist. As they arrive the door is flung open. And for the first time Mum looks into face of the woman who has taken the choice she herself is about to take.

In the evening, Marit and Pam sit in front of the fireplace. They have a lot to discuss. I'm not sure that the same is true of the two brothers.

Of all the family Lionel was the one Dad most resembled. The two of them had been the rule breakers. They had been the first to leave East Africa, and Lionel had taken his role as Dad's surrogate-father and mentor very seriously. Friction between them had been inevitable, especially after Dad arrived in Burnley, unemployed and miserable. Nor had it eased matters when big brother Lionel appeared to have succeeded in creating the life Dad wanted so much for himself. Pam had given her husband two sons. Together they had created a new branch of the Figueiredo line in Europe.

But Dad felt sure of himself now. Marit had come back to him. Happiness was in the palm of his hand. He just had to close his fingers, and it would be his.

BACK IN LYNGHEIM, GRANDPA and Grandma spent an anxious winter. Their eldest daughter wanted to marry this Indian of hers, or whatever he was. She generally did whatever she'd set her mind on, but would this mean that they would lose her for good? Where would she settle?

Marit reassures them. She'll marry him, yes. But there's no way *she* will follow *him*. Her project that spring is to convince her boyfriend that there's nowhere in the world to compare with the coast of Telemark.

"He needs a home," she tells them in a letter bristling with confidence. "Yes, yes, we have lots of plans and we're coming home to Norway. It's the only place I can imagine living in."

But this does not preclude other plans; one being a possible trip to Goa with Xavier's parents, who are now thinking of returning to their village. And wouldn't it be amazing if her parents came too? "There are plenty of cargo ships that go from Norway to India," she advises them, "and you'd get to see most of the world on a trip like that."

But the fifty-year-old woodcarver and Sunday School teacher, Bjarne Walle, and his wife Hjørdis, who had lived their entire lives in Lyngheim and Bamble – apart from the odd shopping trip to Porsgrunn – had no intention of seeing the world, least of all from the deck of a cargo ship. They wanted their daughter home. Perhaps they found some comfort in her theory about why she and Xavier (who started to use his less exotic middle name, Hugo, in Norway) had a firm basis on which to create a happy life together:

"The reason Hugo and I, two such totally different people from opposite ends of the world, make such a good match," she told them, "is that he has no fatherland. He has no traditions, customs, art, music, poetry, etc., as I do. So he'll adopt all our Norwegian ways, something that many Englishmen, for example, would never do."

By Easter the man without a fatherland seems to have given up all resistance. His last months in Manchester have presumably cured him, once and for all, of any desire to turn himself into an Englishman. And Mum has made it clear to him that she, at least, is finished with the big wide world. And as the spring sap rises, so does her longing for home. One warm Sunday in late April her eyes well up at the thought of her family packing the beloved coffee pot and a picnic to spend a day on Rakkestad beach. She has fixed her return journey for some time in June. The plan is to bring Hugo with her. Both of them are ready to compromise: she to marry him, and he to go with her to Norway, on the understanding they manage to find him work. But she is clearly still processing what she is about to do:

"Yes, I am getting a strange sort of husband indeed. Hugo is: an Indian, a Portuguese citizen, British protected with a British passport, born in Africa – pfff... and he's going to get married to a Norwegian. I just hope our children won't ask where their father comes from..."

That summer Marit and Hugo packed their few possessions and took the train to Newcastle where they boarded a boat to cross the North Sea. On their arrival Dad was accommodated in an upstairs bedroom at Lyngheim, while Mum did the respectable thing and stayed at her lodgings in Skien until they were married that September. My grandparents spent the entire summer with their future son-in-law, with no other means of communication than the few words of Norwegian he'd learned and whatever could be said in gestures (although such exchanges must have been somewhat limited, since Bamble folk are not exactly known for their extravert body language, unlike the more flamboyant Goans).

Initially Dad dug up potatoes for four kroner an hour, but he soon got a proper job, first at the Dalen Portland Cement factory, then later at the Øya Shipyard in Brevik. Bamble's first Goan was now a regular passenger on the workers' bus that passed through Lyngheim each morning and evening. As well as working, he did all he could to accommodate his future in-laws; helping in any way possible, showing them the respect that, according to his own deep-seated family ideals, they so deserved.

Weren't my grandparents the least bit uneasy about having a dark-skinned son-in-law? And wasn't Mum's choice of boyfriend at least partly an expression of her need to rebel? She must have felt some pride when she showed off this exotic boyfriend to her friends, and even reveled in the looks they got in the street? But when I ask Mum about this today, I get a firm "no." There was nothing scandalous about a Goan in Bamble at the beginning of 1960s. Dad was different and exciting, but didn't arouse suspicion or strong reactions.

"I think it would be harder today," she concludes.

She may well be right. Dad may have come up against some suspicion and even rejection, but his skin-color didn't necessarily cloud people's perception of him here in Norway as it had in Britain. As much as color divides people, we do *not* fear the unknown as much as we fear what we *think* we know, but don't. Apart from his appearance there was little about Dad to confirm any preconceptions Norwegians might have had about Asians. I imagine they must have been both confused and beguiled by his charm and good looks, and not least by his European ways. Deep down, it is perhaps neither skin-color nor language that separate or unite us, as much as the play of facial muscles, the expressions, the laughter, the gestures, a smile of recognition, a dismissive gesture of the hand, the finer details of non-verbal communication that confirm: We are more or less the same, you and I.

In July they were engaged. Back in Nairobi, Dad's parents and siblings put an announcement in the *East African Standard*. Then Mum received a letter from them welcoming her solemnly into their family, and with it a sari; quite what they thought she'd do with it was unclear. But one thing was certainly still troubling them: "As you know, Marit is a non-Catholic," Michael Joseph wrote to his son. "So please pray for her, pray for the miracle that is her conversion."

Dad had already been pressuring her to convert for ages, in letter after letter, even sending her pamphlets with titles like *Confession and Communion and Prayer for Children*. He had also sent her a little red book entitled *Communism*. Mum not only needed to be saved from Protestantism but also from Socialism, which Goans apparently associated with Norway. But Mum wouldn't hear of any conversion, either to or from anything. She was ready, however, to make other concessions. When the wedding day arrived and the bride and groom walked up the aisle of the *Catholic* Church of Our Lady in Porsgrunn, it was the sari she had chosen as her wedding gown. Which is how a

Norwegian bride walked up the aisle dressed like an Indian princess, while her Indian groom wore a western suit.

It is too dark for the home movie camera in the little wooden dragon-style church, so I have to create the images for myself: The walls melting into the shadows, the rows of faces lit up by the chandeliers that hung over the aisle. Familiar and unfamiliar faces, Sister Irene, Grandpa, Grandma, uncles and aunts. The pastor waiting at the altar. There is nobody from Dad's side, but the residents of Bamble fill the other side of the church, their pale necks bowed, and among them Grandpa standing with his hands folded, just as he has done countless times in the Prayer House. Yet this must all seem strange to him; the incense in the air, the saints gazing down on him, the figure of the bleeding Christ hanging over the altar with the Virgin Mary and Mary Magdalene on either side, all framed by a long, twisting dragon with fire-breathing heads at both ends; Catholic gothic in true Norwegian style. And now Grandpa lifts his head and sees his firstborn walking up the aisle, dressed as he could never have imagined: the white sari with its glittering silver borders lighting up the church.

Do they look happy? Of course, all couples look happy on their wedding day. As they walk out of the church, the camera is ready to capture them, Mum carrying a bouquet of white lilies, Dad with a white rose in his buttonhole. Hats and pipes under the chestnut trees. Grandpa with his shiny greased hair, standing tall in his dark suit. Dad's white teeth, Mum's pink cheeks. She had wanted to bring the world and freedom back home. He had begged her to rescue him. And she had. He'd found a new home in the land where nothing happened. A new life that would contrast sharply with the lives of the family he had left behind in East Africa.

As Mum and Dad were being joined in Hymen's chains in Porsgrunn, Africans in East Africa were about to throw their own chains off. In the autumn of 1963 the British Empire was nearing its end, with all that entailed for Dad's parents and siblings. After Tanganyika had wrenched itself free in 1961, it was Uganda's turn the following year. Change had been longer in coming in Kenya. Only after they had suppressed the Mau Mau rebellion in 1957 did the British begin negotiations with the more moderate Kikuyu leaders, whom it was hoped would form the core of a modern African middle class. White settlers were bought out and their land sold to wealthy Africans, the right to vote was gradually extended, and independence leader, Jomo Kenyatta, was released from jail.

The family in Nairobi was increasingly uneasy. "In December this year Kenya is going to have its independence," wrote sister E. to Dad just before the wedding. "The tension here is going higher as no one is certain about the future."

She had reason to worry. As long as the colonial powers were in place, the various parallel societies lived in peace. How would they relate to each other when the bell jars were broken and the landscape lay open? On December 12, Jomo Kenyatta became President of an independent Kenya. Two days previously, Zanzibar had held its first democratic election, in which the sultanate was turned into an independent, constitutional monarchy dominated by the ancient

Arab elite. It would last barely a month before the Africans from the mainland launched a coup that quickly degenerated into a massacre of Arabs as well as Indians.

For the Goans in Zanzibar January 12, 1964, began like any other Sunday. Everywhere in Stone Town people were getting ready to go to mass at St. Joseph's Cathedral. As the priest prepared for the service, he received a telephone call from Wolfgango Durado, the foremost Goan on the island, who would eventually become Administrative General in the Ministry of Justice. Could the priest refrain from ringing the bells for mass today? Trouble was brewing in the town, and people should stay indoors. But the priest must have thought that his congregation owed God His due, and despite Durado's warning the bells were rung. Catholic families poured out of their doors, in their freshly ironed dresses and shiny shoes. When they were all gathered in the church, Durado telephoned again. Could the priest please hold the congregation back at the end of the service? The streets weren't safe. But God was not the only one to prevail upon the people that Sunday; old habits and certainties played their part too.

What on earth could happen there? In peaceful Zanzibar? Just a few steps out of the church door and around a corner or two, and they'd be home.

Among the Goans shot and killed that day were two sisters; one of whom had only been married for a couple of months, and a brother and sister, she in her twenties, he somewhat older. A young boy, too, was sitting in the back seat of his parents' car when they saw the armed rebels driving behind them, and when his father swerved to escape them his son was hit in the back. That bloody Sunday marked the beginning of Abeid Karum's brutal dictatorship in Zanzibar. The island was now a closed country and would continue to be even after its unification with Tanganyika under the new name of Tanzania in April 1964.

The age of imperialism was over for my family. Portuguese India and British East Africa had ceased to exist; they had crumbled like sandcastles during Dad's childhood, and now the last remnants were washed away. During three of the five years that Dad had lived in Europe, all his homelands were torn away; first Goa, then Tanganyika, Zanzibar and finally Kenya.

Or, this is at least *one* way to see it. Seen in a wider perspective the opposite may be equally true – that my family never had any homeland to lose; at least if we associate the concept of homeland with that of nation or nationhood. For three generations they had lived in a tight-knit community of their own, in a wider imperial world. Where precisely they lived in these vast Portuguese or British territories was of scant consequence; they might just as well have lived in Burma as Zanzibar. Following World War II, the empires were split up and transformed into nations that each demanded a unified identity, loyalty and participation of their citizens. In this transition my family had difficulty in adapting and finding a place to call their own. They belonged to a world of empires, the nation state was alien to them and its borders too restrictive.

Had they tried, they could probably have obtained Indian passports. But what did they have in common with the Indians and their nation building? India had liberated itself from the British and thrown the Portuguese out of Goa, and felt greater solidarity with the African independence movements than with the hundreds of thousands of their own countrymen who had been in the service of the colonial powers or who had exploited Africa for their own ends. Zanzibar, would also have accepted them if they'd been willing to take Tanzanian citizenship. But this option was unthinkable for my family; in reality they lived in fear of being sent forcibly to Karum's dictatorship for as long as they remained on the continent. In Kenya, the new authorities gave non-African inhabitants two years to apply for Kenyan citizenship. Taking up this offer would, however, mean being trapped in a place in which they did not truly feel at home. By the time the deadline ran out most Kenyan Indians, around two hundred thousand, had refused the offer of Kenyan citizenship.

The harsh truth was that now my family became redundant people, mere slag from the grinding wheel of history. They were a people with origins, history, but no territory of their own. The empires that had created them had gone and now they were left standing among the colonial ruins under the scorching sun. Suspicion between the Indians and the Kenyan authorities was mutual. The fact that so many Indians refused the offer of citizenship was interpreted by the government as proof of their lack of loyalty, and over the next few years legislation was introduced with one sole purpose: to push the remaining Asians out of the country.

Where did this hatred stem from? The Asians had, after all, lived in Africa for centuries as traders, financiers, bureaucrats. Never as colonists. A few years after independence, Italian novelist and journalist Alberto Moravia traveled around East Africa. Keenly socially aware, antifascist and anti-imperialist, Moravia was deeply critical of the former colonial system, yet the British he met – *Homo Victorianus* as he called them – inspired less anger in him than the Asian Indians:

"The promenaders were all Indian," he says of Kigoma in Tanzania, "which is as much to say as that the whole of the town's middle class was Indian. Plump, bearded men, dressed in white, wearing turbans."

For Moravia the Indians were the exploitative bourgeoisie in this ex-colony, while the Africans were the proletariat. In other words, the racial divide was synonymous with the class divide, and in his opinion, this was not something that the Indians had learned from the Europeans: "The Indians are racists, not of the present day but from thousands of years back."

Moravia is not the first to point out that the Indian caste system adapted itself easily to the European colonial system. The Indians were accustomed to sorting people by caste, and no matter from which caste an individual might have come, they always regarded themselves as superior to the Africans. As a result the Indians were seen as cynical businessmen who exploited the black proletariat, while sending a large proportion of their earnings back home to

India. They kept to themselves and refused to interact with anyone else; they lived in Africa, but did not belong. So what could be more natural when the European masters had been thrown out of the region than for the Indians to follow them? Evelyn Waugh also preferred the Africans and Arabs to what he saw as the rootless and ruthless Indians. Waugh did not share Moravia's socialist views, indeed, he was a proud racist and anti-Semite; he was just one of many who looked upon the Asians as "the Jews of Africa," summing up his disappointment over developments in Zanzibar thus: "We came to establish a Christian civilization and we have come close to establishing a Hindu one."

The West Indian author Shiva Naipaul, brother of the more famous novelist V.S. Naipaul, however, looked upon the remaining Indians with sympathy when he traveled around in East Africa in the 1970s. For him, they were an invisible people to both white and black – "they only see us when they want to hate us." While Churchill had once talked about "the white man versus the black; the Indian versus both," Naipaul believed that there was a "black and white love affair" in East Africa. While the European Colonial masters might see the Africans as innocent, noble primitives, they regarded the Indians as being clever and useful, but dangerous. A competitor. For the Africans, the Europeans were the oppressors, but they were also worthy of admiration: everything the Europeans had, the Africans wanted too; radios and cassette players had replaced the glass beads and mirrors of yore.

Naipaul's writing belongs, of course, to a distinctly orientalist tradition. For him Africa is a journey into the heart of darkness, his view is clouded by prejudice. Nonetheless he touches on a truth: the Indians of East Africa were the eternal outsiders. Under the British they fulfilled a function. After the collapse of colonialism it was as though they had never existed.

Naipaul, however, acknowledges that the Indians were partly to blame for their own fate, by clinging so hard to their own people: "A Patel remained a Patel. A Goan remained a Goan. An Ismaili remained an Ismaili. A Sikh remained a Sikh. Each looked after his own."

And what strikes me now when I think about the Goans and who they truly are – the product of diverse cultures – is the importance they gave to sexual exclusivity. My aunts tell me that it was unthinkable to go out with anyone from outside the Goan circle, or even from within it if they belonged to a lower caste. The bell jar that made the Goans so secure reinforced the hatred of anyone who looked in from outside. The historical irony is astounding; despite their superior attitude toward the Africans, they never saw themselves as imperialists in East Africa, as "brown bwanas" with civilization-building aspirations. They had been the brown middle layer in the vast colonial cake, with the white above them and the black below. Now that the white layer had been scraped off, they were left on top, causing the Africans to turn their rage against them.

Michael Joseph, Herminia and those children who still lived with them at home could see that life in Kenya was going to get very difficult in the time to come. But never had the question been more pressing: Where should they go?

If Grandfather had renewed their Portuguese passports they could have gone to Portugal. But why would these anglicized Goans choose to live in a backward dictatorship in Southern Europe? Besides, Portugal had closed its consulates in East Africa one by one as independence spread across the continent, adding to the difficulties of getting their passports renewed.

No. The future lay in the U.K. or the United States. But getting permanent visas in these countries wasn't easy; besides, there was the question of money. To make the leap across yet another ocean they were dependent upon others, specifically, the global network of Catholic institutions and individuals – the fellow believers who represented the practical side of universal Catholicism. The way forward was to apply for scholarships or to scrape together the money to send the children to American Catholic colleges as soon as they had passed the Senior Cambridge Examination that qualified them for higher education.

Dad had been the first of the children to go. He was followed by his sister *T.* in 1961, using a scholarship from a Catholic college in New Hampshire in the United States. *T.* had been just seventeen years old, and her first encounters with the West were no less overwhelming for her than Dad's. She sat by herself on the plane over the Atlantic Ocean; the other students were all African and thereby foreigners to her. Arriving at the hotel in New York where she would await her transfer to campus, she took the lift straight up to the 64th floor. *T.* had never been in a lift before, nor seen a television set; the sound of angry voices and gun-battles issuing from the neighboring room terrified her. She stayed in the confines of her Manhattan hotel room for four whole days before finally venturing outside. Come Sunday, she wanted to find a Catholic church, but when she eventually stopped a man to ask the way she couldn't even open her mouth, she stood there frozen with her hands clasped before her as if in prayer. In the end a woman took pity on her and escorted her to St. Patrick's Cathedral on 5th Avenue.

The siblings had lived such sheltered lives under their bell jar that just the noises from outside terrified them. The sense of homesickness was unbearable. And it was no less painful for those left behind. To ease their pain they started to make sound recordings on which they sang songs, talked and told stories about their everyday lives, which they then airmailed back and forth between Nairobi and the United States. Blood-bonds were thus extended across the ocean, between those who had gone away and those left behind. One of these tapes still survives to this day. Recorded by the family in Nairobi on the 9th and 10th of September, 1963; this is the sound of the past:

A click, then a steady buzzing sound that remains in the foreground. Then a voice is heard, as though from a vast distance, like a radio broadcast that barely penetrates the ether. I soon realize that this association is not altogether inappropriate; my uncle, who is talking, is clearly trying hard to reproduce the crisp BBC English tones of a radio reporter, mimicking the British radio shows they listen to so regularly: "Presenting the Figueiredo family album. Dateline: Nairobi, Monday the 9th of September 1963," he says like a true family show presenter. "The first item on our list is a sing song in which each member of the family gives us a song or two. And first on stage is Papa, with his rendering of a three in one combination of songs from the roaring twenties."

A short pause. Then comes my grandfather's slow voice, deep and solemn, laced with a sentimental vibrato:

My girl's a Yorkshire girl –
Yorkshire through and through.
My girl's a Yorkshire girl.
Eh! by gum, she's a champion!
Though she's a factory lass.
And wears no fancy clothes,
Still I have a sort of a Yorkshire relish
For my little Yorkshire Rose.

I can see my grandfather sitting hunched over the recording machine with his eyes closed as he croons. His choice of songs is telling. His repertoire is made up entirely of old English hits, presumably sung all over the colonial world by British men longing for home. But Grandfather had never even been to Britain, he had lived most of his life in East Africa and devoted his best years to a colonial power that had never acknowledged him as their equal and who, when it came to the crunch, turned its back on him. His singing expresses a longing – an unrequited longing. A false hope. Nevertheless, he sings with gusto about his Yorkshire girl, before his son takes the microphone from him and passes it on:

"Ma, the mic's all yours."

Another pause with nothing but a buzzing in the foreground. Then I hear my grandmother Herminia start singing. Her voice resembles

Grandfather's, just lighter and softer. Her tone, like his, is sentimental, infused with a theatricality and pathos I recognize from several of my aunts and uncles. (Something I recognize in myself, if I'm honest). But the song she sings is an old Portuguese ballad, so its sense of longing has a rather different weight. She also sings of an empire which she only ever served and never truly belonged to; but at least her longing is for something that was real for her, for Goa and a childhood in a village on the other side of the ocean, a sunken world that her singing seems to raise from the past.

And so it goes on. One family member after another takes the microphone and sings. "Softly, as in a Morning Sunrise," "Spanish Harlem" and "Evening in Rome"; popular songs, all sung with intense melancholy and the carefully modulated tone that I recognize so well; that reminds me of Dad singing to us in the car on the way to church. The youngsters tend to sing newer melodies, but on the whole there are few generational differences in their repertoire. Music was not something that divided this family, rather it transcended any age barrier, it bridged time and oceans. A few weeks later *T.* will sit in her college room and join in with the family sing-along, while cramming her mouth with the homemade pickles sent by her mother with the tape.

The day after the recording the next daughter, *O.*, waves goodbye to the family and boards a plane to the States to begin at the same college as her sister. Two months later, the youngest boy *J.* sets off for Canada, also to enroll at a Catholic college. The British Empire is dissolving, and so too is the family. Left behind in Nairobi with Herminia and Michael Joseph are the three remaining children, *E.*, *J.* and *M.* The intention is that they too will follow in time.

Herminia took it hard. She had been abandoned by her parents when she was small, and she herself had left her two eldest sons behind in Goa to grow up in the village. Now her children were vanishing from her life one by one. She had once vowed to spell her father-in-law's name with the first initials of her offspring: *A.*, *L.*, *E.*, *I.*, *X.*, *O.* She had gone on to add *T.*, *J.* and *M.* Before the decade was over, most of her children were scattered, thrown carelessly like scrabble pieces across the world map.

Their situation was far from being unique. Hundreds of thousands of African Asians were confronted with similar choices now; sending as many of their children as possible to Europe or the United States in the hope that with education and hard work they would, in turn, be able to finance the next child's education, and then the next, until the whole family had reached safe ground.

All except the older generation, who might decide to return to their country of origin. My grandparents still had responsibilities back in Saligão. After Aleixo's death in 1940, it was Herminia who still felt most tied to their home village. Her mother Elizena still lived in the house in Salmona, and Aunt Ti Filu lived in Tabravvadó; both were entirely dependent on regular money transfers. Thus, the hopes and desires of my grandparents were pulled both to the East and West – to the Indian continent in one direction and Europe and America in the other.

In the winter of 1963–64 they decide to sell all their belongings and return to Saligão to take care of their older relatives and spend their last years in their home village. They will take nothing with them, although Herminia insists that they would at least take their youngest daughter *M.*

"I cannot live without my children anymore," she says. "Let the last one be with me for a while."

In December, Michael Joseph goes to Goa alone to make preparations for their journey. He is away for almost a year. By the time of his return, he has changed his mind, choosing instead to monitor the situation.

In his absence Herminia suffers her first heart attack in Nairobi. Bedridden for months, her thoughts and dreams wander to other countries – to Goa, to the States, to England, and to Norway, where

Xavier has recently had a little boy named, according to tradition, after his grandfather. "I can imagine how excited you all are," she writes to Dad upon the birth of my older brother, adding how sad she is that she cannot see him. "Please give me proper details about how the baby looks, what color eyes, hair, skin he has."

When Mum and Dad send her photographs, they receive a list of advice in return: "His nose looks broad, so please Marit, rub it in position with a little oil every morning, also it's good to apply oil to his whole body in the morning and keep him some time & then bathe him."

Herminia Sequeira de Figueiredo ached body and soul to be there, to be useful. Her hands were made to hold little ones and massage them with coconut oil. She had five grandchildren by this time, all living abroad. The latest addition was the furthest away, which may explain her particular obsession with Dad and his life in Norway. She studied all the photographs Dad sent her of his in-law's house in Lyngheim with its potato fields and chicken coop in the background. Judging from her letters she believed that my grandparents, my Dad, my Mum and big brother all lived together, with Mum and Grandma looking after the house together. She may, out of courtesy, have chosen not to mention the absence of any servants in these pictures.

Most of all, Herminia expresses interest in anything edible, as in the picture of Dad standing on the roof of a boat, holding a freshly

caught fish: "My mouth is watering Xav, seeing the tempting fish on your line, what about making some recheio of it?"

The letters from Nairobi are filled with descriptions of food, especially around Christmastime when Goans came together to dance and share lavish buffets – "sorpotel of pork, stuffed roast fowl and pulao, for dessert jelly milk with canned cherries in syrup & whipped cream." And to finish, mountains of sweets and cakes, "angel ribs, pathies, noddies, jam tarts, pinewheels, almond biscuits." Herminia worries about her son's diet. Can he get cumin and coriander seeds in Norway? And turmeric, fenugreek and chili powder? Just to be sure she sends him small boxes of her own masala mixes and importantly "Goan sausages," the local equivalent to Portuguese chorizo. Thus Herminia tried to keep her family together across three continents, and as long as her health allowed, she sat on her kitchen stool with her mortar planted between her feet.

What mother doesn't worry whether her children are eating enough? What child doesn't long for his mother's casserole? For families scattered across the globe, food gains an even greater significance. Letters and audio tapes may help assuage the sense of longing, but nothing competes with the tastes and smells of childhood. Of all our senses, taste and smell are the most difficult to describe. Perhaps that explains their potency; being pure experience, or memory of experience, they eliminate the need for words, and allow our bodies to speak to us. For the emigrant, food is the fastest way home, although its importance varies between cultures. Where some mark their attachment to their homeland by serving an occasional signature dish, others can't survive everyday life without their own cuisine; they open restaurants and import their own food. Among these food-crazy people are the Chinese, the Vietnamese, the Indians – and the Goans. Perhaps these peoples simply make better food than most, but whatever the case, Chinese and Asian cooking traditions differ fundamentally from those of the West, in taste, texture and preparation. Their food is their culture, identity is kept warm over a gas flame.

To Goans, the pestle and mortar is almost sacred. It even resembles a sacred object, a Hindu lingam perhaps, with its tall elliptical-shaped stone that stands proudly erect in the hollow of a lava rock, like an upturned mushroom. The first thing Herminia did whenever she arrived in a new kitchen was unpack this treasure from its hessian sacks. Then, as she rotated the elongated stone in her right hand, easing the softened mass down into the hollow with her left, and the aromas of spices or lightly roasted coconut rose into the room, each new house became a home.

Perhaps food is so important to the Goans because they are a creole people. Certainly, their unique cultural mix can be traced in the food they eat. Like the chili and the vinegar that make the basis for the fiery red sauce in dishes like vindaloo and sorpotel. The latter was one of Herminia's specialties, and I wonder whether the history of my family, or indeed the entire Goan people, is reflected in this one dish. Sorpotel was originally a rural poor man's dish called sarrabulho from the Minoh Province in the northwest corner of Portugal; a thick soup made from a pig's less appetizing parts, including blood, ears and trotters. In Brazil the Portuguese gave this soup to their African slaves. When the slaves improved it by adding onions, tomatoes and chili, the Portuguese gained a new liking for it, renaming it sarapatel, and taking it with them to India, where further ingredients and spices were added.

Which was how Goan sorpotel came about; the product of a meeting between four continents, cooked until all the ingredients were thoroughly blended and took on a completely new and distinctive character. A good sorpotel should be strong in flavor, although it is not the heat of the chillies that matters most, but their taste. Ideally, dried Goan chilies are used, but I myself prefer Kashmiri chillies, which, as well as their rich, smoky flavor also impart a lovely deep red color to the sauce. Since the seeds are removed you can use a large number, fifteen to twenty or more, adding two or three hotter kinds of chili too. The chillies are soaked in vinegar (preferably palm vinegar, but cider vinegar does the trick) and mashed into a thick pulp. Onions, garlic and ginger are mandatory, as are pepper and cumin, a dash of turmeric, though not too much, and finally a few cloves or a little cinnamon, with a teaspoon of sugar perhaps to round everything off. Then chop the meat, preferably with a high fat content, combined with a little cartilage (pork knuckle is ideal), liver and whatever other pig's offal you like, then cook until it "belongs to the gravy" as it states in one Goan cookbook. To achieve this the meat must be chopped finely enough to make a sauce, but coarsely enough not to disappear entirely.

When the correct procedure is followed and the pot is left to stand for a day or two, the sorpotel takes on its distinct character: the rich, satisfying taste of pork, irresistible throughout Christendom, in perfect balance with the deep heat of chillies, sweetness of cinnamon or cloves and sour tang of vinegar. Like the Goans, sorpotel is the sum of many diverse parts. When cooked, everything blends into one unique, indivisible sauce; a sauce that is unclean in the eyes of others, but to the Goans, is as pure and as red as blood itself.

Herminia's shipments of home-cooking were just one of the many ways that the family kept their connections alive despite distance. In addition to these came the letters, photographs, slideshows, audiotapes and later, cassettes – not forgetting the rosaries and pictures of saints. All these things comprised what I call the "Curry Triangle" that linked those living in East Africa with Dad's and Lionel's families in Europe, and their siblings studying in the States. Years might pass between their meetings, but the family was sustained through the senses, they shared everything that could be seen, heard and tasted. The only thing lacking was physical presence.

As a child, I didn't really understand that the portable cassette recorder that Dad wanted us to talk into was meant to bring comfort to a family in England, East Africa and the United States, that counted me as one of its own. Nor did I know that our home movies had already traveled around the globe before ending up in the cupboard in Langesund. I didn't know that people, unknown to me, had sat smiling at my bowlegs as I toddled across Grandma's lawn, or sighed sweetly when they saw my brothers and I buried under a mountain of Christmas presents and screaming under the heat of the film lights.

"Oh! How cute!"

"How sweet!"

"Oh, I could just squeeze them!"

I was an international sensation before I could blow spit bubbles. I was loved on three continents. In Nairobi the family were dependent on one of the children borrowing a projector from their workplace, making movie nights a rare and precious occasion. Gathering together in the living room in Muthaiga Road they watched the footage of Grandma's flowerbeds, Grandpa's carvings, and our ski trips over snow-covered potato fields, over and over again. And there, in the middle of the exotic Norwegian winter landscape, they'd see Xavier wearing a chunky woolen sweater and a hat with a silly pompom on top. One of Grandpa's carvings could be studied in detail in their own living room, since Mum had sent one of the best examples to her in-laws. Which was how a solitary carved wooden troll came to witness the fall of the British Empire in East Africa. Similar trolls were sent to Lionel and Pam in Burnley, and to my aunt in the United States. This was the Bamble contribution to the Curry Triangle. In her letters, Herminia would quiz her son about what she'd seen on the screen. Did the hens belong to Marit's parents? Who was that man playing an accordion on the roof? And what was their son doing in that field – *have you taken up farming, Xav*? And Marit and her sisters – what beauties!

Less spectacular than the home movies were the photographs. Cheaper to take, easy to send, they were perhaps the mainstay of the Curry Triangle. No sooner had an event taken place – a wedding or birth – than the demand for photographs would pile in. On one occasion, my aunt is full of praises for the composition of the latest pictures Dad has sent: "I like the very natural poses you take," she writes, "I think they are very much more appreciated than the ones where we all stand like soldiers."

I agree with her; Dad's photographs of me and my brothers are rather good. But they also strike me as surprisingly Norwegian. The family pictures taken during my childhood were for the most part informal, capturing a moment around a dinner table, kids playing, my brothers and I buried in the sand with our faces covered in ice cream. This was how photographs were taken in postwar Norway. Formal photographs were the territory of photographic studios. If you set up a pose for an amateur photographer, it was almost always in a humorous vein; a kid making rabbit ears at his mother, a funny uncle lying out flat in front of the others, all designed to lessen the embarrassment of standing stiffly to attention.

This in contrast with the old Figueiredo family albums, which are filled with glossy little photographs of matchstick people in neat rows. The tiny heads that poke out of the white shirt collars and dresses are almost indistinguishable without a magnifying glass. Any natural moment is interrupted in deference to the photographer. The context is rendered irrelevant; the picture might be taken on a lawn, in front of a building, on a terrace, almost anywhere in the world.

The two contrasting approaches to documenting life say much about the difference between the apparent chaos of Norwegian individualism and the Goan order of patriarchal collectivism. That's not to say that the latter's photographs were taken under duress; when Grandfather pointed his camera, I imagine everyone gladly throwing aside whatever they were doing, flocking together and standing to attention. Dad, on the other hand, had to yell at us to get into order, though we generally ignored him, forcing him to snap away without interrupting our play.

In other words, like this:

And not like this:

Or is my memory playing tricks? Was it important for Dad that we stand in a row? I'm sure Mum showered him with advice, but I can't help thinking it came naturally to Dad to adopt the Norwegian way of taking pictures. Dad liked to talk about discipline, but in reality he had stepped out of the ranks long before he left the family home in Nairobi. He was the rebel in the cathedral, the one who did as he pleased. Coming to Europe he'd experienced freedom, and it scared him. Now all he wanted was a new cathedral in which to hide, and he had built that in the form of a family in a new homeland. The only thing that could wreck things now was himself.

WHEN I WAS A CHILD, THE PAST EXISTED as images that flickered across a sheet suspended between the kitchen and living room. Three minutes footage, that was all these black film reels in their yellow tins had space for. But in those brief moments we stepped into a world that was not really ours to see, participated in memories we had no real right to. We were witness to our own origins, to a time before our birth, before our conception, when the world didn't give us a thought and our parents cared only for each other. Then suddenly we are there; a bundle in Mum's lap, a small, startled face, eyes that see without comprehension, sitting in a plastic bathtub on a kitchen table, lying in a pram in a grainy world that glides silently across the sheet behind it. The film lights are too strong, the colors are slightly wrong, and it is this imperfection, this veil-like effect, that makes the home movie the medium of memory and dreams, so palpably close, yet so distant.

Hanging up the sheet was a bothersome affair and the projector had to be borrowed from Grandma and Grandpa at Lyngheim, so it wasn't often that Mum and Dad showed the family archive of home movies. It was a big event, therefore, whenever we gathered for a film night. Especially because we always knew that a fragment of the past would be irrevocably lost. The spool on Grandpa's projector tended to stop at the end of the film, and before Dad could pull it out, the heat from the projector lamp would melt the last frame.

In reality it was only a minor glitch, but magnified up there on the sheet, this final image looked like a major disaster. A raging fire, a mini Hiroshima, that consumed familiar places and people in an instant, melted the frozen faces of our past selves, before everything turned white and we sat in silence, listening to the tail end of the film as it flipped around and around, until Dad got up and turned the projector off. Having to sacrifice a little of the precious past that we were all so determined to relive, filled us, I think, with a kind of trepidation. As though this brought it home that whatever we did, time would ultimately devour our memories, that we would all eventually disappear in forgetfulness, and everything past and present would be gone forever.

Now digitized, these films flicker silently over the screen of my Mac. Short clips follow each other in random order as in a dream. First Mum sitting in tight trousers and polo neck sweater on an upturned washtub in the garden at Lyngheim one summer before I am born. Her hair blows lightly in the wind, she is laughing. In the background I see Grandpa's workshop; I realize she's in the exact same spot as Dad when he was photographed in the snowdrift, but I don't know if this film was taken before or after he came to Norway. Suddenly the light intensifies, turning into a milky membrane that obliterates the summer's day, broken only by tumbling black stripes. The membrane disappears again as the lens turns away from the sun and onto a landscape of skerries. The black stripes continue to fall, but behind them are a pale blue sea, a kayak, and a rock face. And now Dad appears wearing dark glasses and smoking a cigarette, while Grandpa and my uncle walk along the shore collecting driftwood for a bonfire. Dad gives the camera a sidelong glance before turning toward the others, but I can see he's aware that the film is still rolling. Then Mum reappears, sitting in a boat. She's wearing a straw hat and is talking to whoever's holding the camera, flecks of sunlight dance across her face.

I try to imagine her voice, the sounds in the background, the lapping of waves, I long for the heat of this summer day, carried on the wind in a world before my time. I run my fingers over the Mac's membrane-thin plasma wall, making millimeter-deep grooves in its spongy surface. I have to resist the desire to shove my whole hand in; I want to touch, to feel the floating pixels run through my fingers. I want to catch the memories before they burst into flames and dissolve in white.

IN MUM'S FIRST PHOTO ALBUM as a married woman, there are pictures of both my parents as children, taken, of course, before they'd ever met. She has made a montage of them as though the improbable were probable: as if their meeting was somehow fated. But how improbable had it been? Isn't the obvious explanation for my parents' meeting through the smoke of a Kingston pub that history itself had opened a space which allowed for such encounters? And when I say "space" I am talking quite concretely of the first floor room at The Swan, where the International Club met. In the 1960s borders that had been previously closed were being gradually (or sometimes very quickly) opened. As the empires fell apart, people began to move out of their bell jars, crossing the ocean, into the universities, factories and bars in the cities of Europe. In this moment of transition, the shared colonial experience was more important to Kingston's young international students than anything that might divide them. Neither before nor since, have Asians, Iranians, Africans and Arabs regularly mixed in the same clubs. Mum also lived with fluid borders; the shifting borders that marked which ambitions a young Norwegian village girl could or could not pursue. She was undoubtedly adventurous, but had she been born just a decade earlier, it would have been inconceivable for her to go to London, a decade later and she might have gone to university in Norway.

My parents were young at a time when the world was in transition, when everything seemed possible, a world in which old borders were disintegrating and new ones were not yet firm. The first floor at The Swan in Kingston was an historic room, a moment in time, where a postcolonial conservative Goan from Zanzibar and a modern free thinking girl from Bamble felt they inhabited the same world. It was a time of innocence; not that Dad saw it that way as he trudged around Manchester's streets. Mum, though, had embraced the bohemian lifestyle in London with open arms. That this freedom could not last, that the moment when she and Dad belonged to the same world would pass, and that the legacy each bore was more than they could carry together, would soon be clear to her. Perhaps she should have seen it coming, but in reality I think it came as a shock.

On the first page of the family album there's a picture of a female model wearing an apron, which Mum probably found in a woman's magazine; she kept up with the fashions and made her own clothes. She has

glued a photograph of her own face over the model's, transforming herself, like thousands of women before and after her, into the perfect Housewife, the Mother, the Hostess; everything the man-child in the picture could possibly need or desire.

My now twenty-five year old father was, in a way, forced to be a child again. Not only did he have to learn a new language, but also the inscrutable ways of the Norwegian people; it was beyond his comprehension when Mum's relatives met without exchanging proper greetings, barely nodding before sliding into a chair where they sat waiting for a cup of coffee to be put in their hands. In the winter he was dragged off to the mountains to learn how to walk again – on skis. In the home movies we see the rugged landscape of Telemark covered in deep snow, with stunted little birch trees in the foreground, and snow laden spruce trees in the distance. Grandpa glides past in a blue ski suit and wooly hat. Perfectly poised on his skis. Unlike the man who can be seen descending a gentle slope on quaking legs, crouching low, desperately trying to keep his masculine pride intact. An Indian in the snow, like a child taking his first uncertain steps. He takes a tumble at the bottom, but in the next frame he is on his feet again, skis in his hands and a big grin across his face. Having regained his cool, he performs for the camera, laughing and dancing. Finally Mum appears at the door of the cabin, wearing a red and blue ski suit, a hand shielding her eyes from the sharp sunlight.

None of this is remarkable in itself. Dad had to learn to live in Norway. And learn he did. Though he wasn't about to become entirely Norwegian. During their first year of marriage, Mum and he moved into one of the asbestos-clad barracks in Porsgrunn, left by the Germans after their occupation of Norway twenty years previously. Mum was already pregnant with my older brother, Jo Michael, but it wasn't long before Dad had turned the little apartment into a meeting place for any seafarers passing through Porsgrunn. The locals were always ready to help; whenever a cargo ship came into the harbor, and foreign sailors had difficulties finding their way around the village, they'd point them in the direction of the barracks where their local foreigner lived. Once an entire crew of Indian sailors turned up, another time Dad came home with a Polish band who were playing at the *Gamle Vic* down the road.

Dad had never been wholly convinced that he'd ever feel properly settled in Norway. In Britain he had at least been able to speak the language – the only thing that could convince people that he was more than just an uneducated immigrant, that beneath his dark skin he was as good as any European. In Norway the color of his skin would be his only language. Or so he'd assumed. But as things turned out he reaped the best of two worlds: he was almost an attraction among Mum's friends, bringing steaming pots of curry, putting fire in their mouths and fire in their hearts; to this day there are said to be families in Porsgrunn who have curry each Saturday night after being taught to make Indian food by Dad. He represented the big wide and exotic world in a snowy-white Norway, before immigration was a phenomenon or perceived as a threat.

Neither was he cut off from his Catholic roots. Opposite their little house in Porsgrunn was a Catholic church. Dad only had to walk through the big wrought-iron doors of Our Lady's Church, and he was back in the world from which he'd come. Mass was the same the world over, as were the rituals and liturgy. Norway had, of course, once been entirely Catholic. At the turn of the century the pope's men had returned to serve the spiritual needs of Catholic immigrants. Our Lady's Church was built in 1890 for a congregation of some forty Austrian craftsmen who'd been brought over to run a new porcelain factory in town. Later, in the 1970s the Catholic Church would welcome the wave of Vietnamese boat people. When Dad arrived, however, and during my childhood, there was an even mix of foreign and native worshippers in the Catholic community.

In short, it had never been easier to be a Catholic immigrant in Norway. In the Parish of Porsgrunn there were people from all over Europe. Some came and went, like Desmond the Irish sailor, whose jocularity the locals mistook for intoxication and who always wore baggy trousers because, he said, he needed to feel the wind blow through them. Others were married to Norwegians or had come as refugees. Maria had lost all her family in a Nazi concentration camp in Poland and refused to hear a bad word about the country that had taken her in. On the other hand, Helga carried the burden of being born German. Istvan, with his tightly buttoned coat and a face like granite, had fled from Hungary, and Blanca from Colombia. I suspect the refugees from communist regimes found it easier to adapt than those from fascist countries like Spain and Chile, after Pinochet's military coup; the latter were often socialists and at odds with the conservative Catholic Church.

As a child, of course, I had no idea about politics, but I remember being on a tour bus one day with a bunch of kids going to the south coast for some Catholic event. The nuns were sitting at the front, while we sat behind. It must have been the summer of 1976, a few months after the Spanish dictator Franco's death. The news seems to have reached us, since amid our laughter and high-jinks, someone suddenly called out "Hi, Franco!" to a dark-haired boy called Frank. This caused much hilarity, but Frank, who was hardly the most demure chap (he once stole wafers from the sacristy and ate them like biscuits while the rest of us looked on in horror), replied dryly: "Franco is dead." Lord knows why, but this triggered an extraordinary collective response; first one, then another, then the entire bus-full of youngsters, began to chant "Franco is dead! Franco is dead!" What the nuns thought about the Catholic dictator, I don't know, but our raucous confirmation of his passing clearly did not meet with their approval. In response to our shouts, they started to sing a hymn cautiously at first, then more determinedly, causing us to shout even louder. If an innocent protestant had walked along the E18 road on that summer's day in the mid-'70s, which is very likely, he would have witnessed an extraordinary scene: a passing bus reverberating with the angelic sound of nuns' singing and kids loudly proclaiming the death of the Spanish dictator, until the cacophony ceased abruptly when one of the nuns finally leapt up from her seat and cowered us into silence with a stern look.

No other confrontations between God and the wider world feature in my church-going memories, although I am told that a group of Chileans marched up to the priest one day and demanded that the Church should denounce Pinochet publicly. When the priest refused, they came out in protest, saying: "This is just like home, the Church supports the regime!"

The congregation of the little wooden church in Porsgrunn was indeed diverse, but so too were the priests and nuns. The priest who dealt with the protesting Chileans was Norwegian, but most came from elsewhere. The priest of my childhood was a soft-spoken Dutchman named Father Rommelse. The nuns, with fabulous names like Kunigunde, Tarcisia and Ottilie, were all German. Belonging to the St. Joseph's Order, they divided their time between the church and running the hospital.

It was a wonderfully colorful world, the entire globe infused with Norway; its most original manifestation perhaps being Brother Robert, an American Trappist monk who lived as a hermit on the hillside above Lake Tinn in Telemark. Almost a hermit, at least he once told Mum that his solitude was somewhat compromised after the locals had discovered him and began making trips in the hope of coffee and waffles. Brother Robert became Telemark's very own monk, instantly recognizable on his motorcycle in his black leather jacket, and to churchgoers by the chasuble he'd embroidered himself. My sole memory of him is of a Mass he held in a disused workers' barracks that served as a chapel, and where he swung a thurible designed for a far larger church, filling the room with delicious incense until the goats outside, who had their muzzles pressed against the windows, disappeared in a cloud of smoke, and all we could hear was their bleating and Brother Robert's chanting. I have no other memory of this Mass; but then, it is more than I remember from all the school services in Langesund church put together.

Dad was no political refugee. He was just an extraneous piece in the postcolonial jigsaw puzzle. Nor did he have any calling or mission like the nuns and priests. But the Catholic Church offered him a home away from home, a chance to be Norwegian without *just* being Norwegian. What was new to him was to experience a Catholicism that went beyond the confines of the Goan community. In East Africa, to be Catholic and Goan had in practice been one and the same thing. The faith might be universal, but the faithful comprised a strictly limited circle. I'm not convinced Dad missed this tight-knit community, but somewhere deep inside him the fires of despair must have burned, fed by the blue airmail letters that landed regularly in the mailbox, the parcels of pickles that awaited him at the post office, and by the thought of his parents and siblings still floating in the wake of the empire's fall or living a life of virtual imprisonment in Nairobi.

Each letter he received from his mother served as a reminder of his filial duties, not least when she was bed-bound after her heart attack in the spring of 1964: "It seems as if everybody has forgotten me," she wrote. "I have no one to turn to, only my god and my three children who console me."

Do not forget us. Do not forget who you are. Do not forget your duties. He sent money to his siblings for their education, just as his parents expected. But his letter writing grew patchier. Nor was he alone in this. Although the Curry Triangle helped maintain a sense of family, one relocated sibling after another started to feel that they were steadily drifting apart. It was as inevitable as it was unbearable.

"Xavy, writing to you is like writing to a stranger," writes sister O. from the States in the autumn of 1965. "I feel the same has happened as far as the rest of the family goes. It isn't as though I've forgotten them: It's just that I seem to have grown away from that world."

Dad must have understood. The painful tug of his roots, the heavy chains of guilt for his sick mother and the brothers and sisters he hadn't seen for years. No doubt he felt, as did his sister, that they were all increasingly distant to him.

"I think now," she concludes, "I begin to see more clearly why you didn't write home more often and why your letters were so short."

He had a new life that he hardly could have imagined just months before. A homeland, a Catholic community, a beautiful white wife and one son – soon two and eventually three. All the church members assumed we were the perfect Catholic family, despite the fact Mum never converted. Dad must have come to terms with that, after all, he had come a long way to achieving what his big brother had achieved in Burnley.

But how were Lionel and Pam really doing? Not quite as Dad imagined. Pam had converted to Catholicism for her husband's sake, but now it was his turn to convert, becoming, of all things, a Jehovah's Witness. For my Goan grandparents, their son's apostasy was a minor catastrophe, and for him it was the first step on the road to divorce. Lionel was also living in tougher conditions than Dad; not only did Lionel live in a provincial town in a country where racism was rife but one where the old conflict between Catholics and Protestants was still alive and well. How much this two-fold alienation weighed on him, I don't know. But it's possible that he was made to feel his color even within the church walls. And for a Goan this must have felt contrary to nature, to the Catholic Church and God's Law: after all, it was in church that Goans were equal to the Europeans.

Dad, on the other hand, had come to a country that had barely experienced immigration, and where the old hatred of the Catholics was largely forgotten. Although absence of outside threat is, of course, no guarantee of happiness, and although I can never know what was going on in his head or between Mum and him, it's hard to understand what caused his rage to flare up again. But it did. The violent words in his letters now took the form of smashed glass, broken furniture, punched doors and walls. After a few years of marriage it was as though he lost all control of himself. In private, at least. In church and in company he was the same charming man, always the life and soul of the party. But in the car driving back, the shouting would start, and it would continue at home. He was constantly dissatisfied and could explode at the slightest thing. Mum had to beg for housekeeping money, she sewed most of our clothes herself. His need for control over the family was boundless, whether he was happy or angry. He began hitting her. She was scared but told nobody. One didn't in those days. She could do nothing right, and neither could we, his sons.

The boundless freedom, the lack of roots to hold him down, the absence of bonds to tie his strong arms. He had no voice in the chamber of his heart to tell him enough was enough. And still they came; the blue letters, the boxes filled with food, the photographs and home movies from the family he'd left behind, from those who were still locked in Africa. No doubt, the Curry Triangle's packages did not just bring Dad comfort, but also a sense of powerlessness. They were a constant reminder of everything he had lost, of the family for whom he longed and to whom he owed everything, and who were now living in a state of desperation.

Why, in this state of grief and longing, he didn't take better care of the family he had created – of Mum and my brothers and I – is beyond my comprehension. He had gotten everything he wanted. He had every reason to be optimistic. The future lay before him like a bright Norwegian summer's day.

But that was not enough. We were not enough.

HERMINIA DREAMED OF SNOW. Lying in bed after her heart attack in the spring of 1964, she used the book about Telemark that Mum had given her to lean on when she wrote her letters. Then she'd leaf through it, looking at the pictures and trying to work out the precise location of Lyngheim. As she drifted off to sleep she entered a strange and alluring winter-white landscape.

"I dreamed," she writes to Dad, "that I was going to Norway in a new kind of transport, never seen before. I was very happy, but when I had pain I was afraid and thought maybe I was going to the next world, but my god saved me."

The Kingdom of Norway and the Kingdom of God; two dreams that floated into one for my grandmother. She longed for those mysterious white vistas, but they could also turn into something fearful when she was gripped by pain.

Over the summer her health improved, but her heart grew no lighter. She was worried about the old folks back in Saligão, and about her children in the States who were struggling through college, working on the side to pay their way and help their other siblings. Back in Muthaiga Road it was *E.* and *I.* who now provided for their parents and their little sister *M.* Herminia did the only thing left to her: she sat in the kitchen on the stool Dad had made her, grinding spices, cooking and making preserves, either alone or with the children, since they could no longer afford a servant. And in the Norwegian corner of the

Curry Triangle the packages of prawn balchão and Goan sausages continued to arrive: "Let me know if you want any recipes," she writes to Dad in an accompanying letter. "Do you get red chillies over there?"

The following summer the last of her sons still at home left for a six-week trip to visit Lionel in London and Dad in Norway. As he packed his suitcases, she stood in front of him with armfuls of mango chutney, pickle, curry powder and peradas.

"Ma, please!"

Some hours later when his suitcases were checked in at Embakasi Airport their weight was well in excess of his limit. Luckily an indulgent official turned a blind eye, and a few weeks later Herminia could write triumphantly to Mum instructing her to add some hot oil to the pickle if it had dried out, but not to the chutney, which was made with syrup. What wouldn't she have given to be in Norway preparing the food for them herself; when cars passed on the road below her house, she used to imagine it was the roar of a plane that she was aboard. She knew her youngest son would return to her, but she also knew that he, along with *E.* and *M.*, would soon head west too; and that it would be forever.

No, Herminia's heart was certainly no lighter. And while her son was away, Michael Joseph fell gravely ill, so close to death that the priest gave him the last rites. In the dark times that followed Herminia was alone with her youngest daughter. In the evenings she'd take up her pen and pour out her troubles to her son in Norway.

In the autumn of '65 Grandfather was restored to life, and their youngest son returned from Europe. Soon after, their daughter *T.* returned from the States, the first girl in the family to have completed a college education. No sooner had she returned home than the battle to get out again began. Before *T.* had left the States, an American couple had given her money to apply for a Green Card. Suzanne and David Grant were just two of the ordinary Americans, who, out of pure generosity of heart, helped the siblings.

"I don't know how to repay you," was all *T.* had been able to stutter when they offered her this gift. "You don't have to," she was told. "Just pass it on."

But a Green Card wasn't of great use in Kenya. *T.*'s British Protected Person passport having expired, the authorities refused to let her leave the country. She needed some sort of travel permit. Day after day she and Grandfather trekked from office to office but were repeatedly met with resistance from Kenyan officials. Her failure to apply for renewal of her British Protected Person passport is probably explained by the fact that it had been issued in Zanzibar. And if there was something she really feared, it was to be sent there.

Added to this, *T.* was very reluctant to leave her parents in Nairobi: "I suppose knowing how close we came to losing both Pa & Ma makes it harder to think of leaving. If only we were in England there would be a chance of reunion, but otherwise I don't know when & if I would ever see them again."

In this, *T.* put words to something everyone was thinking, expressing a worry that could be summed up in a single word: passport. This little book that could confirm one's citizenship was vital; not only to get into another country, but to get out of Kenya at all. The question was which passports they could obtain. Of those who had managed to get out first, Lionel was luckiest. He had traveled to Britain in 1960, before the British had tightened their immigration laws. When he met Pam he already had full British citizenship. Dad was lucky too. His worries were over on the day of his marriage to my mother, which would eventually secure him a Norwegian passport. The children who traveled to America, *T.*, *O.* and *J.*, left East Africa as British Protected Persons of Zanzibar, but since their passports expired after the liberation of Zanzibar, but while they were still in the States, it remained unclear for some time where precisely they belonged (in their letters they describe themselves stateless). The two sisters eventually got American citizenship, while *J.* had less luck: when it came to his turn to apply for a Green Card, he was informed that his cohort of immigrants would be expected to join the military and the war in Vietnam.

J. did not want to go to war. The price was that his dreams of going to the States were destroyed. Instead, he settled in the U.K., before moving to Holland later, where he became a Dutch citizen.

Unsurprisingly my grandparents in Nairobi started to lose track; "What passport have you got, Xavier?" Herminia asks in one of her letters at around this time. In another she sighs over the homelessness that has dogged her entire life: "I have no place anywhere in this world, I have been wandering all my life."

In the midst of this postcolonial chaos, her own mother, Elizena, dies in Saligão. Ever since Aleixo's death Elizena has lived alone in the house in Salmona, but she has walked through the village and past the rice fields every day to visit her sister Ti Filu in Tabravvadó. During these last few years the two elderly sisters have had only each other; soon after the first is laid in her grave, the other takes to her bed and prepares for a speedy reunion.

Back in Nairobi Herminia confides her distress at this in a letter to Dad that November. "I am living a tortured life," she says, "aunty has been like a mother to me, and I can't look after her."

A few months later, Ti Filu dies too. Herminia had worn black when her mother died, from now on she would wear nothing else. However, aside from her grief and self-reproach it was of some comfort that she and Grandfather were now freed from their duties in the village back in Goa. From now on they could turn their gaze westwards, to their own and to their children's future. And if any further incentive was needed a letter arrived in the spring of 1966 informing them that Marit was expecting another child. Herminia invested all her hopes and feelings into the forthcoming event, throwing herself into knitting and cooking.

"About the names, you can choose any you like," she writes generously in a letter to Mum. "I will only point out just a few: Cedric, David, Gerard, Glen, Ian, Wynn (pronounced Win), Richard, Oscar, Terence, Keith, Kenneth, Osmund, Lester." The name my parents chose was, of course, Ivo Bjarne.

The evening before I came into the world, somebody in Muthaiga Road got ahold of a film projector, and once again the pictures of Norway rolled across the screen. Not just once, but several times over. The family was now determined to emigrate. They spent 1966 looking for a way out of East Africa. In Burnley, Lionel and Pam had begun working to get them into Britain through the Family Reunion Association. But to do this, they had to have a valid passport – it wasn't so important *which* – but they had to have a passport. Lionel and Pam decided to try the Portuguese route from Britain. Portugal had closed its Consulate in Nairobi, so they applied to the Portuguese Consulate in London for the passports to be renewed. This strategy proved successful. If everything went according to plan now, the family in Nairobi could soon travel to Britain as Portuguese citizens.

Herminia's letters seem brighter now, more hopeful. Not even a minor setback in her health that June can dampen her spirits. When *T.* leaves for the airport, Grandmother's thoughts travel with her, along with the food and knitted baby clothes she has sent. (*T.* made a plane trip to Norway before heading for America. She had been invited to be my godmother and held me at my baptism in Our Lady's Church. She can be seen in the home movie like an oriental dream walking beneath the chestnut trees outside the church among the local Bamble-ites who smile at her shyly before averting their gaze.)

Herminia is making plans. Perhaps they can all get together in England? Or perhaps she and Michael Joseph could settle in Portugal despite their previous reservations, after all she speaks the language fluently. Michael Joseph was born in Zanzibar and was thoroughly anglicized, but even he eventually agrees that Portugal might be a better option than England. What did the cold and foggy island-kingdom have to offer an elderly Goan couple? Portugal might be backward, and a dictatorship, but it was a Catholic farming culture, not unlike the Goa they knew, and the weather was closer to what they were used to. As too, Grandfather pointed out to Dad, was the culture and food: "The wine, good salad oil for cooking, Portuguese sausages, Bacalao (salted fish which you can prepare by adding dry peas and other vegetables). Even cheese and butter is very good." Besides this, Grandfather had heard that rented accommodation and servants were cheap in Portugal – refugee or not, Grandfather's sense of class was alive and well; they would, of course, have servants again, if they got to Europe.

For Herminia, such details were of minor concern. All she wanted was to be closer to her children and to the grandchildren she had never seen. Dad had sent her a recording of my voice, but the tape had gotten damaged, and all she could hear was a crackling sound and the distorted noise of a baby crying in the distance. Herminia had had her fill of sketchy recordings and grainy pictures, what she craved most was closeness.

She sends clear instructions to Dad: "Please, please start talking to Baby in English, right away," she writes shortly after my birth. "Don't talk to him in Norway [sic], as he will learn the language with others."

In January 1967 she has another heart attack. Fortunately, it is only a minor one again, but she is bedridden for a month. The book about Telemark is brought out again, and as she falls asleep at night, the snow and mountains reenter her dreams.

"I just can't wait for the time to come. I feel like flying, just now, how anxious I am to see my beloved children and grandchildren and also to meet your parents Marit, dear. To be in Norway? Oh, how I long to see that beautiful country, which I have seen so often in my dreams."

In June, Michael Joseph, Herminia and their youngest daughter *M*. receive their Portuguese passports and temporary British residence permits from Lionel. They are now free to leave Kenya, and hopefully, in time, travel to the States. However, they decide to postpone their trip until *M*. has passed her Senior Cambridge exam in November. Besides this, *E*. and *I*. still do not have passports; why it hasn't also been possible to obtain Portuguese passports for them, I have no idea.

Herminia is getting increasingly impatient: "About my Jo Mike & my little Ivo Bjarne, how I long to see them. How sweet of Jo Mike to talk about his granny, my heart aches for him, he is so very cute and beautiful, Little Ivo is also growing so very beautifully."

That autumn, her health goes into decline. Her blood sugar levels are unstable and she loses her appetite. When she does try to eat the food comes straight back up. The doctor visits her three times a day and gives her an injection of insulin.

At nine o'clock on the morning of the 18th of November 1967 she falls asleep for the last time in her bed. No more longings. Just white dreams.

DAD IS HUNCHED OVER THE KITCHEN TABLE sobbing. He is clutching a blue letter. Mum rests a hand on my shoulder to comfort me, so that I may, in turn, comfort him. I've always believed that it was about my grandmother that Dad cried that day, making this memory of him also my sole memory of the grandmother I never met. But I realize now that my mind has played tricks. I was barely one and a half years old when Herminia died, so it's impossible that I should remember the events surrounding her death. Nonetheless the image of Dad at the kitchen table clings on. And I think I know why – this is my earliest memory of him crying.

In the spring of '68 our parents bought the large, white timber house in Langesund. Soon afterwards my little brother Kenneth was born. The family was complete and the scene of my childhood set; thirteen rooms, an outhouse and a garden in a peaceful village along the coast of Telemark, with Dad's world of the Catholic Church half an hour to the North, and my grandparents in Bamble half an hour to the southwest. There are no letters describing Dad's first year in Langesund, only home movies and photographs. But these do not show everything. Nobody films after nightfall. I only have the vaguest dream-like memories to cling to from here on. One of my earliest being of my parents' bedroom. That is, I've forgotten the room itself, all I remember is getting out of my bunk bed, dizzy with a fever, wandering through a seemingly endless kitchen and opening a door that is as heavy as a castle gate, into the long hallway where the walls swim toward me, and seeing the bedroom door far, far away at the end. I can still hear the noises that greeted me. Dull thumping sounds from an adult world. And with each thud my heart beat a little harder, and the darkness closed in a little tighter.

In the morning I could see the results of the night's work; Mum's averted face as she laid the table or stood over the sink. The results of uncurbed freedom. As Grandfather and the remaining children fought to escape East Africa and find a new home in the West, Dad was already well on the way to destroying the home he had created there.

IN JANUARY 1968, DAD RECEIVED A LETTER from Nairobi: "Conditions out here are getting rather stringent with non-citizens now being pressured politically," his younger brother *I.* informed him. "Certain visiting classes are due to apply for working permits which purposes a 'quit the country'-order."

The Kenyan authorities were determined to make life difficult for the country's Asian population. Non-citizens were now obliged to apply for a work permit, while new legislation put restrictions on where non-Kenyans could trade. In reality, the laws were designed to push the last Asians out of any official posts, and out of business. As my uncle *I.* suggested, the Kenyans were pressuring them to "quit the country."

The British response to this was to tighten their own immigration policy to prevent an invasion of Kenyan Indians. One of the strongest opponents to immigration, the Conservative member of parliament Enoch Powell, looked to the ancient poet Ovid to find words to express his fear of the Asian hordes: "Like the Roman, I see the Tiber foaming with much blood."

In Nairobi *E.* and *I.* finally got their passports; British, no less, through an acquaintance in the immigration department. *O.*'s papers were also in order; she had made her way home from the States after completing her college education the previous autumn, but had a valid visa to return. But still the family didn't leave; Grandmother's death seems to have put the brakes on their plans. In the new year, a grief-stricken Michael Joseph returns home to Saligão to think about the future. He's can't even contemplate staying, not without Herminia. He spends his days wandering along the beach in Calangute, trying to see a way forward. What if he settled in Portugal after all, so he could be closer to his children in Europe at least? Back in Muthaiga Road *M.*'s application for a college scholarship in the States is refused, and *E.* is promoted to the job of secretary to the staff manager of her office. A sense of loyalty to the familiar seems to hold them back. Uncle *I.* had always put other people first; in particular, he was the one who had made the greatest sacrifices for his parents. In a letter to Dad he concludes: "Actually I'd rather pack my lot in & get out right now before conditions worsen, but my boss who is the director is actually pleading for me to stay on."

So they hang on for a while longer. It isn't until early August of the following year, that *E.*, *M.* and *O.* finally leave for Embakasi Airport and board the plane that will take them out of Africa for good. Going first to Europe, to visit the family in England and Norway, they go on to Boston, Massachusetts. Here, *M.* starts at Emmanuel College while her two sisters find jobs. I'm not sure if it is a coincidence that they chose the most Catholic city in the States, but Boston was to become the family's new center in the years to come.

There were only three family members left in Muthaiga Road now; my Grandfather, Uncle *I.* and a new edition to the family; the young and beautiful *F.* Uncle *I.* had married *F.* during the previous summer. She came from an old landowning branch of the family in Goa, but had grown up in Uganda where her father had been a businessman, politician and Portuguese consul. Her family belonged to the Goan upper class who never broke their alliance to the old colonial rulers; the Portuguese flag still flew over her father's offices in Kampala. They were about to lose everything. In January 1971, Idi Amin led a coup and immediately introduced a regime of fear in Uganda. The following year, Amin announced that God had come to him in a dream and told him there was no room for Asians in the country. On August 4 he gave them ninety days to get out. More than 41,000 Indians, including approximately 3,000 Goans, fled the country and were held in refugee camps worldwide. This time the United Kingdom was among those who opened their doors.

Meanwhile Zanzibar's dictator, Abeid Karume, was holding his residents prisoner. Here too, life was getting dangerous for the Indians, just as my family had feared; and even more so for the Arabs. Following the introduction of the Forced Marriage Act it became illegal for Arab and Indian women to refuse to marry African men. This law was the most dramatic expression of African hostility toward Arab and Indian sexual exclusivity, and unsurprisingly it created panic. Young girls swallowed glass to avoid forced marriages, many families smuggled their marriageable daughters away from the island in double-bottomed boats.

East Africa had once been my family's promised land. Now it was extremely unsafe. The situation wasn't as drastic in Tanzania or Kenya, but events in neighboring countries spread fear throughout the region. Who knew what would happen next?

On February 28, 1972, *I.* took his father, his wife *F.* and their little daughter, and moved to Boston. The family's borrowed life on African soil was over. All they took with them to their new home in the States were their dreams of Goa and memories of Herminia, whom they'd left behind in a cold grave in Langata Cemetery to wait for a reunion in another life and place, where nobody would ever be homeless again.

AT NIGHT AS A CHILD, I LIE IN my little bunk bed, facing out toward the room. Whenever I sleep, I always have the same dream, night after night. I am sitting in the stands of a large sports field. In the middle of the field is a brick wall, and standing in front of the wall, some distance away, is Dad. He is young, as young as I remember him back then. He is dressed in sports gear and is poised to sprint, but just as he's about to take off he turns to me. He says nothing. Just looks at me with serious eyes. Then turning his gaze straight ahead again, face impassive, body tense, he runs full bore. His skull meets the wall with a thud, a shudder goes through me, the same shudder as when my glass of milk skips across the breakfast table, when Dad's fist meets the tabletop and its impact penetrates into the very core of my being. The same shudder. The same gasp for air.

Still in the dream, returning to the starting block, he looks at me again. I realize that he's about to repeat this whole ghastly exercise, he must repeat it, that's what his eyes tell me. He is obliged to run his head into this wall again and again, and with tears in my eyes I get up and shout that he mustn't, that he must stop. But he just calmly goes back to the start, nothing can be altered, he has to do this, and I realize that I'm the one making him do it. I am his only audience, and it is for me that he must repeat this bloody contest time after time.

Not long ago, I remembered a joke that Dad told me when I was little. I remember laughing till I cried, even though the joke wasn't particularly funny. Laughter comes so easily to children. But here it is anyway:

A man runs his head against a wall several times in quick succession. A second man stands watching him for a while, before he eventually asks the first man why he's doing it. Doesn't it hurt?

Yes, answers the first, it's very painful. But it is so lovely when I stop.

That's true. It's lovely when it stops.

I REMEMBER SO LITTLE from my childhood. My body remembers, but not me. When I want to write about it, it's as though I'm entering an attic in pitch darkness. A bare light bulb sputters intermittently in the ceiling, now and then I get a split-second's glimpse of what's hidden in the corners, or stacked against the wall. So fleeting that I'm not sure afterwards what I saw. Not all memories are real, which isn't to say they're not true. I've had a memory, for as long as I remember, of Dad standing in the middle of the kitchen at home, between the dining table and sink. He is screaming at the top of his voice. Mum is there too, but he pays no attention to us; he might as well be standing in an empty landscape. Arms hanging limply at his sides, eyes staring, as though he'd just seen something horrendous. He screams, without stop. I watch him from the doorway. Or is it from my highchair at the end of the kitchen table? A strip of milk oozes over the table. Then stops. Broken spindles of the rocking chair in the living room, like ribs torn out by giant claws, Mum's smashed typewriter, and little letters strewn across the floor.

I know I was in fear of him. Of whatever it was that moved inside him. He was brash and unpredictable in anger, excessive in happiness; even when we played it felt as if he had to win the game, as though he was fighting something I couldn't see. But I had no way of fighting back. Nor could I cry with him. So I gave him the only thing I had: laughter. I laughed, joked, larked about, and he accepted it all greedily.

Those pictures in the album of me sitting on his lap laughing. They bring it back to me now.

The violent play-fights. On the bed, on the living room floor, the strong fingers between my ribs that massaged the laughter out of me. How I squirmed in their grip, laughed until I could barely breathe, my lungs gradually draining of air while my laughter turned into something close on tears. Those hands held me in their iron grip. There was no choice but to laugh. The brute force that was applied. The bird chest. I was that laughing child, wild, joyful. That crazy kid. I laughed until I was thirteen. Then I stopped.

I've carried this picture in my head for years. But only now do I know what happened to him before he arrived in this country. The weight he carried on those young shoulders. Only now do I understand what this picture shows.

Those strong hands. I wasn't the one who was held hard by you. It was you who were holding onto me.

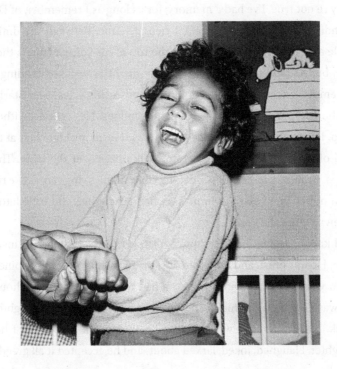

WE FLED. THREE SLEEPY BOYS in our pajamas and overcoats. Head-lights of a car coming to a halt. I don't know who was driving. Not her. We drove to Lyngheim, to the woodcarver in the forest. We fled, and we fled again, until he finally moved out, but even then we weren't safe.

One night he came back, I was thirteen years old and woke up to the sound of metal against metal outside the window. The night air felt cold and strange in my mouth. The street was empty apart from the man under the streetlamp holding a sledgehammer, slamming into Mum's new partner's car. I don't know what I thought, except that I noticed how bow-legged he was standing there, and that I remembered somebody saying that I had a slightly bow-legged walk too. Each time the sledgehammer met glass or lacquer it was as though a faint electric shock hit my face and spread like a vibration through my body.

Did he notice us? Did he throw a hasty glance toward the house and see us at the window, as he raised his arms to strike again? Or had he simply finished his night's work? Whatever the case, he suddenly threw the sledgehammer aside and ran. Quick steps down an empty street. And he was gone.

A FEW WEEKS LATER, WE BOYS visited him in his studio apartment. The first thing I noticed was his finger, injured when he'd driven into the ditch that night. Dad's damaged index finger looming before me. Not wagging cheerfully, as my aunts' did, but pointing straight up in front of two dark eyes.

"This," he said, "is *her* fault."

When we didn't answer, he took a step closer, his gaze fixed on us.

"This. Is. Your. Mother's. Fault!"

Just that. Nothing more. He even robbed us of the possibility of forgiving him. And it was in the ensuing silence that I made a decision. Just as I had when I stood before the mirror in Wales as an eight-year-old. The feeling, or rather, the realization that I was standing before something inalienable, that could never be changed, made me make a clear declaration – not aloud, I wouldn't have dared do that – but quietly to myself. I decided in that moment to shut him out. If I was going to emerge from my childhood in one piece, I had to keep him out of my life. For years I continued to visit him every other weekend. I somehow assumed that it was my duty. I think my brothers felt that way too; I don't know why, we probably had no idea of what the alternative might be. Only as an adult did I break contact with him completely. But from this day onwards, when I was thirteen years old and stood with Dad's disfigured finger looming before me, he was a stranger to me.

He would have to carry his own life; I had enough with my own.

NORWAY – SPAIN

In Steinvika, just beyond the pebble beach that we went to each summer is a narrow bay where, in stormy weather, the waves are thrown meters into the air. With a gentle booming sound the water is sent frothing in all directions – not with every wave, but when the outgoing current meets the incoming current far out at sea, causing a wave to gather force and return to the shore with added impetus. When Dad told me about his lonely evening walks, it was here that I imagined him coming, to the place where I'd go with my minor sorrows. As a boy I discovered a spot on the mountainside that remained dry, however high the waves came. Here I could stand and look down into the swirling water, without being washed away or dragged into the depths. The onshore wind and curve of the bay always deflected the water from this spot, so that I could lose myself in the foamy white cataclysm below, as close to death as I could come without dying, as close to fear without fearing it.

It's a long time since I've been there. I rarely go to Langesund these days. The years I spent there seem so distant to me. Scattered on the desk before me are Mum's and Dad's letters, virtually all underlined in soft pencil, the bottom drawer is filled to the brim with family photographs, all neatly sorted, my shelves heave with books about Goa, East Africa and the British Empire, alongside ring binders, boxes of home movies, cassettes, recipes and other ephemera I've collected. I'm exhausted, tired of living in my childhood and in the twilight before my own time, tired of breathing life into dried ink and frozen faces, into memories that dissolve the instant I grab them.

The last letter I have from Dad to Mum is from London, and dated July 22, 1973:

"I like it here, and feel at home with my people, although I'm longing to see my children. I somehow feel they are more yours than mine in the sense that you have given them such a lot and they know so little of my background."

Dad was probably in Britain to visit Lionel. He'd spent the last decade establishing himself in Norway. Only a year after marrying Mum he'd gotten himself permanent work in a reputable shipyard, a line of work he continued until 1976, when he started work on the construction of Norsk Hydro's chlorine factory at Rafnes. He always left with impressive references. Meanwhile his father and siblings had settled in the States. When Michael Joseph, *I.*, his wife *F.* and their little daughter landed in New York in early March 1973, they went straight to Boston, where the rest of the family were waiting with pots of steaming hot chicken curry with potatoes and okra, and noodles with mushrooms and bacon.

After four months in their new homeland F. writes to Dad: "This is a truly great country. We don't miss Nairobi too much now. It was hard though to forget the big functions, the house gatherings & the cheap living. Yet the U.S.A. offers so much more of everything & there are many opportunities to make a quick buck if one is prepared to work very hard. We feel in our hearts that we should have come out here long before instead of enduring all the frustrations of the work permit system & the insecurity of not being a welcome race." It seemed that even Michael Joseph was settling in: "Papa is getting very americanized. He is now wearing buckled shoes, colored shirts & wide ties."

The family's long journey was at an end. But not Dad's. In 1977 Mum filed for divorce. I was ten, Dad was thirty-eight. In all the years that followed he would continue to live like a man who'd gotten divorced the week before. He didn't rebuild his life. Or make a new family. He just wandered eternally from apartment to apartment, from woman to woman, from country to country. His life came to resemble a coming-of-age novel in reverse: homeless, home, homeless.

Dad had destroyed his family, now he was unable to adapt. Mum's demand for a divorce was a manifestation of the times; the revolt against authority that marked the beginning of the end of the patriarchal hegemony in the West.

Mum found the strength in the end to break out, but she also had the spirit of the time on her side. Dad did not. Mum was in the first generation of Norwegian women to break ranks. She was a journalist, and always where the action was. In the early 1970s she was asked to sit on Bamble's Arts Council and was involved in the grassroots arts movement that was spreading across Norway at this time, arranging folk music events, a dance group and art association. In 1975, Women's Year, she joined the Labor Party. She became a socialist, a feminist, and filled our home in Langesund with artists and musicians. Eventually she became an artist herself, setting up her own studio; enjoying some success with her paintings and postcards of buxom women and chubby men, not dissimilar to Grandpa's wooden carvings. And like Grandpa, she wrote books; in her case, travel books, which surprised nobody.

Dad was a conservative through and through, a child of the colonies. Everything he had learned about being a man and husband proved useless, and he had no new perspectives with which to replace the old. He had destroyed what was most holy to him. Now he had nothing. Could a family simply dissolve? Could something that was joined by God be rent asunder? Could a man be expelled from his home? What is a man without his family? Nothing.

He started to drink.

I didn't really understand what was happening. Least of all *why*. I was a child, and for children things simply are as they are. I never asked myself why Dad was always dissatisfied with us and who we were, or why he got so angry when he cried, or why he didn't stop before his rage overflowed into shouting and violence. Now I think he no longer had any choice. That he had, long ago, done what we all perhaps crave deep down; to give in to the siren song within our nature. To simply let go. To stop holding back. To let everything run together; thoughts, words, feelings, the fibers of our muscles, the strength in our lungs. The relief, the elation of being a whole human being, if only for one ecstatic moment. Least of all did it occur to me that Dad's rage was about something he felt he'd lost and that he could never find with us. And why should I?

Throughout my youth, I visited him every other weekend at various places he rented or owned. I played the obligatory table tennis matches, endured the endless girlfriends, socialized with their offspring. I sat and watched the minute hand on the clock drag through the hours as he slept off the booze on the sofa. During all these years, which I will not describe in detail – just as I've not described the positive aspects of my childhood, or the other threads that comprise the waft and weave of my life but have no place in this story – I not only distanced myself from Dad, but from everything he stood for, from his story, and from his people. Apart from when the birthday cards arrived from my aunts and uncles in the States, or on the odd occasion when Dad persuaded me to accompany him on a picnic with the Norwegian Goan Association in Oslo, a small group of Goans with Norwegian husbands or wives and coffee-colored children, who, if my memory serves me right, seemed as disinterested in our common heritage as I was.

After I'd taken my university entrance exams and left home, I only saw Dad sporadically. In the end he disappeared from the country. The old millennium drew to a close, and a new one came in. Where he had lost his love, I found mine. A new life was founded, children were born, who were given their mother's surname, to Dad's added chagrin. Slowly but surely I pushed him out of my consciousness;

the childhood nightmares, the strong hands, I locked them all away. And I could because I was young. I'd never been good at phoning him, and eventually he stopped phoning me. In fact, the pact I'd made as a thirteen-year-old took its own natural course, with little effort on my part. I just quietly let him sail his own way. Which is how things continued until the summer of 2011, when I suddenly stopped, turned back, and looked behind me.

About a year after my visit to my aunts in Boston, one morning in June 2012, I do the unthinkable: I send Dad an email and ask if he wants to talk on Skype. I have no idea what to expect, I no longer know him. I am sitting at my desk in the living room in front of the bow window in the center of Oslo, and he is in his apartment in the Spanish town of Alfaz del Pi, where he now lives. Minutes later I get an email back.

"I tried calling u, but you did not answer. Tell me when u can skype. Love Papa."

He writes to me in English. That's how it's always been: he writes in English, and I reply in Norwegian. When we speak it's generally in my mother tongue. And now, the ringtone sounds from my Mac-speaker, followed by the sound his voice.

"Hei, det er pappa."

I recognize the hint of melodrama in his tone. His picture still hasn't come up on the screen. He probably hasn't found the video feature, so all I can see while he talks is a mirror image of myself. It occurs to me that I ought to have put on a shirt, I don't want him to see me like this in my thermals, I have no wish for him to see my middle-aged man's body, the way it is now. Then his image appears. He is sitting behind a pendant thing that dangles from his reading lamp, the white wall and bookshelf in the background tell me nothing I don't already know. His apartments have all looked the same, indeterminately modern and void of any personality.

He looks older, and there's something about his teeth, which I suddenly remember from our last meeting five years ago. It was in a cafe in Oslo, neutral ground, chosen by my brothers and I so as to avoid any attempt at intimacy. The same strikes me now as it did then: his teeth are somehow shorter or smaller than before. He has, I realize suddenly, got false teeth, and it occurs to me that at some time in my life, not too many years hence, a dentist will place a hand reassuringly on my shoulder and tell me that the time has come, that my mouth must now be cleared of its last natural fixtures. Death begins as a disassembly. But shouldn't his dentures at least fit? Dad doesn't have the face of an aged man that comes with a complete absence of teeth. Instead, these new teeth cause only a slight, and thereby bizarre, distortion of the familiar; as though his lower jaw had been replaced with the corresponding body part of another, much smaller man. It takes only a minute alteration to the familiar for us to see things as though for the first time. Which was how I saw Dad that day in the café, and how I see him now on the screen before me.

We sit here making conversation of the most elementary nature. He finds it hard to understand what I say, I don't know why. Surely he can't have forgotten his Norwegian – perhaps his hearing has started to go. Or perhaps it's just his way of protecting himself from the uncomfortable fact that we have so little to say to each other.

I speak slowly and clearly: Is it warm over there?... It's very warm here... Yes, a vest... Thinning hair... Yes, time passes. Time passes, I say.

Sitting here with my headphones on, I feel as though I'd joined a Norwegian language course. Nothing meaningful is said. I try to catch Dad's gaze, but it's impossible on Skype; the camera lenses are above our screens, so we're obliged to choose whether to look directly at the screen to see one another, or whether to peer up into the lens so the other person can see our eyes. Since it feels more natural to look down at each other's faces on the screen, we sit there with lowered eyes like two coy schoolgirls. I don't look him in the eye for even a second; to do so would mean asking him to look up into the lens, it's impossible on Skype to look into each other's eyes simultaneously, we just have to look at each other by turn. Thinking about it now, that's how we've always looked at each other.

After we've hung up, I know what I've got to do. I can no longer put off the inevitable. Although I still try, of course, for as long as possible, until events force me out from my comfortable chair.

A couple of weeks later I get another email from Dad. Our Skype call has clearly rekindled the hope that he harbored in my youth, and that I know deep down, he never quite gave up on. The hope of reconciliation. Could I, he asks, contemplate visiting him in Alfaz del Pi? He'll pay for my ticket, he'll even cover my expenses, if only I come and stay with him for a few days. No strings attached, only three or four days sharing his world.

Everything in me rejects the idea. But I can see that I have, in reality, invited myself. I have meddled in the unnamable, tugged at the strings that bind me to him, while doing everything possible to avoid meeting him face to face. I have journeyed through his life, and then, being the historian I am, I have tried to bury myself in my sources. Spread out on my desk before me, are the letters, photographs and other historical documents. I have squeezed as much life out of them as I can, now they lie there like a heap of dry autumn leaves.

Enough letters. Enough photographs. It is time to travel again.

DAD MOVED TO THE SPANISH COSTA BLANCA in the early 1990s. Designated forty years earlier as a destination for package tour holidays by General Franco, by the time Dad arrived in Benidorm it was like an open-air museum dedicated to the early days of mass tourism; with blaring discos and vending machines along the promenade, for a few pesetas, you could buy a pack of condoms and a fake leopard skin thong for a night on the town. The area attracted permanent residents too, all of whom were fleeing something, ex-colonials from the shattered British Empire, those deemed traitors after the war or other shady sorts. Others weren't so much fleeing *from* something, as *to* something: hoping for a life of greater freedom. Others again were simply escaping the long, dark winters of Northern Europe; retirees with pensions in their pockets.

The old village of Alfaz del Pi and the harbor area of Albir below it turned into Northern European pensioners' towns long ago. The Norwegians have created a little corner of Norway for themselves here. With the El Vikingo restaurant at its center and a good supply of traditional Norwegian meatballs and newspapers, they can enjoy the cheap wine and sunshine without being unduly bothered by the fact that they're living in another country with another culture.

One evening in early July, I board a plane to Alicante. Up in the dark and empty void, I feel nothing can touch me. Only when the cabin door opens and the hot Spanish night air hits me, do I feel it. Like a fist grabbing at my intestines and squeezing. There is no way back now. Minutes later I am in the arrivals hall, scanning the usual semicircle of people waiting, ignoring the searching eyes of chauffeurs with their name boards. I spot him getting up from a plastic chair in the corner. There is an over-eagerness about his movements. I note the joy in his eyes and respond with a smile, and instantly remind myself of the stewardess who just waved me goodbye. We hug and exchange a few words about the flight. He has a young Ukrainian girl with him, whom I soon realize is his cleaner, driver and general assistant. I sit in the back seat of the car and stare into the deep night that the headlights barely manage to sweep ahead of them. From the front seats I hear the lame attempts at communication between Dad and Kristina as he tries to give her directions despite not knowing where we are, and she tries to protest in her broken English.

It is well past midnight when we reach Alfaz. We drop Kristina off at a street corner and drive to an apartment block on the outskirts of Alfaz. The two of us are now alone.

On his front door I notice a porcelain plaque that says "Familia de Figueiredo." A pang of guilt shoots through me. As the door opens, I find myself staring at a wall of photographs of myself, my brothers and my daughters. Pictures I've seen before, on other walls in other homes in other countries. They are all at least twenty years old, from when my children were small, and I still hadn't lost contact with Dad entirely. I look at the portraits of my younger self and realize that I live here in this apartment, that I have been part of his life for years. But only up to a certain age, as though I were a dead son, a young man torn away in his prime, living on as a shadow on the wall.

One of these pictures is a portrait of me as a thirteen-year-old taken by my eldest brother, now a photographer, when I was still his favorite and only model. It is taken with a soft lens, I am sitting with a bare torso on a sheepskin rug, eyes turned heavenwards like some sort of St. Sebastian. I catch myself feeling a vague regret at my own demise, quickly followed by the impulse to run out of the door I have just walked through.

I do not. The plan is to spend four days with Dad before I go back home.

In the morning he takes me to his various haunts; the pub on the corner, the pub a little further up the street, the breakfast place by the beach. We have lunch at La Pensionista before driving to the covered market El Ciste for a shandy. That's pretty much it. Norwegian, German and British pensioners everywhere; a woman hobbling on crutches, a bare-chested man with a huge tanned belly and a bypass scar like a shriveled red snake twisting its way under sun-bleached chest hair. Between Dad's various watering holes, the sun burns over a landscape of asphalt, gaudy advertising boards, withered grass and hard white earth. This is where Dad has chosen to live, amongst the red-faced Northern European pensioners who have turned their backs on their homelands in their old age, to spend their days drinking between meals and eating between drinking; living a no-man's-land existence that has robbed them of their last topic of conversation; namely the weather.

Refugees. Though, on reflection, these Northern Europeans are like colonists here, parading their affluent bellies, served by the crisis-battered Southern Europeans. Where many refugees entering Norway bring little with them and send as much as possible back home, these Norwegian emigrants come with riches and spend all they have here. From a global perspective I suppose all this has a balancing effect. I can't help but see an exquisite irony in this, but I let it pass. I am here to meet my father.

My first impression is that Dad has found a kind of peace here; a calm that I imagine only faith and resignation can give. We sit side by side on his beige leather sofa, and he permits me to turn my voice recorder on. He seems surprised by my newly awakened interest in his life, but is happy to have the chance to talk. In the office I find another ring-binder containing yet more letters, as well as a family album and five cassettes labeled "Goa 1977," all of which he says I can take home with me. Dad is surprisingly interested in Mum and about the man who entered her life as soon as he was out of the door. Are the parts for the old '54 Mercedes still in the basement? Are they happy together? No bitterness, no accusations.

Seeing Dad is like meeting myself after the passing of the storm, when everything has been destroyed and calm can settle over my life. The atmosphere between us is friendly but tense, and I soon notice a rising restlessness in his eyes and body; as though he can't quite believe this harmony can last.

The next day he has a hectic schedule planned for us. Immediately after breakfast he insists on taking me to a Russian restaurant by the beach in Albir, where Kristina has an extra job as a waitress. From this moment on Dad seems to lose his grip. First, he indulges in a little light flirtation with Kristina as she gives us the menu. Then, when she next passes our table, he stretches out and pinches her behind. She gives out a little squeal, a squeal of insecurity and economic oppression. After the meal Dad blows his nose on the linen napkin. We go without leaving a tip. And so it continues. We've barely set foot in his apartment again, before he suggests we go to his regular pub around the corner. We are greeted by the owner, Sebastian.

"This is my son, Ivo."

"So I see, Hugo, so I see."

Then to the post office, to check his empty mailbox. He introduces me to the post-lady.

"My son, he's here from Norway."

Then there's the trip to the optician-lady, followed by the bank-lady. He is on first name terms with all the people who work in the shops and businesses he frequents. He flirts, he jokes, but I think to myself: Is this it? Is this all he's managed to achieve? A life without any real friends or family, lacking closeness and commitment, just hola amigo from the bank to the pub?

In the evening we drive to what I assume is his last regular haunt, in the little village of Calpe, half an hour's drive north along the coast. It is here, to the seafood restaurants in the little marina, that Dad takes guests when he wants to make a special fuss over them. It's only when we've parked the car and set off along the quay toward the rows of parasols and awnings, that I notice he is drunk. I say nothing, but when we sit at a table and he orders a bottle of red, I realize I've walked into a trap. Dad is a proud drunk-driver. For years I refused to get in a car with him when he'd been drinking. But I've forgotten this, and now I am stuck here. I know that he'll never hand his car keys over to me.

I try hinting. Perhaps he could go light on the booze since he's driving? A shadow crosses his face. His eyes darken. His gaze is blurry yet steely.

"No!"

It's as though the strength has been blown out of me. The voice that issues from my mouth is that of a twelve-year-old, so weak compared to his manly tone. I do exactly as I did all those years ago – the only thing I can do in the face of this big, strong, intoxicated father – I reason with him diplomatically, determined not to let him see my pain. Like a shot he answers:

"YOU do not tell me what to do!"

He says nothing more for the rest of the evening. It is a quarter past eight, and the food still hasn't arrived. Eventually two overly smiley waiters turn up, each carrying a huge pan of sloppy paella, which they place before us. We eat in silence, interrupted only by the clink of cutlery and the sound of slurping as we suck the juices out of the crayfish claws. When we leave the restaurant an hour later, the bottle of wine is still on the table untouched. He maintains his silence in the car home. I hold my tongue too. Something is happening inside me. I sense his masculine presence beside me. In the corner of my eye I observe his hand on the gear stick. His body seems to fill the car. He is driving fast, wrenching at the wheel each time we veer toward the center lane markings. He has my life in his hands. Just as he did back then. The silence weighs on my chest. I know he has no choice. I know he has to do as he does. I hold my breath. If I exhale the windows will explode, if I inhale I will be filled with this evil. I wish I didn't have a body right now, I spread my fingers so as not to feel my own skin. I was wrong. Dad's rage has not gone, this darkness runs too deep. I should have known – nothing disappears, we carry our burdens for all time. Emotions weigh so little, Dad is so strong and can carry so much, far more than I. Darkness is closing in, he drives even faster. We put the kilometers behind us as we race through little towns with bright neon signs and deserted streets. On the beach below, the parasols and deckchairs have been stacked up for the night as though the sole fortification along Europe's border against the poor third world were made of woven plastic and aluminum poles. The third world of Dad's childhood. We turn off from the main road. He avoids hitting the speed humps by swinging the car to the extreme left and into the oncoming traffic, then swerving back to the right again. The past two days suddenly crowd in on me; the cramped apartment, the bed linen that smells like Dad, the pubic hairs in the shower and toilet bowl, all the things which to my surprise and relief I've been able to endure. Now I feel my entire body is infected. A sense of hopelessness grips me now, even though I hadn't come with any great expectations.

Back in Dad's apartment I ask him the question I've been preparing for the last fifteen minutes. I have recovered my composure, and won't tolerate any argument or discussion about what's happened. All I know is that I've got to get away.

"What do you say? Should I leave here tomorrow?"

A carefully formulated question. I am threatening to leave but push the decision onto him. He looks at me uncomprehendingly.

"Leave, why?"

I meet his gaze.

"Ah, that." He waves his hand dismissively and turns to go into the living room.

"You talk to me as though I was a child. I don't like that."

And that's it. The subject is closed. Not a word about the two hours of demonstrative silence, about the hazardous drive home. Nothing has happened; that is, it's all in my head. He's smart, I must admit. With reluctant admiration I watch his back as he goes over to the drinks cabinet. I could leave then and there, check into a hotel or sleep at the train station. But I'll stay just one more night; prisoner to my own sense of decency. I can't make a polite escape until tomorrow morning.

Sleep is slow to come that night. The din of Benidorm's nightlife can be heard in the distance. A wind has blown up outside, but it is stuffy in here even with the fan on and the window open. My door is firmly shut, but the draft makes it rattle as if someone were trying to get in. I remember peering at the clock at about four, so I must have fallen asleep.

Any sensible person has a terror of their parents. The only way to survive childhood is a timely escape. I am lying in bed in Dad's apartment in Alfaz del Pi. It is the morning of my third day. I can feel his presence on the other side of the door. I know that he's lying on the sofa with his head on a sweat-soaked pillow without a cover. Mindless programs roll across the TV screen. He is waiting for me to emerge so we can spend the rest of the day together. I was wrong. There is no peace here, not even resignation. He is as restless as ever. If he seems calmer it's just because there's nothing to do. He doesn't shout because he knows no one will hear. But the rage is still there, like an animal in hibernation, ready to spring to life as soon as it is fed and nourished.

And my presence is nourishment.

I have decided to leave one day earlier than planned. Everything in me wants to go. Yet I feel an unexpected sadness at leaving him here, in the land where pensioners come to die. But hasn't he wrought his own path toward a lonely old age? Why do I have these qualms? What do I owe him?

I toss in bed, quarreling with the physical urge to get up. When I finally go into the living room, Dad is ready with the car keys in his hand. He understands that our meeting is over for this time. During the short drive to the train station I am deep in thought. My bad conscience at abandoning him refuses to lift. But isn't my self-flagellation hiding something else? An uneasy thought is forcing its way into my consciousness. Is it really just a sense of guilt that nags at me? Don't I also feel a touch of admiration for Dad and his reckless freedom? Am I perhaps one of the circle of obedient servants, seduced, despite my better reason, by his negative charisma? Enthralled at the thought of being able to grab what I want, regardless of any consequences. When I visited the family in Boston, Uncle *I.*'s daughter told me about a car journey that she, her father and Dad had taken one winter across Maine. Of all his brothers, Uncle *I.* had been closest to Dad back in East Africa, despite their temperaments being polar opposite. Where Dad was assertive and dominant, Uncle *I.* was selfless and timorous, a Martha child. Now he was sitting behind the wheel, visibly nervous because Dad was committing a traffic offence by drinking beer in the backseat. As soon as Dad saw his brother's agitation, he began to click his beer can provocatively, his enjoyment rising in tandem with his brother's discomfort. Finally Dad announced that he needed to get out for a pee. They parked the car near a large heap of snow, but instead of going behind it Dad climbed to the very top and did his business in full view of everyone. While Dad's brother cringed with embarrassment, the sight of her urinating uncle seemed to prompt admiration in my cousin. She was still a child when this episode took place, and of all the family she would be the one to maintain the closest ties.

When my cousin told me this story, I was startled at my own reaction. I could relate to her admiration. In fact the image of Dad standing on the top of a heap of snow and pissing for all the world to see, shameless and free, filled me with a strange sense of pride; the same feeling perhaps as when we were kids and claimed the highest pile of snow as our own, defending it from our playmates, with no other purpose than to see the world from its highest peak and to prove our dominance. To be King of the Castle.

Until, that is, another kid pulled us down and took our place.

As we park the car and walk along the platform of Benidorm's modest train station, I feel sure that I'm leaving a doomed man behind. Dad is an Icarus, a falling Tower of Babel, a sinking Atlantis, a man drowning in a sea of tears. He is slowly dying, and dying alone among strangers. Why on earth has he chosen to exile himself in this cheerless place? Yet I can't dismiss the thought that he belongs here in some way. Here, in this colony of Norwegian pensioners in Alfaz del Pi, he can do as he pleases, live as he wants, help himself to what he wants, without anyone protesting. Once again he is sovereign, just as in his childhood in East Africa. The only difference is that he is now one of the colonists.

Viewed thus, he has rediscovered his childhood paradise. A hellish paradise perhaps, as a paradise usually is when we return to it. Still, he has in some sense come home. As the train doors close, I see him waving from the platform for the last time, and reciprocate with the last smile I have. Then come the tears.

SOME WEEKS LATER, LYING on my bed at home in Oslo, I look through the plastic bag of letters and photographs I brought back with me from Spain. Shortly after my return my brother converted the five cassettes I found in Dad's wardrobe into digital voice files. They are now waiting to be played on the Mac beside me. I have no idea what they contain, beyond what is suggested by the penciled labels on the cassettes: "Goa 1977." It's a sunny summer's day outside my window, a fresh breeze plays in the blinds. I am back here in my own world, back in my own life. Yet it is with trepidation that I put on my headphones, turn on the Mac, and press play.

The whirr of a cassette tape. A click. Background noise. Then Dad's voice: *Year, nineteen-seventy-seven. On the fifteenth of November I was at Heathrow Airport awaiting Papa, who was coming from Boston.*

Dad seems to be reading some sort of report. But about what? For whom? I haven't listened for long before it suddenly becomes clear. The recording is indeed a report that Dad made for his siblings during a trip with his father to Goa in November 1977; barely a month after he'd reluctantly signed his divorce papers at the town hall in Skien. Soon the reason for his trip also comes clear. After living for years in the States with each of his kids in turn, Grandfather has decided, at the age of seventy-seven, that he wants to get remarried. Through connections in the village in Goa, he has found himself a suitable wife, just as his father did before him. And now he wants to get married in

Bombay, where there is a large Goan community. His children have clearly sensed trouble, and Dad has taken on the task of accompanying Grandfather back to his motherland; not just to avert a crazy marriage, but to sell the family house and arrange Grandfather's will.

From the moment they land at Santa Cruz Airport in Bombay, Dad feels overwhelmed by the city: *Thousands of people. Communications are bad. Cannot rely on anybody.* The controlled aggression in his voice tells me he is tense; it seems he needs someone to blame – whoever listens to this tape in the future – for the situation in which he finds himself now. Almost every night while they're in India he takes out the cassette recorder and gives a precise account of the day's events. No detail seems too trivial; he is determined to document everything for his siblings, particularly his handling of the marriage plans and the making of the will.

After the first night in a transit hotel near the airport, he goes through Grandfather's pockets and absurdly heavy suitcase. The suitcase proves to contain a typewriter, which he desperately tries to persuade the old man to leave behind. In the jacket he discovers a copy of a telegram Grandfather has sent, and a letter from a certain Don Manuel Machado, the man who has set up the contact between Grandfather and his prospective bride, Annie Fernandez.

"The lady was shown to me by Valdimir, sister of Mons Sequera of Arrarim," writes Machado. "She's a widow with no children. She's working as a teacher on a small salary of 200 rupees a month. She's well built and strong, she's fifty years old. She will look after you and give you good nourishment. Fair and beautiful. Before marrying you, she wants to know how much money you are prepared to give her, should anything happen to you."

He then instructs Grandfather to put his house in Tabravvadó in the bride's name, or to transfer an amount equivalent to its value into a bank account.

In the unlikely case that Grandfather doesn't fall for Annie Fernandez, Machado adds, there's no reason for him to give up all hope of marriage:

"After seeing her, you will make up your mind and then fix the ring," he says. "She is believing me and coming forward to get married to you. If not, Valdimir is prepared to marry you. Number one will look after you till your death."

On the envelope is a handwritten note: "To the postmaster in the U.S.A. Please deliver the letter to the address at once. Someone died and so he has to fly to India."

Don Manuel Machado is clearly a crook, although not a very smart one.

The following morning Machado doesn't even turn up at the hotel as promised. Dad has to call a taxi, and following the vague directions given in his letter, they weave their way through the streets of Bombay. Grandfather is dressed in his best suit and very excited at the prospect of meeting his bride-to-be. His son, by contrast, is very stressed. They drive around for nearly two hours, they take several wrong turns and have to stop to ask the way. At one point Dad gets out of the car to ask for directions. When he turns around again, the back seat is empty. Grandfather has vanished without trace into the bustling crowds of Bombay. An elegantly dressed, elderly gentleman with white hair, lured by the dream he once had of his twilight years, the dream of a comfy chair on a cool terrace, shaded from the shimmering heat, a woman's footsteps, a glass of Feni on a tray, freshly ironed shirts on a Sunday morning. The heat, the air filled with the aroma of foods and spices, these are as they should be; but not the noise, the roar of mopeds and endless honking of cars, the crowds, the chaos. Grandfather, this is Bombay not Saligão! You will die here! But here comes Dad, dashing through the streets, somebody points at a concrete block of flats, a staircase leads up to the first floor, to the second, and there he is, Grandfather.

"Papa, this is the wrong building, what are you doing here?"

Soon after this episode their driver finally thinks he's found the right place and pulls up in front of a drab concrete residential complex. Grandfather strides forth, every inch the splendid groom. People stream out of their houses and flock around him, adults and children alike. They must think he's a modern day Croesus from America; one of their own who has crossed the ocean, made it big, and has returned to bestow riches upon them all. Somebody directs them to Machado's apartment. Inside he greets them from his makeshift bed on the floor. He informs them that they are expected at Mrs. Valdimir Pinto's house at four o'clock that afternoon, and that the fair Annie Fernandez will be present. Machado's room is horribly stuffy and overlooks a very noisy road, but Dad and Grandfather have no option but to wait.

As the clock strikes four, the sound of tires on gravel can be heard outside. They go out to the taxi and are taken a short distance to Mrs. Valdimir Pinto's house. The Pinto residence is close to The Sacred Heart Church in the old Portuguese town of Santa Cruz. It's not a bad district, but the house is clearly at the wrong end. An aging woman in dirty clothes is waiting for them in the doorway. Dad realizes that this is Mrs. Pinto; the woman who has so generously offered to be an alternative bride should Grandfather be dissatisfied with Annie Fernandez. Standing behind Mrs. Pinto is a retarded boy who turns out to be her son, and her adult daughter, holding a baby, a urine-stinking bundle, in her arms.

Dad's voice on the tape sounds tense again. He is describing the events of the previous day, but he is still filled with revulsion. He is sitting on the floor of a strange house in Bombay. There is barely any furniture, the air is hot and stagnant. He knows that none of these people wish him well, but he has no choice but to talk to them. Grandfather has given promises; verbal agreements have been made. The four of them – Grandfather, Dad, Don Machado and Mrs. Pinto – sit in a row against the wall to wait for Annie Fernandez while the Pinto children stand staring mutely at the elegant old man with the white mane.

Suddenly she appears in the doorway. Annie Fernandez. Dad finds her neither "fair" nor "beautiful" as promised. *A fattish woman around fifty or something, I don't know, but, er, she's so very shy, she sits in the living room and everybody's there.* Eventually this unprepossessing woman plucks up the courage to whisper a few words. *I felt like being sick, when that woman told me that she likes me already and started calling me 'son'.* But shyness soon engulfs Dad's new mother once again, rendering her silent. Finally, she nods at their hostess and they both disappear into an adjoining room.

When the two women reemerge, it is Mrs. Pinto who does the talking:

"How much is Michael Joseph earning in pension?"

"Look, this is not important," Dad answers, "we don't bother about the money. The most important thing here is that you can look after Papa."

There's a crackle and then the tape breaks off with a click. Opening the next track, I find that we've skipped forward a few days, and Dad and Grandfather are already in Goa. So, what happened to the negotiations with Mrs. Valdimir Pinto? How did they escape the clutches of these marriage-crazed women and their dodgy agent in Bombay? Had Dad really intended to abandon Grandfather to these people? I search among the papers I brought back from Spain and find a copy of a letter Dad wrote to his siblings that describes the India-trip in detail. From it I can reconstruct the next twenty-four hours or so in Bombay. As I suspected, Dad does not really enter any negotiations; he is diplomatic and more clear-headed than the tense voice might suggest. His sole intention was, of course, to bring Grandfather back.

Nevertheless, Dad decides to let the old man spend one night with Mrs. Pinto. In his letter he explains that he needed time to arrange the practicalities of the trip ahead, first to Goa and then back home. He may also have thought that since Grandfather represented such an investment to these people, they'd have the wisdom to treat him well.

It was a decision he may have regretted when he turned up next morning to find his father asleep in the bed, with Mrs. Pinto lying on the floor with a threadbare blanket over her, and her daughter, still with her baby in her arms, urine streaming onto the floor, without anyone batting an eye. Dad feels something rise in his throat, but controls himself. Mrs. Pinto wakes up and gets up from her makeshift bed. She explains that Grandfather has agreed to the marriage and that everything will be clear when Don Machado and Annie Fernandez arrive in an hour. But when they are all finally gathered, Dad makes a polite but firm announcement on behalf of himself and his siblings: He dismisses the idea of any marriage, thanks everyone for their kindness toward his father and gives all three of them – Don Machado, Mrs. Pinto and the former prospective bride, Annie Fernandez – one hundred rupees each. Then taking his father's hand, he leads him to a taxi waiting outside.

Two days later, father and son are in Saligão. They head straight for the only house still in the family's ownership, after Aleixo's property in Salmona was sold. The shabby old house stands wall-to-wall with the Santa Ana Chapel in Tabravvadó. It is now inhabited by Marie, an orphan Hindu girl who was originally taken in by Ti Filu to look after her in her dotage, who has lived here alone since the old lady's death.

Dad is back in the land of his forefathers. He was a child of ten when he was here last. Later, as a young man, he was ready to sacrifice himself for this country, to bring his Norwegian sweetheart here and to join a new generation of settlers. He chose Norway instead. He has fulfilled all of his father's and grandfather's expectations, broken through the barrier of the immigrant, overcome racial prejudice and made a new life in Europe, with an education and high income. Now he is divorcing his Norwegian wife and his sons are slipping away from him. His siblings are scattered across the globe, his childhood homeland in East Africa has long been lost to him, only Goa remains unchanged in his imagination.

But now that he's actually here, he can't bear to stay in this house. Not even for one night. *Dirty. Shocking hygiene. Bad lighting, can't even write a letter, no lamps, there's no furniture, there is absolutely – you know, you just come to a – where you feel like crying to start with, and in the end, you sort of build up courage and continue.*

In short: *The house is a wreck.*

He leaves Grandfather in Marie's care, finds a taxi and moves in with an affluent relative in one of the larger villas in the village. But further disappointment awaits. One evening he wanders into the club where the village men spend their evenings playing whist and drinking Feni. The grinning faces that greet him, say it all: *Papa's marriage here has been a big joke, everybody's laughing, typical Goan mentality, but it... hurts me.*

Village-folk are all the same. Rumors have been going around for ages, and this has only been made worse by Grandpa *bragging and talking big* about his trip to Saligão.

Another break in the tape. Crackles. A new recording. Voices in a room. Echoey. Hard brick walls and tiled floor. A hot afternoon perhaps, in a spacious living room. An elderly man and much younger woman are talking in a language I recognize as Konkani, the Goan language that bears no resemblance to either Hindi or Portuguese. One of the voices belongs to Grandfather, and I assume the other belongs to Marie, who can't speak English. Until this I've only heard Dad's voice, now it feels as though an endless space has opened up between myself and the events on the tape. As if in a dream, I hear Grandfather's melancholic voice, I picture his sweeping hand gestures, his white mane nodding. The woman laughs. My old grandfather's voice, droning away in this alien tongue makes me think of an ancient shaman sitting by a campfire. Then a familiar voice cuts in.

"You're talking too fast, papa, you're not talking loud enough."

Dad doesn't understand Konkani, the language of his ancestors. Grandfather grumbles, but reverts to English. The shaman disappears, to be replaced by an articulate British Empire bureaucrat. But then the tape starts to break up. Only fragments can be heard now.

"My own father got married again... times do not change, YOU change... you see, my son, I have a vast experience..."

The rest is drowned in crackling and background noise. I let the tape run for a while more. Nothing. On the last tape Dad is talking with the wealthy relative with whom he has been staying. The clinking of glasses suggests that they are sharing a bottle of Feni. The cassette recorder is running in the background, no doubt they've forgotten it, until it switches itself off with a clunk.

The time capsule closes. I am back in my bed in Oslo. A tram can be heard rumbling past outside. I lie there staring at the ceiling, thoughts and emotions racing through me. This wasn't what I'd expected. My father rescued his father while his own life was falling apart. He'd crossed continents and oceans, he'd been selfless, he'd been decisive and assertive. Was this really him? I'd tried to spend just four days in Alfaz del Pi, the backwater where he's ended up in his old age, and I'd only managed three before making my escape.

Yet it wasn't this realization that brought tears to my eyes, but a little comment in Dad's letter to his siblings: "Papa in the end listens to me because he has NO CHOICE, and I make him laugh on top of it by cracking these old jokes."

Old jokes, a gentle nudge, laughter. Love. Was it that simple? For Dad, it seems it was; and everything suggests that he had the old patriarch in the palm of his hand.

Or did he?

One more fragment of conversation can be made out on the tape. I'm not sure where they are here, although I presume they're still in Saligão.

"You're sick of the place, aren't you?" says Dad in a rather flippant tone.

Grandpa sounds offended, but his reply is restrained, his tone that of an imperious old man:

"Don't say that I am sick of the place. It's my birthplace."

"That's a lie. You were born in Zanzibar."

"You can be born anywhere," Grandfather retorts, "but I am a person of this soil. You see? I love this place. But since my children are in America, I would like to return. And secondly, to keep me company until I die, I'd like to marry."

"Keep you company? You've got your children to keep you company." Dad tries to maintain his humorous tone, but Grandfather refuses to budge.

"Will my children be at my bedside? No... the children are working, they have their own lives. You see..."

Pause. He continues:

"... unless... YOU sacrifice... my son?"

"I don't mind sleeping by your bedside," answers Dad, as though Grandfather's question isn't quite serious.

"You see, if my son Xavier sacrifices to be with me, then I would love to be alone."

"You come to Norway then?"

"No, no," he chuckles, "too much winter! Hahaha."

Grandfather may have been stubborn and confused, for all I know he may even have been suffering from early stage dementia. But he was canny enough to know that a man is nothing without his children, and that the way into their hearts and spare rooms might be a trip to India and the threat of a prospective bride from the slums of Bombay.

Michael Joseph Conceição de Figueiredo died in Boston in October 1982, surrounded by five of his beloved children. He was laid to rest in Fairview Cemetery, 12,657 kilometers from Saligão and 11,572 kilometers from Langata Cemetery in Nairobi, where his wife Herminia had lain for some fifteen years. That's how it is; people who travel all of their lives, who travel for generations, are forced to leave their dead wherever they may be at the time. Our lineage rests in these scattered graves, like so many beads on a string across the globe. Great Grandfather lies in an unmarked grave in Goa, his first wife under a weathered stone in Pemba, while Grandmother lies in Nairobi and Grandfather on the East Coast of the United States. When I bury my father on European soil one day – whether in Spain or in Norway, I don't yet know – the string of beads will be complete. My father's family has traveled for three generations, always living on borrowed land and forever moving on. But it's nice to think that it's been their habit to leave one of their dead before they go, a pledge to their host country; a body to give nourishment to the earth that, for a while, gave nourishment to them.

The price they paid is that their host countries repeatedly failed to recognize them. On Grandfather's death certificate is a box headed: *Race (e.g. White, Black, American, Indian, etc.) Specify*. My aunt must have been in some doubt when she filled it in. None of these categories were quite appropriate. For lack of a better alternative, she wrote in a hasty hand: *White*, followed by her signature.

AFTER MY ESCAPE FROM DAD'S APARTMENT in Alfaz del Pi, I was convinced that I had seen him for the last time. I thought my next trip to Costa Blanca would be to collect his coffin. But that wasn't to be. One day that winter, the portrait of an exotic woman appears on my Facebook profile. She is about forty years old and is posing in something reminiscent of traditional American Indian dress, with a border and embroidery and a feather headdress. She is holding the hand of a delightful little girl of about three or four, also wearing feathers on her head.

I send an email to my brothers:

"Our stepmother is a Red Indian!"

When precisely Carmen came into Dad's life, I'm not sure. But it couldn't have been more than a couple of years before she sent me the picture of herself and her daughter, along with a friend request. Dad was now in his seventy-fourth year, thirty-one years older than his girlfriend, who turned out to be from the Philippines. The reason I hadn't met her in Spain was that she hadn't yet visited him there. Rather, he'd always been the one to travel to her. Indications pointed to a relationship where he had the money and sought love, while she needed the first and offered the latter. A form of global exchange, perhaps; but the question was, who was using whom.

In the next few months after my return to Oslo, I barely heard from Dad. During the autumn I sat at my desk working on a manuscript that was painfully boring, but which I had to submit. Winter came, miserable, cold. Dad had told me he that was going to the Philippines for Christmas, and after accepting Carmen as a friend on Facebook I was able to follow his life in Baguio City, where she lived with her extended family. Pictures of beautiful, smiling women, laughing children and vital young men. Carmen's brothers? No elderly folk, except a grey figure I assumed to be the mother. And Dad, of course, sitting in a living room or a kitchen, posing with Carmen in front of a military monument in a park, or standing beside her in a bakery wearing a purple striped apron and matching headgear, making pierogi dumplings while the baker doubles up with laughter in the background. Or posing in a pull-off on a country road, in front of a landscape that is doubtless more picturesque in reality. Most of the pictures are taken at parties or family dinners, where two characters stand out. The first is the customary whole pig, roasted and glazed, then sitting proudly, soon to be half-eaten, its glossy grinning head like an over-sized ship's figurehead on a sinking galleon. The other is little *L.U.*, Carmen's daughter, with the confident smile of a spoiled child as she lounges on everybody's lap or clings on Dad's neck.

In one of the photographs they are sleeping in the same bed, *L.U.* with one leg over Dad's chest. Her face reposed in sleep, contented, safe. I feel a stabbing in my chest.

Early in 2013, just after New Year, the message came that Dad had fallen ill. It wasn't easy to figure out precisely what had happened from Carmen's English, but we understood eventually that he'd suffered a serious diabetic attack. Hardly surprising, since he'd stopped taking his medication long ago and began most days with a whiskey and sour or a rum and coke.

Had Dad finally succeeded in forging his own destruction? Was he at the end of the road? He was lying in a hospital somewhere in the Philippines, somewhere in the world, among strangers in a foreign land. He had talked so warmly about his girlfriend and her family when I visited him the summer before: "They're just like Goans," he'd said.

"They live with their families within a strong Catholic community."

But NO, this certainly had little to do with any warm Goan circles. Rather he had fallen for a fantasy, he was chasing a dream of what might have been, just as my Grandfather had done when he decided to find a new wife in Bombay.

Was this where Dad's story was going to end? Out in this seemingly empty void? Or perhaps things weren't as bad as they appeared at first glance? While we didn't know which hospital he was in, we could do little. Carmen was our only source of information, though what exactly she was trying to tell us, it was hard to say.

At about this time she sends a picture via Facebook. The picture shows Dad lying in a hospital bed, looking gaunt. Sitting beside him is Carmen with *L.U.* on her lap. The little girl has her usual mischievous smile. Carmen is making a v-sign for the camera with her right hand. In her left hand, above the bedridden diabetic, she holds a plate full of chocolate cake topped with lashings of cream. It's as if she wants to say: "A bit more cake, and the money is mine."

This picture is shared widely; among my brothers and sisters, aunts, uncles and all the siblings in the United States and Europe. And since I'm the one who has resumed contact with Dad, I am the one among my brothers who gets a stream of e-mails from our Boston Aunts. *Ivo, what is happening? You must go to the Philippines and get your father out of there!* I know full well what the family expects of me. I know what my duty as a Goan is. And in a quiet moment I also realize that this duty stands true universally. Dad holds the last card, the trump card: Fetch me, or I'll die.

Once again I put off the inevitable. I call Dad on his Spanish mobile, with no answer. Then a few days into February, I get a message from my aunts telling me they've been on Skype with Carmen and Dad. The only problem was that Carmen hadn't managed to turn on her microphone, so that she and Dad could hear my aunts, but my aunts couldn't hear them. I imagine my aunts yelling at the little window on the computer, a silent, flickering image of an unknown place somewhere on the planet, where their brother lies limply on his sick bed, in the hands of people who may, or may not, wish him better. He tries to answer them. Do they see his lips move? Can they read his eyes?

I click on Carmen's Facebook page, scroll through the pictures, studying them in detail, stopping at one that seems to have been taken at dinner last Christmas. Dad is sitting hunched at the heavily laden table. He is surrounded by Carmen and her family. Their cheeks are aglow with laughter and wine. The only guests not laughing are Dad and the roasted pig that lies prostrate on the table with its trotters in front of it, squealing mutely, eyes empty, like Dad's. Carmen leans over toward Dad, laughing, and lifting a fork-full of food to his mouth. But he doesn't open his mouth, he just sits there with a dead expression. He is unshaven, he doesn't have his teeth in, and his mouth hangs loose at the corners. I don't notice my tears until everything goes misty. He has the same expression in every picture, and I now notice how thin, how broken, he seems. Something is seriously wrong. Has the time come to book a flight?

Not long after, I receive a short e-mail from Dad. He is well, it says, there's no reason for concern. Has he written this e-mail himself? It's impossible to say; he *may* have, being such a stubborn man. But uncertainty nags at me. I should go, but I don't want to. A few more days pass. I get another email from Dad saying that he is going back home to Spain alone. Carmen will not be accompanying him; she has problems with her travel agent, whatever that means. So perhaps the situation isn't that critical after all. I consult my brothers. We agree to wait and see how things pan out.

One morning at the beginning of April, an email arrives from one by my uncles, telling me about a rather worrying phone call he's had with Dad. He does not mince his words: I *must* go to Alfaz del Pi. A fresh wave of emails follows from my aunts in Boston. And when I eventually relent, things go apace. I cancel the Berlin trip I had scheduled and book a flight to Spain for the next day.

It's nearly a year since I saw Dad last, and I can't say that I'm looking forward to it.

The plane lands in Alicante in the late afternoon. I pick up my rental car and drive straight to my hotel in Altea, a ten-minute drive from Alfaz. My plan is to maintain some distance to whatever awaits me in Dad's apartment. Besides, Altea's little streets and beautiful squares are far preferable to the faceless town of Alfaz. At one of the restaurants on the square, in front of the church, I order an entrecôte steak and a bottle of red wine. My aim, to knock the edge off my nerves.

The next morning I drive into Alfaz. I park the car and walk up to the front entrance of Dad's apartment block. I'm about to ring his doorbell, but I can't find the courage, remembering the shrunken figure in all those pictures. Am I going to open the door and find him dead? If so, there's no rush. I walk to the bar on the corner and sit at the counter. Dad's a regular here. I recognize the bartender from last year and judging by his smile from behind the tap he remembers me too. Sebastian is one of the many Eastern Europeans who are stuck in a crisis-ridden Southern Europe. He's a qualified psychologist, but he serves alcohol to Scandinavians instead. At least, the bar is his own. Sebastian is clearly a hard-worker, with the look of a man to be trusted. He puts a Corona on the counter and looks at me seriously:

"You must prepare yourself for a shock. He isn't the man he was."

I don't answer. How precisely does one prepare for a shock?

"I knew him as the man he was, you know," continues Sebastian. "A thoroughly decent man. Before he lost it. His dignity, I mean."

Sebastian's words spur me to do what I should already have done. I pay for my beer, walk the few meters to Dad's apartment building and ring the bell once, twice, three times. No answer. Eventually, a young woman comes and lets herself in through the main door, I sneak in after her and take the stairs up to the third floor. My heart is thumping as I walk to the end of the corridor. I recognize the plaque on the front door that says "Familia de Figueiredo." I ring the bell and footsteps can soon be heard within.

SOMETIMES WE OPEN A DOOR that ought to have remained closed. There are thresholds we ought never to step over, choices that are irrevocable. And we know that immediately the door is opened, the step taken, the decision made, nothing will ever be as it was before. I was prepared for this when I pressed my index finger on the bell to father's apartment in Alfaz del Pi that April morning in 2013. But that the sight hidden behind that door would also alter the past was more than I could have foreseen.

He stands before me wearing nothing but his khaki camouflage underpants. The first thing I notice is how thin he is, just skin and bone. His hair sticks out wildly, his bushy grey beard is unkempt. He has the bottom set of his false teeth in, but not the top, giving him an exaggerated underbite. His gold-rimmed spectacles sit crookedly on his nose. He looks at me with a trusting, inquisitive gaze, and in a flash an unlikely thought, or word, enters my head, which I would never have associated with Dad before: it occurs to me that he's rather sweet. Like a puny, little monster.

"Don't you recognize me, Dad? It's Ivo."

A moment's confusion. Then his mouth breaks into a wide grin, exposing his lower teeth.

"My gosh, Ivo!"

He stretches his hand out to me, and just as I grab it, my nasal receptors send signals to my brain about the acrid smell emanating from inside the apartment. I look deep into his eyes. I have seen eyes like this before. Eyes that look without seeing, that search without finding.

"I can't believe it," he continues, still smiling. "You know Ivo? That's my son! My son's name is Ivo. How do you know my son?"

He'd probably exhibited signs of dementia when I visited him the year before, but I'd not noticed it through my tears. I don't cry this time. As I enter the apartment and realize what a state he's in, my own feelings evaporate; there is no room here for any father-son confrontation, what's needed now is a bucket and mop. The minute I think the thought, it's as if the darkness I've carried inside me splinters and dissolves.

For good? I don't know, and I don't have time to reflect on it. Dad is malnourished and totally dehydrated but, due to his obvious state of inebriation, in an excellent mood. I grab my mobile and ring for help.

Half an hour later two nurses arrive from a private home care service I've managed to find. They wash him, get some food into him and then put him to bed. Meanwhile I look around the apartment. Everything is the same as it was when I was here last, the neat piles of bills and letters. In the bathroom I find his collection of aftershave, twenty-six bottles in all. On the bookshelves are eight bound volumes of Time-Life's *Planet Earth*, a postcard of the bleeding Christ and another of the Virgin Mary in prayer. A photograph of Dad in a bar flanked by three busty blondes stands alongside Mel Gibson's *The Passion of the Christ*. No doubt about it, this is the apartment of a Catholic divorcee, a believing sinner, Hail Mary and Bloody Mary in one. You might be forgiven for assuming that the little bottle of black liquid in his office contained holy oil. But it doesn't. The label reads: *HYDRO. First oil sample taken from the Oseberg Oil Field, December 1988.* Dad has been homeless for long periods of his life, a man born of empires he was forced to seek a foothold in the brave new world of nations. And he did very well for himself in Norway; first, in the proud Norwegian shipbuilding industry as it entered its twilight years, and later contributing to the development of Norway's state-owned oil industry, the very basis of the country's comprehensive welfare state.

Did he see an irony in the fact that he ended up working with Norway's oil pioneers, one of the most successful nation building teams ever? I have no idea, but I can't help but envy his generous pension.

Although, perhaps to say he *ended up* is misleading. The truth is, Dad never fully identified himself as a Norwegian. He could easily have stayed in Norway after the divorce, established a new family perhaps; he had a good job, friends, a church where he felt at home. Indeed, he did stay for a number of years. But when he realized that his relationship with his sons would not improve, it was as though any attachment to Norway disappeared. Here in Spain he tended to avoid Norwegians. When I asked him about this last summer, I got the impression they bored him. They were, he declared, "too Norwegian." I think in a way he'd reverted to being what he'd always been: a world citizen, a man betwixt worlds.

I find pictures of Carmen everywhere in the apartment, on her own, or arm in arm with Dad. Displayed on the sideboard are two porcelain plates; one with a picture of Hong Kong harbor with Dad and Carmen posing beside Mickey Mouse and Donald Duck, the other of them standing in front of an aquarium of exotic fish in Underwater World on Langkawi Island, Malaysia. On the shelf over the cooker in the kitchen I find three big jars labeled *Xacutti Masala, Goa Aug. 2002*. I can taste Dad's hot chili prawn curry in my mouth. Almost unconsciously, I start to decide what should be kept and what thrown away. I assume he can't come back here. I have found my Dad emaciated and dehydrated in his own apartment. He looks like a skeleton and has lost any notion of who he is. Sebastian had suggested Dad had lost his dignity too. But dementia is a disease, and surely nobody loses their dignity by being ill unless someone takes it from them – as Sebastian has with his thoughtless comment.

I spend the next days partly with Dad, partly driving around Alfaz del Pi looking for a permanent solution for him. Surprisingly quickly I find a private nursing home, which seems more like a hotel than an old age people's home. Father's pension instantly guarantees him a place. Then I retrace our steps from the previous year, visiting Dad's regular haunts, including Sebastian's bar and La Pensionista. I contact his cleaner Kristina and wander along Avenida País Valencià and visit the post-lady, the optician-lady and the bank-lady.

Nothing has changed. Alfaz del Pi remains a plastic parasol paradise, the land where the sun never goes down and pensions never run dry. Everything is exactly as it was. And yet not. I get the impression now that Sebastian the bar-owner and Sonia the bank-lady actually care. And it isn't long before I come across people who have known Dad for years. Mostly Brits, who, like him, waved goodbye to their homeland long ago to find freedom. *To enjoy life*, as one of Dad's old flames says. *Simple as that*. I meet them all, one after the other, at La Pensionista; Dad's old buddies and girlfriends. Older guys with open shirts and flashy sports cars, seventy-year-old party girls with smoky cockney voices and a glint in their eyes. And the more they tell me, the more I see how wrong I have been. Dad is well liked here, and has been for years. In this frail, little community where some undeniably run aground, there are also those who bother to notice others when they stumble. And I'm ashamed. Not because I think I was totally mistaken last year, but because I failed to see everything. Perhaps the most important things.

With Dad in the nursing home, I have his apartment to myself. I conclude that it's too soon to start throwing things out, but since I have one day left before going home, I decide to go through his apartment thoroughly. I find his entire life neatly arranged in ring binders in his office. His tenancy agreement for the apartment, bills from his electricity supplier, gas supplier, water supplier and bank statements. And a letter from Carmen:

"Dear my Darling!!! 19 of December around 8am I am going to Pangasinan with 3 children because this moth time to plant rice is going there to help my mother because darling we have a farm in Pangasinan..."

I read this last sentence again. We have a farm, does she mean...

"... we have 14,000 square meters and I am start to belt my house all so in Pangasinan, I won't took out a money from your account to use to me house if it's okay to you I need Php 120,000,000, so all money that you give to me I am invest to farm in Pangasinan!!!"

Reading this letter I am reminded of an e-mail Dad sent me last year – or was it a phone call? – telling me that Carmen had named a litter of piglets after him. Far away in the Philippines there was a litter of piglets all called Hugo. I glance at the pile of bank statements on the window ledge, glimpsing the balance from four years ago, and from it I subtract the figure that Sonia, the bank-lady, told me is Dad's current fortune. The latter amount is significantly lower than the first. What's happened to the missing money? Granted, he's traveled a great deal in recent years, but this alone can't explain his expenditures. I'm aware that he's bought a car and an apartment for Carmen. I know a regular stream of money has gone to her and her family. And now there's a house and a pig farm of 14,000 square meters. How many pigs can be housed in a farm of 14,000 square meters? And are all the pigs still baptized Hugo?

For some reason, I can't get these pigs out of my head. I see them wallowing in the mud in a clearing in the jungle, on a pig farm of what I presume is a considerable size by Philippine standards. Aren't they my step-brothers, these little pigs who bear my father's name; these pigs who now control his fortune, who give a yield on his investments in sheer meat?

I've never expected to get a penny from Dad. Nevertheless, I feel a pang of irritation at the thought of these Philippine pigs who are, at the thirteenth hour, munching on my legacy. But envy is a contemptible emotion, especially between man and pig. As far as I'm concerned my brother Hugo-piglets can live in peace, and I'm sure they won't waste a thought on my brothers and I.

Carmen, however, has not forgotten me. Some days after my return from Spain, a message appears from her on Facebook. She asks how things are with Dad and says she plans to visit him soon. I reveal as little as possible, least of all his precise location. Communications between us continue for some weeks. She insists again and again that she'll go to Spain, her travel plans growing increasingly detailed:

05.05.2013 14:20 Carmen Rodrigo dear ivo this month i am plan to come in europe on may 18 can i visit your dad in hospital and is possible i have a relative in barcilona i can stay there I wont to see hem. regard Carmen

She has promised to visit Dad in Spain for several years but has never done so. And he's repeatedly sent her the money for flights. I've taken this as proof of her less than honorable motives. But when she persists in saying she wants to go, I start to believe her.

In early June, however, we decide to eliminate her from his life. My eldest brother goes to Spain to remove any trace of Carmen from Dad's apartment and to close the landline so she can't call him, if he should return after all. He does a thorough job. Photographs, albums, papers, applications for marriage and permission to stay in Spain, letters, postcards, telephone numbers, are all put out of sight. We systematically remove Dad's girlfriend from his memory, while informing her that the staff at the nursing home will turn her away if she comes.

But Carmen does not give up:

02.07.2013 11:12 Carmen Rodrigo Hi Ivo. sorry i just read your email to methank for that.you know ivo maybe you don't understant me allso what i meant to say Im not after the money or something from your dad I just won't to see him eventhough he will not recognize me enymore. but why not the staff will not let me in? Ivo why did you do this to me and your dad I thing we are all humans that we got hurts. I really still want to travel to spain nobody can stop me to visit your dad. I think you will not kill me rigt? I do hope you will understand this matter? my best regards love Carmen

Yes, Carmen, I think I understand. And no, I will not kill you. And I realize we are all human, and that we can all get hurt. And I get a pang of guilt whenever I think I may have done you an injustice. That in my European arrogance I have perhaps turned a Filipino woman who is maybe too loyal, too much a Catholic, and too submissive, into a gold-digger, a cheat and a whore. But that's how it is, Carmen. There is simply no room for you in this story. You must go.

And little by little she does indeed disappear, the messages on Facebook become less frequent and eventually cease. Neither I nor my brothers are particularly keen to pursue the issue, far less to go over to the Philippines and throw a big family out of their home. And what on earth would we do with all those little Hugo-pigs? Slaughter them? Set them free and watch them run joyously, grunting into the jungle?

As for Dad, he stopped talking about Carmen on the day he went into the nursing home. It's as though she had never existed. All that remains is a mute profile on Facebook, wallpapered with pictures of Dad, like a digital mausoleum marking a forfeited fortune and perhaps a lost love.

AM I AT THE END OF THE ROAD NOW? In a way Dad's story is certainly at an end, he will spend the rest of his life in an old people's home in Spain. It doesn't seem too bad. The home itself is reminiscent of a huge Spanish villa, surrounded by a garden of fragrant orange trees, and enclosed by a transparent fence of tempered glass. In this bell jar Dad is like a king; he flirts with his carers, does the rounds of the other old folk in their wheelchairs, joins all the day trips and is the first to sign up for bingo night.

Nobody knows what he really feels, but he expresses nothing but gratitude and joy. All his sons visit him regularly, alone or with our children. When we leave, he stands at the window, smiling and waving goodbye. His brothers and sisters come too, and his old friends regularly take him to the dinner-dance at Albir International Singles Club. (I went with him once and will never forget the sight of forty British pensioners, all single, all with ever-lasting tans, out on the dance floor and cooing in unison: *why must I be a teenager in love*. I spent the entire evening waiting for my chauffeur, a grandmother with tireless legs, to grow bored of dancing. (None of the old ladies invited me up.)

You could say that Dad has drawn the long straw. He is the center of attention *and* we've come running. Added to which, he is convinced that he's living in the home for free, saving a heap of money each month.

He never cries.

But I do. After leaving Dad in the old age people's home in the summer of 2013, I felt empty inside. I'd lived in fear of him as a child, later I'd felt only anger. For the last couple of years I've spent most of my time digging into my family history. What had I really expected to find? An answer as to why Dad was who he was? I have come to see him as a child of the colonies, broken by his encounter with the land of the colonist, the bell jar man who couldn't survive the freedom outside, the creole who won a place in the white world but who disintegrated because of the absence of boundaries. But history alone did not doom him to this fate; his siblings didn't go the same way. There must have been something about him that separated him from the rest, a lack of borders or boundaries within *him* that were intrinsic to his deeper nature. But I don't want to delve that deep, nor do I have the capacity to do so. And that's fine by me, I have no need to own his soul. But what about mine?

When I first started working on this book, I'd lived my whole life without giving my cultural identity much thought. I was Norwegian with a touch of the exotic. A bone fide Bamble Indian. Then life caught up with me in the most banal way possible. I was in my mid-forties, my two daughters had grown up and flown the nest. Nothing stood between me and the work I loved, the woman I loved, the life I wanted. Nothing but a sense of unease that regularly drove me out of my office chair and sent me pacing the city streets aimlessly. Without warning, I'd find myself gripped by an acute discomfort, an intense desire to throw off my shackles and run. At night I would dream that I was running effortlessly through the forest. When morning came, I would stand for ages looking at myself in the soft light over the bathroom mirror. Inspecting the fat that had begun to collect under my skin, the same wobbly belly that I'd seen in the gap in the saris of Pakistani women on the street. I may not have inherited an Indian nose, but I have the large earlobes that hang over the shirt collars of older

Pakistanis and Indians like heavy drops of meat.

Had my earlobes grown longer? My hair had certainly gone grey long ago, and it had started to go thin on top, although my body was still covered in black, curly hair. Had this grown thicker over the years? Once again I was back in front of the mirror, just as I was that day as a boy in Wales.

"I am Ivo. I am standing here."

I was the same, and yet not. But whatever the case, I was heading straight for a classic midlife crisis. This would scarcely have warranted a paragraph, were it not for the fact that this all-absorbing experience of change, this sense of being homeless in my own life, created an unexpected bridge between myself and the man I had excluded from my life for so long. His disintegration became my disintegration. I could no longer see clearly what was what. And if truth be known, I still don't. But, at least, I now dare – indeed, after my investigation of my own roots – I am *forced* to ask the question of who I am with greater frankness than I have ever done before.

Who am I?

All I have to do is close my eyes and look back, follow the paths of my genes, history's waft and weave, the tension of lifelines that disappear into the dark behind me, and I know: I am a Brahmin, a proud member of the caste of priests. A lost son of the Portuguese colonial powers, a bastard child of the British Empire, born in the aftermath of its fall. I am stateless, I am Norwegian, an immigrant who never migrated. A fisher-farmer from the coast of Telemark, a Catholic and a Prayer House child, a little fish in Jesus' net. I am a privileged functionary from East Africa, the blacks are my servants, then my masters. I flee. I am endlessly returning to a homeland in which I have never lived. I am a postcolonial man, I am brown, I am white, I am Norwegian – though not quite as Norwegian as before I started writing this book. Skin color separates people, blood unites them. But blood is not just red, it is thick. I look at my fingers as they flit over the keyboard, fingers that can scoop up dhal in a piece of chapati, that can sift rice or catch water to pour over my head, as people do when they wash in the river Ganges. I see myself in my aunts, the beautiful sari-clad women of my childhood, and they see him in me. Like them, I am reserved, yet temperamental and emotional, regularly crossing into sentimentality. And I fear everything, except animal fat. When I make a pot of sorpotel, with pickles and Chutneys on the side, I don't just eat it, I do as Dad and his siblings do, I attack my food with deep concentration. The chili rips through my body, beads of sweat collect on the bridge of my nose. Norwegians do not sweat like that, chili makes their faces red and bloated. But not mine, not ours. We sweat on our noses, we Indians, we Catholic Goans. Subjects of long dead empires, we are homeless and long for a home which no longer exists, but which was perhaps alive for Dad when as a child I observed him kneeling in church with his eyes closed, listening to Father Rommelse chant as he held up the chalice in the shard of light from the stained glass windows high above; a warm, hazy light that touched Christ's crucified body in the background, settled gently on the priest's hands and melted into the sacred words *mysterium fidei*. The mystery of faith.

Dad's journey is drawing to a close. But not mine. In December 2013 I board the plane once again. I have journeyed through Dad's life, traveled to all the places on the African continent in which he lived. I know the colonial kid, but have not yet visited the place where it all began, the place of origin, the dream land that Dad has carried within him all his life, the very source of his life. And perhaps mine.

GOA

I HAVE SEEN PARADISE THROUGH the window of a plane. Below me a coastline, where in some places, soft green mangrove forests lead to the ocean's edge and in others the land is divided from the sea by clear strips of white sand or black lava rock. Here and there the landscape is pried open by rivers whose estuaries look like open fans from above. When I was little I heard stories about this country, and recently I have read about it in books and letters. Now that I'm finally coming here myself, I expect the dream-like picture I have formed to evaporate in the sharp light of reality.

But it doesn't. The feeling of unreality persists as I walk down the steps from the plane, dazzled by the heat and the shimmering light that makes everything look like a vision. I have not spent many days here before I register a heightened sensitivity to the world about me. It's as if the halo of light that touches the whitewashed houses, the aroma of spices rising from the stands along the road, mixed with the exhaust fumes from lorries and mopeds, all activate dormant senses in me. The crashing of the waves against the rocks between the beaches of Baga and Anjuna reverberates through my body as I drift off to sleep at night. Everything, near or far, seems so palpable; the distant green-blue hills are as vivid to me as the cracks in the tiles under my feet. The air feels hot and almost viscous in my mouth.

It is still unclear to me how I might fit into this landscape and among its people. Yet it seems very clear to Savio de Souza. Savio, a distant relative, has invited me to his restaurant, comfortably set back from the row of noisy bars along the Calangute beach. We spend the evenings in the garden with a glass of whiskey and soda and a plethora of Goan snacks, the steady crash of waves on the beach in the darkness behind us. Savio is a deeply serious man with a burning sense of patriotism, and the conversation is invariably the same. In one instance he leans toward me with a look of quiet determination:

"You know that you are a son of a homeless man, don't you?"

During the monolog that follows, I become intimately acquainted with Savio's view of the world: that is, of Goa. As he sees it, the Goan culture is neither Portuguese nor Indian. Goa, he insists, with one finger pointed at my face and his other hand locked around my wrist as if to ensure I don't wander off before what he says has sunk in, has been subject to two empires, Portugal and India. The Goan culture is unique unto itself, and a Goan is only truly at home when he bows down and scoops up a handful of his forefathers' soil. Thousands of emigrants who have sought happiness in other countries have failed to tell their children about their roots. These people, he says, are traitors, and their descendants have been thereby rendered homeless.

He pauses, loosens his grip on my wrist and looks searchingly into my face. I nod in agreement, while three words echo in my head: Blood. Homelessness. Soil. It is as if Savio has read my mind. He blames neither my father nor me for having forgotten who we are; he adds in more conciliatory tones, it is my grandfather he blames for not having pointed us the way home. There follows a lengthy exposition of Goa's history and social structure, the so-called *communidade* system: Since time immemorial, he explains, each village has been ruled by a village council made up of the male members of families whose lineage can be traced back to the village founders. These descendants (Ganvkars) have joint ownership of the land, and with the help of the income from their tenant farmers (Mundkars) they ensure the wellbeing of the entire village, the maintenance of the temples, the execution of public works, medical services and crafts. Any surplus profits are then divided between them. The title of Ganvkar is hereditary and exclusive to the male line. Thus, the Goan village has been both a collective and a feudal society, ruled jointly by an upper class.

Savio's monolog is interrupted only by his abrupt orders directed to the waiters who slip invisibly in and out of the dark with more snacks and whiskey and soda. He is talking with growing intensity, and I don't think the whiskey's to blame so much as subject matter, and that he himself is among those who can call themselves Ganvkars, with an ancestral line that can be traced back to ancient times. And I soon realize there's more:

"Are you telling me that I am a Ganvkar too?"

"I presume you are, because all Brahmin families in Goa are Ganvkars."

It's all making sense to me now. My distant relative on the opposite side of the table, this conservative, patriotic Goan whom I have just met but who has nevertheless welcomed me with such hospitality, is telling me that I ought to return to Saligão and take my place among the village Ganvkars and claim my annual dividend from the earth. Further, I should demand the return of one of the two family residences, the first being Ti Filu's old house in Tabravvadó, which my grandfather inherited but which Dad donated to a retirement home for priests in 1977 when he went to Bombay and Goa to rescue Grandfather from his crazy marriage plans. Dad and his siblings had all agreed to this, since none of them wanted to return to Goa. Seen through the villagers' eyes, Dad had done what too many emigrants had done before him: he had thrown away his inheritance and signed away his duty to history and the community. But, says Savio, the damage is not irreparable. As Michael Joseph's grandson, I can easily challenge the bequest and get the family house back.

In other words, everything is in place for my honorable return to the village as my home. The ancient roots are poking out of the ground, I need only to grab them.

Even before Savio is done talking, I notice my thoughts start to wander. Almost against my will, since what he is saying is undeniably fascinating. But my mind is elsewhere; I'm back with my Norwegian grandparents in Lyngheim as a child. I can recall the scene in detail, exactly as I recalled it when, aged twenty-something, I received the news of Grandpa's death. During the funeral and later too, this particular scene played itself over and over in my head. I don't know why, perhaps it reminded me of the close bond between us. We are all sitting out in the garden, enclosed by the hedge and the workshop where Grandpa used to sit and carve his trolls. It is summertime and Grandpa wants to jump over the hedge, presumably to show us how fit he is. He breaks into a sprint over by the tall birch tree by the driveway, runs over the gravel path, and speeding up with a grunt he crashes right through the hedge. Everybody laughs, but I can see he is embarrassed. He probably wants to laugh with them, after all, it is rather funny, and trivial too. But he can't help it, he's hurting. And I am the only person who sees it. Grandpa and I.

The sound of a cricket cuts through the night. I am transported to the cemetery in Saligão that I visited yesterday, rows of graves bearing my own surname. I had not expected to find the name "Figueiredo" itself. Someone had told me that my great grandfather's grave had been removed long ago. While Savio talks and gesticulates, I recall the white church, Mãe de Deus, where my grandparents' request to be married was refused because the priest thought they were brother and sister. I climb the bell tower, standing for a while at the top, gazing over the landscape. The church is surrounded by a stretch of sunken rice fields; during the monsoon they fill with water, but now they are dry. Palm trees stand like soft brush strokes against the sky, behind them green hills, and hidden below the trees narrow roads twist their way between whitewashed houses with gardens and verandas, where the old folks sit and rock as they wait for a visit or a letter from a son or daughter in Canada, the United States, Portugal.

On my way out of the church I notice the tall, narrow honors boards along the walls of the side entrance, filled with the names of various benefactors through the years, stipulating the sum each has donated to the church. Might it be possible? I scan the boards one by one. In a column with Portuguese names I find the inscription:

"Xavier Hugo De Figueiredo & Sons."

Black writing on a white background, crudely framed. Each new name written in the same script, making it impossible to distinguish those applied a century ago from those added in more recent times. My name has arrived home ahead of me. After all, what else can I call this place? Home, if not for me, then for those who have received me, who have welcomed me with open arms back to the village that I've never seen before, for which I've hardly spared a thought. The place where a title may nonetheless await me, and with this an annual lump sum to which I've had a claim since I was twelve years old; my share of the profits from the *communidade* land – my *zohn*, as it is called in Konkani.

When I ask Savio what I have to do in return for this title and money, he just throws his hands in the air. Nothing at all! It is my birthright! No strings attached! The Ganvkars in this province are traditionally Catholics, the Hindu tenant farmers are from lower castes, it is their destiny to spend their days in the paddy fields, fulfilling their duty to my people. And to me? Is this still how the communidade system works? Does my eventual zohn still rely on the labors of the tenant farmers in the field?

If so, I know exactly what I shall say to each and every one of them: Cast off the yoke! I, the Brahmin of Langesund, the Norwegian Ganvkar, release you from the iron law of karma; I am, in any case, a *Catholic* Brahmin, a pork-eating Brahmin, a wandering self-contradiction in this land. So hold your head high, stroll down to the beach and take a dip in the sea, then go home and make love to your wife. And when you get up the next day and go to work, know that you can keep my share of the profits.

A FEW DAYS AFTER MY MEETING with Savio I am on a bridge, driving across the Mandovi River. Below me to the right, the river opens up to the sea, with Goa's modest capital Panjim (renamed Panaji after the liberation) nestled between crags and vegetation on the southern shore. On the other side, the river stretches inland. Behind the distant hills where it divides, lies the abandoned city of Velha Goa that was once known as the Rome of the East. This is where it all began. And it is here that I ask the driver to take me.

It feels decidedly wrong to enter Velha Goa by car. For centuries the river was the only way into Goa's old capital. It was here that Vasco da Gama came ashore on his third major sea voyage in September 1524, then as the Portuguese Viceroy of India. From the waterfront, where the ships unloaded their cargos of spices, silks, Arabian horses and porcelain from China, the Rua Direita ran the few hundred meters into Christianity's most magnificent city east of Constantinople. Almost everything is gone now, hundreds of handsome buildings with white facades, red tiled roofs and large overhanging balconies have vanished; they have collapsed, or been torn down, or swallowed by the jungle.

The instant I see the first buildings peeping between the trees, I ask the driver to drop me off, and I stroll down to the river. At the old harbor, now barely more than a ferry stop, I turn toward the lost city. I start along what's left of the Rua Direita, the stretch of road that was once filled with jubilant crowds whenever a new Portuguese viceroy was appointed. Passing under the old arch I gaze up at Vasco da Gama himself. He didn't get much joy from being a viceroy, dying just three months after his inauguration. But here he stands, looking across the river, rendered proudly in stone, in his full regalia. As if nothing had changed in Velha Goa. Further up is the city square, where carpet makers, goldsmiths, jewelers, spice traders and money lenders once stood, as tightly packed as the trees and bushes that grow here today. To the left I find another gateway that leads nowhere; this is all that is left of Yusuf Adil Khan's Palace, the last remains of the city that was here *before* the arrival of the Portuguese.

The heat rests heavy over the town square. The Senate and the Palace of the much feared Inquisition might once have cast some welcome shade, but they are now gone. Across the square, however, are the Sé Cathedral and St. Francisco Church. The city has not disappeared entirely. Here and there, spread over a vast area, between trees, old ruins and empty streets, a handful of churches and monasteries still rise high with much of their splendor in tact. Like lonely giants they loom over the palms, giving visitors an overwhelming sense of past grandeur. Of European grandeur, one should add. Will Rome look like this when the Baroque churches and palaces have been brought down, a city of ancient ruins? Goa has always given the European traveler a sense of being in all times and places at once. My literary companion Evelyn Waugh, who came here in the Christmas of 1952, describes the climate as milder than an Italian summer, while the whitewashed churches reminded him of being in Mexico, were it not for the Arabian boats in rivers and ports.

When Somerset Maugham was here some years earlier, he found it hard to identify with the Christian faith as he saw it practiced here. During a Mass in the Basilica of Bom Gesù, he felt sure that he heard mysterious, pagan undertones in the singing of the native church choir. A priest confirmed his suspicions:

"'We're Christians,' he told me, 'but first of all we're Hindus.'"

I am walking around in an exotic world, which nonetheless feels strangely familiar. Perhaps this is as it should be? This is the Goan experience; an indeterminable familiarity, universal and unique, whole yet divided. On the other side of the square I find Bom Gesù. Once inside the cool church I loosen my damp shirt and amble over to the side chapel that houses St. Francisco Xavier's sacred body. It can just about be glimpsed in its casket of silver and glass high up on the jasper catafalque decorated with reliefs of bronze and marble. I have come too soon; next year the coffin will be taken down and carried over to the Sé Cathedral to be exhibited to believers. The tradition of displaying the saint's remains began in 1782. A growing conflict between the Jesuits and Portuguese State, together with rumors that the saint's remains had been swapped for the body of a more recently demised Jesuit, prompted a decision that the coffin should be displayed to the public. In recent times, these displays have been held every tenth year, and next year, the pilgrims will stream once again to Velha Goa from every corner of the world. Today there are only a handful of pilgrims and tourists here.

I also feel that the place in which I now stand is holy. For my family, for Dad. His patron saint lies here, his protector, the miracle corpse, the spiritual center of my forefathers' world. But am I overwhelmed? Is time suspended? Have I come home? Not exactly. The sense of magic I experienced in East Africa, when I put my hand on a gravestone, or rested my face against a rusty locomotive, does not, for some reason, work here. As a Catholic apostate my encounter with this relic has almost the opposite effect on me than it presumably has on believers. I have been so fascinated, obsessed even, by the legend of the saint, that it seems almost banal to stand here with my hand on the catafalque, squinting up at his shriveled remains in the casket way up high.

A sense of defiance rises in me; a resistance to being pulled *too* far into the Goan dream – a dream that was, until recently, utterly foreign to me. And why do I repeatedly return to these bygone British authors; to Waugh, to Somerset Maugham and Graham Greene, with their dreamy depictions of Velha Goa's picturesque decay? And didn't I do the same when I was in East Africa? Don't I see the arrogance of these men who trotted about the globe marveling at all these strange foreigners with their un-British ways? More than anything they loved to stand here, surrounded by the ruins of Velha Goa, gloating over the decline of this other bygone empire. Richard F. Burton, who came here in the late 1840s before traveling to East Africa, was convinced that the Portuguese empire had fallen because the races had been allowed to mix. His notions about race were simple, of course; to him all non-Europeans were "niggers." Not even the Catholic faith had, he thought, brought anything worthwhile to the Goans. "Their superiority to the heathen around them" he said, "consists of eating pork, drinking toddy to excess, shaving the face, never washing, and a conviction that they are going to paradise."

The reason for the stagnation of Portuguese India clearly lay elsewhere than in the mixing of races and consumption of toddy and pork. Yet the narrative chosen by the Portuguese themselves is scarcely more believable. Burton was a great admirer of Portugal's national poet Luís Vaz de Camões, and translated his epic poem about Vasco da Gama's first trip to India, *Os Lusíadas* (1572), some of which Camões had written here in Goa:

> Lifting across the Orient waves they came.
> In India's seas already they perceived
> The sun's bridechambers where he is born aflame.
> ...
> That it was Heaven's will, he knew aright.

For Camões, Goa was a paradise that God had bestowed on Portugal. And this image persists to this day, with many choosing to portray the Portuguese Empire as a Catholic realm free of any racial division. But this is not altogether true. Even though Admiral Afonso de Albuquerque, the second Portuguese viceroy of Goa, is reputed to have encouraged his men to find local wives, the social hierarchy in Goa was never color-blind. The Portuguese were at the top and the African slaves at the bottom, with the Goans ranked by faith and caste between the two.

Camões and Burton are not, of course, credible as historians by any standards. They saw what gave meaning to them in their time. Nonetheless, why do I find it so easy to see the world through their white imperialist gaze? There is no escaping it; my gaze is helplessly white, despite the density of pigment in my irises. This has never been clearer to me than on my travels in Africa and India. Though, whether this white gaze is necessarily Norwegian, I am no longer sure. This trip is my pilgrimage, a search for my own story, Dad's story, the story of a family and of a people. From the moment I fought through Pemba's jungle and lost my way in Stone Town, the world of the Catholic Goans – or rather the world from which they sprang – has gradually formed a membrane over my eyes. I have searched for my clan, and in doing so I have stepped imperceptibly into the bell jar. I view the world with the white gaze of the Goans, as much as that of the Norwegians – perhaps more.

If this is correct, the Goans are not "half people." Rather we are a double people; we share the British and Portuguese notions about ourselves, their thoughts are our thoughts. We are a mimetic people, orientalism's flesh and blood, born and trapped in a no-man's land between "us" and "them."

The strange thing is that despite being aware of all of this, and despite the disappointment I feel at seeing St. Francisco Xavier's body, I continue my pursuit of these dreams. Because there is something about Velha Goa, something about the old Portuguese-Indian world, which feeds into a shamelessly erotic romance with ruins. I experienced the same thing when I visited Lisbon the year before coming to Goa. It was autumn. I stood in my loft room and watched the last of the sun's rays touching Alfama. Every major city has its own distinct color. Just as Rome is brick-red and Paris a sandstone gold, Lisbon is a white city, despite the colorful tiled facades of the houses, a testimony to the Moorish influence. Viewed from one of its many high vantage points, the city is white, brilliant white, in the low autumn sun. I walked through the narrow streets past Lisbon's Sé Cathedral, and down into the city square. While Velha Goa is a dead city, Lisbon very much alive. Yet if you look up, as I invariably did, it is impossible to overlook its quiet decay; the grand mansions with their broken windowpanes and cracked tiles. I think anybody visiting Lisbon will be gripped by the aesthetics of decay. A tranquility rests over the city and over those who live and work here, in the wings of a drama long over. I experienced these people as proud, as they tended and cleaned the remains of this by-gone splendor, which I imagine they neither believe in nor wish would rise again.

One day I accidentally found myself in Igreja de São Domingos, a church in the heart of Lisbon. I stood gazing up at a vaulted church ceiling with its rows of granite columns on either side of the aisle. High up I saw a row of grimy windows; no colorful saints with their eyes turned toward heaven, just dull, white glass. The magenta lime-washed walls were peeling, the thick marble floors cracked. Only the pulpit, and the finely decorated altar that gleamed with gold, had avoided decay. I felt I was wandering through a crumbling history. Never had the past felt closer to me. And perhaps the priest and his little congregation huddled in the front pews felt the same, as they celebrated mass as though God and the Portuguese Empire still ruled the world. As though someone had shut and sealed the doors in mid-service four centuries ago, and they'd continued with their rituals, heedless of the outside world, as the building slowly crumbled around them.

Someone jolts my arm. I'm back in Bom Gesù, where more believers and tourists have found their way to St. Francisco Xavier's coffin. The perspiration has dried on my body, and my damp shirt feels cold against my skin. I must get out. I don't belong here. I am a foreigner, an imperialist – a double imperialist, since not only do I see the Goans through a mythical veil, but their Portuguese masters too. Everything is a tangle, a web of myths, a whir of thoughts, it is impossible to think straight in this place. I hurry toward the door, the sound of my footsteps filling the church, before I reenter the sunlight and heat. On the other side of the square, I find my driver resting under a tree. We drive on to Margão, South Goa's largest city. I am going there to meet a man who can tell me my family's history from the dawn of time – or, at least, from a thousand years ago or so. Something tells me that this dream is not yet over.

THE OLD PRIEST WELCOMES ME into his office in an annex to Margão's Baroque Holy Spirit Church. We sit opposite each other in plastic chairs in this plain, unadorned room, with bare white walls, furnished with only a desk and filing cabinet. Somebody places a bowl of vegetable soup in my hands. I eat it dutifully. It all feels rather awkward. Above our heads hangs a fan, redundant since the breathable brick walls mean the room is comfortable without it. The sinewy old man with white, smoothly combed hair and eyes that dart behind thick glasses was born in Saligão and can tell me everything I want to know about the village's history. He speaks English with a strong Indian accent. Any important point is emphasized with the characteristic wave of an index finger.

Is this really the man to give me the truth about my origins? My doubts are aroused long before my soup bowl is empty. But, that aside, here is the story the old priest tells me, about who I am and where I come from, retold to the best of my ability:

Long, long ago our ancestors came from the north and settled in the fertile and water-rich lands between the sea and the eastern edge of the vast Deccan Plateau. These people were Aryans and Brahmins, they were lighter-skinned and brought civilization and religion with them. In total sixty-six families arrived and settled near today's Curtorim, before spreading in all directions. Sixteen families went to what is now the province of Bardez north of Goa. Later the plague caused these sixteen families to split up and become further scattered. Four of these families settled in what would become the village of Saligão.

The old man peers at me over his glasses:

"The first is Porob Salgãocar, then comes Naik Salgãocar, third comes Sinai Salgãocar and the fourth one is called Dhond Salgãocar."

His tone is solemn. The pride he takes in his story and our shared origins is obvious:

"We were known as the Aryans! We were the superiors!"

He skips a few centuries, millennia, historical and mythological time merge into one, my brain is going into a spin. We? We're Aryans? Superior? To whom? The old man goes on. We weren't the first people in this land.

"There was already the Mahr. The outcasts. They were the originals of Saligão."

The Mahr, or Black Indians, were Goa's indigenous people, who had lived here since time immemorial.

"The Mahr and all did not have any religion. They believed in spiritism, and they believed in their ancestors. They had their ancestors in a block of stone and they were adoring that."

So this indigenous population was conquered by our people; the light-skinned Aryans. We knew little about farming or fishing, but brought our gods and weapons, and chased the Black Indians to the edges of the village. Here they would provide a living bulwark against outside enemies, the first to fall in any attack.

"The Black Indians had to accept that the four families were now the Lords of Saligão."

The Lords of Saligão, that's who we are. It has certain ring about it, I admit, even if we are only talking about a small village that, even today, has no more than about five thousand residents. But the old priest is not finished yet; his smile tells me that the best is to come. One of the four families, Porob Salgãocar, brought the sal tree – *Shorea robusta* – with them, the favorite tree of the god Vishnu. They planted a grove of sal trees and called the village Sailém, before building a temple dedicated to the goddess Sharvani on a nearby hillside, close to a natural spring where they could perform the ritual cleansing that was required before entering the holy sanctum. It was this place, with its grove and holy temple, that would eventually be called Salmona, and it was here that the village of Saligão would eventually emerge. And further more, the old priest concludes triumphantly, this is the place of my roots:

"Now, Figueiredos in Christianity they belong to the first family, that is Porob Salgãocar."

So, I am not only a Brahmin but a descendant of the founders of the village, the Porob family, who planted the trees that gave the village its name. The founders of the temple by the spring are my ancestors; I am Ivo Bjarne de Figueiredo, Lord of Saligão, Aryan, Brahmin and Ganvkar.

I can't deny that the old priest's story made an impression on me; indeed I sat transfixed, listening like a child at its teacher's feet. I see the light-skinned Brahmins, the Aryans walking through the forest, descendants of the old high-culture in the north that apparently disappeared thousands of years ago when the Saraswati river dried up; I see them sitting around the campfire at dusk, or standing bowed over the earth as they plant the sal tree. I see them wash in the spring which is so close to where Aleixo Mariano de Figueiredo, one of their descendants, will build a house hundreds of years later, knowing in his heart that he has continued the legacy of the past, just as I would have done if I were to choose today to turn back home to Saligão.

IT TOOK A LONG TIME TO WAKE UP. How long can we walk about in a dream *knowing* it is a dream? How long can a historian deny his own discipline? There was nothing left of my people in East Africa but dreams, the traces of the life Dad and the family had once lived. There were so few; perhaps that was why the remains that I did find seemed so weighted with meaning, the presence of history so real. In Goa, the past exists in the present in a completely different way; the Goan Catholics' dream about themselves lives on today, around dinner tables, in newspaper columns, in day-to-day politics, and in their conflict with the Hindu Indians, who threaten their way of life.

It wasn't as if I'd come unprepared. Over the last two years I'd read copious books and talked with a vast number of people, mostly exiles or their descendants whose images of their homeland have been passed on and fixed, made into a shining myth. I knew that the mythological *Goa Dourado* was not the same as the other Goa, *Goa Indica*. But I didn't know this other Goa, I had no counter-history. An astonishing number of the books I'd read were steeped in precisely the same myths that I found in the versions told to me by exiles, and that I also dragged around with me. Slowly other stories began to surface as I met with Goan Hindus, members of lower castes, and later when I returned to Oslo, from international Goan scholars who emailed me recommending research articles, all contributing to the painstaking process of the historian's everyday labor, which will not be told here.

We are who we believe we are. There is some truth in that. But what about others? What happens when we also turn other people into who and what we think they are?

Perhaps this is of little importance to the exiles; they carried a myth with them that gave them the strength to go on. It's a different matter entirely, however, for those who still live in Goa. They also need the myth, but now that I've been here myself, in the real Goa, I cannot allow the old priest's story to stand unchallenged. There is no road back from knowledge. An *alternative* history – or story – of my people (not denying there are many more), might read like this:

The Catholic Brahmins originate from the first territories conquered by the Portuguese, *Velhas Conquistas*. Created in the image of their conquerors, they also became co-creators of the empire, and indeed, of themselves. As a land-owning aristocracy they were the favored subjects of their colonial masters. While they themselves were masters who wielded power over a nameless host of peasants, fishermen, craftsmen and servants. To bring coherence to all of this they created a beautiful myth of origin. But the old priest's story is just one version of this myth; the most common involves one of Vishnu's incarnations, the hero *Parashurama*.

According to this myth Parashurama shot an arrow off India's coast, and where it fell the sea receded to reveal the landmass that became Goa. Parashurama decided to create a tribe of Brahmins to rule over this new country. When they failed to live up to his expectations, he destroyed them and fetched the noble, light-skinned Brahmins from the north. It is a myth that supported the Goans' sense of privilege, legitimizing their control of the villagers, and eventually strengthening their association with the white Europeans. Even the status of "Brahmin" may be something they constructed themselves as late as the last part of the 19th century. And it was a myth the Portuguese encouraged. Indeed, they built on the ganvkar system, favored the Brahmins (most of them Catholics, though not all), educated them and inculcated them with the Portuguese culture and mindset. What they did *not* do, however, was to develop or industrialize Goa; instead, it remained a stagnant agrarian community until the Indians took over in 1961. But when my great grandfather emigrated it was not only because of any lack of future prospects, it was also as an educated empire builder. This explains how the family's identity could shift in just one generation from Portuguese to British. The masters might have been new, but the task was largely the same.

Today there is little left of the Catholic Brahmins' power. The immigration of Indian Hindus rendered the Catholics a minority in Goa long ago. Among those who remain, some want to preserve the communidade system and the legacy of the Portuguese, and they continue to fight for a "special status" for Goa. My relative Savio de Souza is such a man. It is a lost cause. After the liberation in 1961 the authorities drove land reforms through, strengthening the rights of tenant farmers. A modest amount of village land is still in the hands of the Ganvkars. The income still rolls in, but not from tenant farmers as before. Instead the money comes – a few hundred rupees annually to each of the Ganvkars – from the sale of farmland to the Indian government or to the farmers who can now demand to buy the ground they cultivate and live on.

The Ganvkars are consuming their own legacy, and for each rupee handed out, their power shrinks. Like a fallen aristocrat who sells his furniture and artifacts while the dust settles in his empty halls. My generous thoughts of allowing the Hindus to keep my share is utterly redundant. The Indian state has taken the situation in hand long ago.

Myths fell like crushed oyster shells from my eyes. I became wiser, but also poorer. Since if my family needs these stories about themselves, so do I. Like it or not, I see myself in them. The Catholic Goans who live here in Goa have much of the same reserve and warmth that I recognize in my aunts and uncles. Being so European in their lifestyle and character, they seem liberal compared to the Indians. They enjoy both wine and pork, the women show their cleavages and wear bikinis on the beach, something you'd rarely see an Indian do. In Bollywood films the clichéd "loose woman" is often a Goan; with a short skirt, a defiant glance, and a big cross hanging around her neck.

The God-fearing Goan women who I know are far from loose. Their passion is well under control, and they portion it out in gentle hand movements and quick glances. Far less fettered are the passions of the local Goans when the conversation drifts onto the subject of the foreigners who are flooding the border, in increasing numbers each day. The beaches where hippies danced naked in the burning sun a few decades ago have long been taken over by pale Russians, and coy Hindus who, unable to swim, stand fully dressed in orderly rows, clinging to ropes that stretch out into the water. For Indians elsewhere in the country, this former Portuguese colony is a local Europe, and those who can, purchase holiday homes here. For the Goans it is not tourism itself that they feel threatened by, but the huge influx of Indians. Speculators who build hotels illegally along the coast, or buy land and drive up the property prices. Politicians who invite the poor and outcast to settle on communal land in exchange for electoral votes.

The Indians brought Goa into the modern age. They broke the back of the ganvkar and communidade system, initiated progress in industry and commerce, brought electricity to villages, made education more accessible. But modernization has brought new problems with it; cynical industrialists, corrupt politicians, property speculation, pollution, poverty and crime.

Catholic Goans observe this with rising concern. While their young people continue to emigrate, the Indians stream in, filling the beaches, roaring through the narrow lanes on mopeds, endlessly beeping their horns, churning up the red soil, the dust of which settles on the baskets of spices and sari fabric in the market booths and floats onto the Goans' porticos and terraces. A huge amount of sweeping is done in this land, a frustrating battle has to be fought to keep the dirt from one's own little patch. India may be in chaos, thinks the Goan, but my terrace is clean.

Although, of course, they do not do the sweeping themselves; my people have servants for that, as they watch on with their hands behind their backs and shake their heads dolefully, before settling into their wicker sun-loungers, closing their eyes and letting their minds drift back to times of yore.

It is to this sinking Atlantis that I am welcomed back to put my house in order. Because the Catholic Goa is a truly threatened culture. Soon the Goans will put their brooms away for good. The end is nigh, the writing is on the wall. One day I was in Savio's car, he had to slam on the brakes for a cow that was wandering across the road. "It used to be pigs!" he roared, not without a hint of irony.

According to Richard F. Burton, Panjim could be recognized as a Christian town by the number of pigs infesting the streets. The pigs are now gone, but a clearer sign of decline is the number of beautiful Portuguese-Goan villas that have been abandoned and left to decay. Set back from the noisy streets, they are not always easy to spot as you rush past in a taxi or tuk tuk. But they are still there, hidden behind the clouds of red swirling dust from the road, deep in the shadows of the overgrown trees, in what used to be well-tended gardens. The sea green or azure blue painted windows are bolted and blinded; here in the shade, the sunlight no longer penetrates oyster shell panes to fill the rooms with dancing shadows. Nor are the rooms ever filled with dancing people these days. Instead, the houses stand in silence, like sleeping turtles, their low roofs sagging toward the ground, closed in upon themselves, as though waiting for better days when the uncouth newcomers will leave and their rightful owner return. A Mascarenhas, or a de Souza, or a Figueiredo, or a Pereira; a family man in freshly pressed beige trousers and white short-sleeved shirt, a well-groomed beard and perhaps a Stetson. With a wife who has white streaks in her hair, and squeaky clean children, the boys in short trousers and white socks, the little girls in white dresses. Four, five or six children, a gardener, a kitchen girl and an *ayah* for the little one. But the houses slumber on, the exiles who should have returned to them with education and wealth, have stayed in their foreign lands or ventured further west.

Portuguese Goa is vanishing, shrinking like St. Francis Xavier, as each autopsy prior to the display of his slowly diminishing body has ruthlessly confirmed; toe by toe, fiber by fiber, he is vanishing, until nothing but dust and memories will remain.

Do I have any place in this apocalyptic tale? I am Norwegian, a foreigner in these parts. Yet I know now that I am also something else, and this recognition forces me to choose where my loyalties lie. With the myth or the reality? Goa Dourado or Goa Indica? And, just as importantly, I must ask if I have anything in common with the Goans here, or is my place among those exiles, whom Savio declared homeless?

AFTER MY VISIT TO THE OLD PRIEST, I am ready for what has always been the aim of my journey. I will look up the family's old houses in Saligão – Ti Filu's house in Tabravvadó, where Herminia grew up, and Aleixo's house in Salmona, and the holy spring where it all began.

But does the legendary spring still exist? Did it ever exist?

A kindly village woman named Anita tells me that it does indeed. I cling tightly around her waist as her moped swings through the narrow crooked roads of Saligão. Portuguese houses and gardens on either side, some well maintained, freshly whitewashed, with mustard yellow, turquoise and blue oyster-shell windows. Others on the verge of collapse. But everything seems so peaceful surrounded by the lush vegetation. Shrubs and flowering bushes burst forth, stems twist and stretch toward the sky, and big trees spread their heavy branches over the red earth. A veil of smoke in the air. A tranquil and idyllic quality reigns in Saligão, such a contrast to the raucous Calangute just kilometers away.

I try to imagine my elderly aunts coming out of the doors, leaning over the fences and gossiping with their neighbors. Aunt *E.* with her black leather cap. The picture doesn't seem quite right. What about Dad? He couldn't have endured this uneventful idyll for more than a week. Two if he was near a bar on Baga beach perhaps.

Our moped climbs steadily up the hillside, through the district of Salmona, then a little further, and we've arrived. I find myself at the end of a blind alley, looking across a pool of water surrounded on three sides by stone walls and with steps leading down into it. On the far side, water flows into the pool through a rusty pipe. Behind it I glimpse a narrow rivulet of silver that disappears into the jungle. The sound of birdsong can be heard. This is the holy spring, the mythical source of my village and my clan.

"We used to come here all the time," says Anita. "From all over the village. Your grandfather too, and his father before him."

They came here to bathe, to light a bonfire and spend time together. Since then, the authorities have built a landfill site further up. The water that was once considered to be purifying is now polluted. The only people who come here now are kids who want to party in peace. Empty beer bottles are strewn everywhere, plastic bags float in the sludgy grey water. It's difficult to imagine that there was ever a temple here; the only sign that this has been a holy place is a white cross at one end with a portrait of the Lord himself facing toward the pool.

I stare down into the filthy water, thinking of St. Francisco Xavier's shriveled up body in Bom Gesù.

"Perhaps we should look for the house instead?" I ask Anita.

Like so many properties owned by exiles, the house Aleixo once built for his mother and himself stood empty for years. The last permanent resident was Aleixo's second wife, Elizena, but after her death in 1965 the house was abandoned again. Today, it belongs to an elderly local couple. Coming from the village, they are, says Anita, familiar with the history of the house. They and their neighbors know my family well, she says, as we park the moped at the side of the road, they even know that Dad is divorced from his Norwegian wife. The villagers keep abreast of anything concerning the village, and the village forgets nothing, not even me, though I've never been here before.

We walk through a gate surrounded by red-flowering bushes and up a narrow path of terracotta tiles. The house sits perfectly on the hillside, with its wide roof and covered terrace. Where there were once tall, slender doors along the facade, which might have been opened to let in the light and air, there are now windows. Not oyster-shell windows, but glass with wrought iron grills. For many Catholic Goans the replacement of these old windows is a sore point; there was no need for any bars on the windows in the times of the Portuguese, they say, any more than you needed to lock your door at night. Oyster shells are a symbol of the safety in old Goa before the Indians invaded.

We find the elderly couple sitting on the terrace. Anita introduces me, and they cast a curious glance at me. Then they burst into conversation. The stream of chatter is interrupted only by the occasional burst of laughter and shouting, all in Konkani, with a little Portuguese and English thrown in. I can only make out a barrage of names, of places and relatives, from far in the past and even further across the world: Great Grandfather Aleixo, Michael's son, or not, grandson, that was it, and wasn't Joachim, Michael's half brother the godson of the present homeowner's mother, and did I know that the old woman's oldest brother had known Aleixo's mother, Maria Santana Zatã, who was the great grandmother of this house?

I nod and smile politely, but while the others talk and gesticulate, I imagine a tree growing up between them; a family tree rising at record speed, fertilized by memories and stories. And soon its branches spread to protect the people beneath them from the scorching sun. Buds open anew as the neighbor, an elderly man who was lurking behind the garden wall, joins the conversation and gives the talkative pair a welcome opportunity to repeat the entire roll-call of names and places, and then to make further additions and corrections that have sprung to mind.

At least I assume that's what's going on, since I can only understand snippets of their conversation. But eventually I get the impression that the family tree has reached its full height – not that that's any cause for the chatter to stop. After all, from our family tree there are roots that reach out to other families too; an intricate weave of fiancés and godparents, acquaintances and neighbors. What was the name of those people who emigrated at such-and-such time, and what happened to the house they left, which house, ah, yes, that one, or those people who went to... where was it again? (laughter), Canada, no, Toronto, yes, he became a doctor, a doctor you say, not bad.

Just when I'm sure I've been forgotten and start to surreptitiously back off toward the moped, the conversation halts as abruptly as it started. Everyone turns to me. They've finished placing me genealogically and geographically. Their glances invite me to step into their circle and to share the cool of the village tree's broad swaying canopy. And I realize that whatever I might think, whatever objections my inner historian might have, I am one of them, and I always have been; ever since the dawn of time when four families chased away the Black Indians and planted the first sal tree in the heart of what would one day be Saligão.

THERE'S A PICTURE FROM THE 1930s taken behind Great Grandfather's house; I recognized the spot immediately when the old couple showed me around the property. The photograph was sent to me by a relative – funeral cards are no longer my only visual source for these older family members.

The woman sitting in the front on the left is Elizena Sequeira, sitting

on the right is her sister Ti Filu. The man in the center is Aleixo. The composition is clearly aimed to draw our focus onto this patriarchal figure with his shock of wavy hair, yet it is not toward him that my attention gravitates. There's a force in this photograph, heightened by the play of light and shade and by the careful retouching, which draws the eye not in one, but in two directions. Toward the two children kneeling at the adults' feet.

Are they people? Or devils with luminous eyes? Do they even have souls?

Roland Barthes suggests that there are two ways in which to look at a photograph. We can see what the photographer set out to capture, reading the image according to its creator's intentions, admiring or despising the subject. But often there is something in the image that shatters this harmonious method of observation. A disturbing element, which ruptures our view, something unintentional and random that shoots out of the image like a dart, knocking the observer off balance. Like these children with their luminous eyes. It's hard enough to look steadily into one pair of eyes. Here two pairs of eyes draw my attention, causing my gaze to glide back and forth over the picture in a vain attempt to see into both at once.

I know who these children are now. The girl on the right is still alive. I have met her.

The photograph was taken some time after my great grandfather retired as postmaster in Pemba and returned home to Saligão. Ti Filu was childless, and like any single person in India it was vital she plan for her old age. Aleixo and Elizena faced this problem too, with their children and grandchildren still in East Africa. Who would take care of them when they could no longer manage? Aleixo suggested they go to an orphanage in Benaulim and each choose a Hindu child, whom they would baptize and raise on the understanding that they would repay their benefactors by caring for them in the future. The two children were given the names Raphael and Marie, and while Raphael went to live with Aleixo and Elizena in Salmona, the girl went with Ti Filu to Tabravvadó.

But to return to the photograph: it's not just these children's eyes that grab me, but the awkward tension in their bodies, their submissive pose at the feet of their guardians. When we compare the demeanor of these foundlings with that of the two smartly dressed boys in the back row, my uncles Lionel and *A.*, this picture speaks volumes about religion, caste, poverty and charity in this country. There's a word (or rather two words) in Konkani for children like Marie and Raphael. Poskem for the girls, posko for the boys. Children who are adopted, but under special conditions. Many Catholic families took in orphans, who then spent their entire lives in their benefactors' service, without pay, rights or privileges, or even a seat at the family table. This arrangement was seen among Catholic Brahmins as an expression of Christian charity. But seen from the viewpoint of the unprivileged, and those who have fought for greater social justice in India, these children were treated like serfs, at the mercy of the host family, bound by a lifelong debt of gratitude that they could never pay off.

Marie fulfilled her duty, taking care of Ti Filu until her death. Not so Raphael. He disappeared one day and was never heard of again. The family version of events is that the boy had evil blood in his veins, but what exactly was he guilty of?

The day after my meeting with the elderly couple in Salmona, I went to Tabravvadó to visit Marie. She still lives in the house in which Herminia grew up with Aunt Ti Filu, and where Uncle *A.* and Uncle Lionel spent so much of their childhood. The house that Dad donated as a priests' home, and which Savio thinks I should reclaim, stands wall to wall with St. Anne's Chapel and is more dilapidated than my great grandfather's house in Salmona. The garden is overgrown, but a couple of the oyster-shell windows are still intact, with beautiful ochre-colored decorations in their frames.

Marie is standing on the stairs when we arrive. She smiles and bows with a humility I don't recognize from anyone else in the family. She leads us into a sparsely furnished living room and little kitchen; the rest of the house was given over to the retired priests, but all these rooms stand empty now. In the kitchen I peep behind the stove. My aunts have told me about a hatch in the wall that once led into the church; if anyone in the household was ill or otherwise unable to go to Mass, they could open it, kneel by the stove and participate in the service. The hatch is now gone, bricked up long ago.

Marie doesn't seem at all keen to talk about Raphael.

"This is not a story to be told," she says, before mumbling something about him being seen in the cemetery at night. Marie has lived in this house for years, ever since the death of Aleixo and Elisa, supported partly by the family and partly by her own endeavors. When she opened the door to me, I could see she'd dyed her hair and made an effort to smarten herself up. But it's not easy to disguise poverty, it is in the walls and the newly mopped floor, and engrained in the grubby bed that serves as a couch. And it's in her body too somehow, no matter how clean. I know what she's waiting for, and after rejecting an unappetizing meal as politely as I can, I pull out the five thousand rupees I've been told I should give her. She accepts it without a word, but her eyes shine like a child's.

Five thousand rupees is the equivalent of about sixty dollars. I feel the shame burning in my cheeks, it must surely be visible. I bow my head, thank her and go.

Marie belongs to the same generation as Dad and his eldest siblings. But she has never been their equal. She presumably has a place under the villages' swaying trees, but after my meeting with her I wonder if I belong there after all. And what about Dad? When he came to the village to rescue my grandfather from his marriage plans, he couldn't bear to spend even one night in Marie's house. *Dirty. Shocking hygiene. Bad lighting, can't even write a letter, no lamps, there's no furniture...*

I know more about Goa now than Dad ever has. But I also know that his trip out here in 1977 – at around the time of his divorce from Mum – meant a lot to him. From a letter he wrote to me some twenty years later, (a carbon copy of which I found among the papers I brought back with me from Spain), I realize that this trip was also an attempt to fulfill a duty he felt he'd neglected.

"As you may or may not know, I've done very little for my father in his old age, while my siblings have taken care of him," he writes, for once in Norwegian. "He was never 'shipped' off to an old people's home, since it would have killed him. After the separation I promised myself that I'd do my part."

He goes on to write more about his trip, but with no mention of my grandfather's wedding plans. Instead, he tells me that he has not only donated the Tabravvadó house to the priests' home, but has ensured that Marie can continue living there for as long as she wants. He has also organized a place for her in a nursing home, which she can take up in the future, if and when she needs it.

Marie chose to stay in Tabravvadó. Dad's visit may not have brought any further improvement to her life, but at least she was secure in her old age. As for Dad, he returned to Goa several times in the 1990s, but almost certainly never considered moving here. He came to do his part, not to invest his life in this country to which he felt so drawn, but in which he was ultimately a stranger. As am I. The welcome I received in Salmona may have been warm, but after my meeting with Marie I felt nothing but pain, a sense of sad resignation coupled with a realization that this society was too brutal for the likes of Dad and I, its laws too cruel and intransigent. When my family emigrated to East Africa, they lost much of their status as Brahmins and the privileges they'd had in the village. Looking at it now, I think there must have been a certain liberation in this.

Although, in reality, things weren't so very different for them on the African continent. After all, they still had people below them – the Africans – and their loyalty to the colonial master was unchanged.

So when did my family finally walk free of a society based on cast-iron hierarchies?

In a large villa, pleasantly set back from the busy road between Margao and Panjim, lives a man who knows more about breaking bonds than any other Goan I know. The villa is, in fact, just one of Fitz de Souza's residences; he and his wife Romela spend part of the year here and the rest in London and Nairobi. I join them on the roofed terrace overlooking their garden. We sit at the table, Fitz at the end, while Romela goes in and out of the house fetching tea and little dishes of food. As she goes back and forth she answers her husband's questions, gently correcting him and supplementing details. Fitz sits ponderously, slightly askew in his chair. He is eighty-four years old, but his gaze is quick, his conversation lucid. He grew up in Zanzibar, the son of a captain who fought alongside Lawrence of Arabia against the Turks during World War I. In 1942 his father took the family and moved to the Kenyan mainland, just as my grandfather would eight years later. Kenya came as a shock to the thirteen year old Fitz. Although the division between peoples, religions and races had been noticeable in Zanzibar, it was nothing compared to the systematic racism he saw there:

"The nuns and the priests were running schools for whites only, libraries for whites only, hospitals for whites only. Even in church all the front places were kept for Europeans only, Indians in the back, Africans were told to go to another church for Africans only."

Fitz would eventually decide to challenge this status quo. After graduating as a lawyer in the U.K., he returned to Kenya in 1952, and immediately entered the fight that would change East Africa's destiny. That year the British declared a state of emergency, which led to the infamous Operation Anvil in 1954 to crush the Mau Mau uprising and get control of the Kenyan liberation movement. Fitz joined the defense team for Jomo Kenyatta and other liberation leaders. Together Fitz, Joseph Murumbi and Pio Gama Pinto would make up the Goan troika in the Kenyan liberation movement.

Such men were rare among Goans. While the colonial world was on fire and the winds of freedom blew across the old, European empires, most remained loyal to their masters and continued to live their segregated lives according to their masters' design. Segregation had no place, however, in the liberation movement. Here Goans, Indians and Africans came together in the fight against the common enemy. Murumbi himself was a *half-caste*, with a Goan father and African mother. When liberation was achieved, however, Kenyatta's Asian allies were disappointed. Instead of a true multicultural state, one-sided africanization and a one-party state would be established in postcolonial Kenya. Murumbi reached the office of Vice President before retiring in 1966 to become an art collector. Fitz also became a member of parliament before he also stepped down four years later. Pio Gama Pinto did not get that far. He was shot and killed in his car in a political attack on February 24th, 1965.

When Dad's family first came to Nairobi in 1954, Fitz de Souza and Pio Gama Pinto were their neighbors, so that for a while they shared the same courtyard in the Parklands district. When Pio was killed later, Grandmother wrote to Dad: "Xavy do you know Mrs. Gama Pinto? Her son Pio was shot dead this morning (he is Rosario's brother) for political reasons."

This rather vague statement is the only reference to the Goan freedom fighters in my family's letters. They barely knew Pio, since he spent most of the '50s sitting in jail. But Fitz was a family friend. His mother was godmother to one of my aunts, and it was Fitz who pulled strings so that the first of my aunts could go to America and study. Yet the political situation, the struggle against British imperialism, does not seem to have had any resonance for my grandparents.

It is strange. I can't count the number of East African Goans who have told me they stayed out of politics and civic life: "We kept ourselves to ourselves" is the phrase I hear repeatedly. This does not prevent them from being proud of their reputation as the trusted servants of the British and as the "backbone of the empire."

Did it never occur to them that they were part of an oppressive regime? Under the state of emergency in Kenya, for example, more than twenty thousand Mau Mau rebels were killed, as opposed to thirty-two white settlers and a few hundred British soldiers and police officers. Nor did it stop there. In the hunt for Mau Mau sympathizers, the British interned more than seventy thousand Kikuyu in concentration camps and subjected them to torture, forced labor and murder. While the French had their Algeria, and the Portuguese unleashed bloodbaths in Angola and Mozambique, the Mau Mau operation in Kenya was the British dirty war during the breakup of colonial rule in Africa.

Nobody has investigated the role of the Goans in this war. They were rarely out in the field, but in their work as bureaucrats in the Police and Prison Departments, the Public Work department and elsewhere, they were undoubtedly part of the apparatus of power. It would have been difficult, particularly in the small District Commissioner's offices in areas where the Mau Mau were active, for Goan bureaucrats to avoid any involvement in the British persecution of Kikuyuans. On the other hand, what could they do as long as they were subject to the British, albeit in more privileged positions than the Africans?

So were they victims or accomplices?

"They were both," explains Fitz. "They were victimized by the British, because they were not given equal status with the British people. But they were told they were not Indians, that they were special people. And they believed that."

They were caught between sides. According to Fitz, the Goan prison guards could be more brutal than the Europeans. On the other hand, some Goan officials secretly supported the African liberation movement, smuggling messages for them in and out of the country.

The question that started to loom large as Fitz talked was not new to me. What exactly, I wondered, did my grandfather do during the Mau Mau War? I had sat in the reading room in Nairobi and leafed through the yellowing copies of *Colony and Protectorate of Kenya – Staff List* from the years when my family lived there, but had failed to find his name. A phone call to one of my aunts solved the mystery: Grandfather never took permanent work after his arrival in Kenya, only short term contracts that his younger brother got for him in the tax department.

But how should I view Grandfather's professional role in East Africa? He was a very ordinary official who lived in a society where people were sorted by skin-color, in which one did one's job, and then went home to one's family. Besides, I remind myself, I must not forget that the imperial world, with all its parallel societies, the land of bell jars, as I've called it, was founded on political passivity. Democratic participation belongs to the nation state; in an empire, loyalty goes to the colonial power and to one's own circle. Ultimately, our judgment of the subordinates' role is reliant on our perspective on imperialism: European colonialism has traditionally been seen from a purely European point of view. It was the Europeans who created empires and shaped the world according to their vision. More recently, however, colonial theory puts greater emphasis on the idea that empires are also created from below, not least by trusted subjects like the Goans.

But if the Goans were co-creators of the British Empire, just as they had once been co-creators of Portuguese-India, weren't they also co-responsible?

When I broach the subject with most Goans, my questions are usually greeted with a vague shake of the head and a slight look of unease. Just as when I ask them what caste they belong to. It is as if they are ashamed to have been a part of this society at that time, which now feels so distant. I'm always rather surprised at this reaction. It seems that what is a mystery to me is no less a mystery to them: how could these people live seemingly untouched in the middle of a seething cauldron of violence and racial hatred?

When it comes to Dad, I expect he knew Fitz as a family friend, but I doubt he had any strong opinions about African liberation. Dad had already left home as a nineteen-year-old, before the situation got serious. The initial rush of excitement that came over him when Goa was liberated in 1961 passed quickly, and East Africa's freedom struggle was never his struggle; on the contrary, African liberation shattered his childhood world. Instead, he fought his own lonely battle with the British masters, manifest in the scornful faces of Manchester's employers and landladies. During my childhood in the late '60s and early '70s the winds of liberation had arrived in Portuguese Africa. Had Dad even heard about Sita Valles, the Goan revolutionary martyr from Angola, who looked her killers straight in the eye when she faced the firing squad in 1977? Or the revolutionary Goan journalist Aquino de Bragança, who became an adviser to Samora Machel, the first president of the newly liberated Mozambique, and died alongside him when his plane crashed in 1986?

No, Dad's East Africa was a childhood kingdom. His real homeland, Goa, was a memory given to him by his parents. He belonged to a family that protected itself, adapted to circumstances, and did its best to improve its lot. Dad was in turn adept at this, just as all my family were.

They did not make revolutions, they survived them.

While Fitz talks, his grandchildren run past us heading for the swimming pool in their swimsuits, laughing and taking no notice of us. But I notice how the old man's gaze follows them out into the garden. Romela comes out carrying yet another tray, she refills my teacup, her slender fingers around the pot. I grab my cup, drink and as the warmth spreads though my body, I realize that I long for a father who challenges empires. A rebel, not for his own ego, but for others. A freedom fighter. The irrationality of this thought, its lofty vacuity, make me cringe. I turn back to the old man. I know he is sizing me up as he talks, he's met people like me before. Journalists and writers, all well or less well prepared.

Fitz fixes me with a steady gaze. I meet it undaunted. Not because I am well prepared for our conversation, I am not, but because I know that this old man will show me precisely the respect I deserve. And that's enough, it's all I need right now.

*

Most people need to feel they belong somewhere. Fitz de Souza is perhaps an exception. As I left his villa, I thought I'd met a man who had overcome the longing for any homeland, who had found a sense of belonging in his ideals and made his life's journey into his home.

If this is true, the opposite can be said of Savio, whose home is inextricably linked to his ancestral line, to the earth and to the traditions of Goa. I understand Savio's feelings toward those who have turned their backs on their homeland, I understand his despair in the face of obliteration. But it stops there. It is easy to sympathize with a minority group fighting to maintain its way of life, its ancient lineage, its familial community, its sense of duty to the soil. But this presupposes some kind of purity, a right to belong that one either possesses or not.

"No one is forcing this on you," Savio explained as we sat that night drinking whisky and sodas in his garden restaurant. "It is your choice. But it is there for you to take, if you want it."

But how can I choose my father's legacy without betraying my mother's, and everything I am and ever have been? In all these tribal notions about blood and soil there is no answer to that question.

Purity is an absolute. Everything that is not clean is unclean. A form of pollution. And what is my father's legacy really? My great grandfather abandoned the soil, yet he spent his final years here and was buried in the village cemetery. Grandfather also turned his back on the soil, and though he dreamed of returning, he eventually chose to die among his children on the other side of the world. Dad married a European and betrayed both blood and soil.

And I? Well, nobody in Goa has ever heard of the Bamble Indians. I am a guest here and will never be anything more.

Nevertheless, Savio's words have left their impression on me, as have my meetings with the old priest, with Marie, Anita and the elderly couple who live in Aleixo's old house. They have all embraced me as one of their own, let me enjoy the warmth of the old ancestral hearth, they have given me a fleeting taste of belonging to one place and to one community where my right of residence has been earned through generations.

I am by no means untouched, but my legacy does not lie here. Rather, it lies in what Aleixo took from this place and gave to his children.

Although Catholic Goans seem in many ways to be one people no matter where in the world you meet them, there will always be a difference between those who went away, and those who stayed. For many families, this separation happened twice over. First in their departure from Goa, then, a generation later, in their departure from East Africa. In both cases those who stayed had to live under a new set of rules that threatened their culture and way of life. But while those who stayed in Goa were able to maintain their close ties to the earth and traditions, it was different for those who stayed in East Africa. I met several such people on my journey, and it seemed that the higher the caste they belonged to, the more uncomfortable they felt after African independence. They talked constantly about the good old days when the British kept order, much as the Catholic Brahmins in Goa talked about the days of the Portuguese with such longing.

This perspective was not always shared by Goans from lower castes. In Zanzibar I talked at length with one couple; she was of a lower caste, from a tailor's family, while he was a Brahmin. For them, Karume's bloody revolution not only brought an end to British and Arab domination, but also to the iron rule of the caste system: "If it weren't for the revolution," they told me, "we would never have gotten married."

In my family people were not exceptional like Fitz. They were like most people, or should I say, like most Brahmins. But they did not cling to a dying colonial dream in East Africa. They moved on. And when I look at my family's journey as one, I'm in no doubt that, for them, every step toward the West was a step toward a better life with greater scope. From being the foremost people in the village of Saligão, they became the British favorites in East Africa, high status servants, not wealthy but secure, for a few years at least. In reality they were never anything more than a little cog in a vast imperialist machine, and when everything collapsed, they were stripped of everything but their drive and self-esteem. As it was, they seemed to internalize the legacy of their homeland; in East Africa being Goan went from a purely geographic and cultural sense of belonging, to an inner quality – "we *are* Goans" as my aunts said. And what you *are*, you can take with you wherever you go.

In a way then, I'd say the exiles gained more from the legacies of Portugal and Parashurama than those who stayed in Goa. Including Dad, who hardly knew the Parashurama myth and could speak little more Portuguese than the three words in his own name.

But even if we know who we are, we still need a place in which we can *live* as that person we are. The place my family has moved toward for three generations has always been the place that all emigrants seek. East Africa can be likened to an America for Aleixo and his two wives, Ermelinda and Elizena. Herminia may have been caught between two worlds, but Michael Joseph and most of his children reached the actual

America. They experienced the American dream as it was meant to be, and were near perfect immigrants; hard working, modest, clear about the expectations their new homeland had of them – respect for the Constitution, the flag and the American way of life. Beyond this, one was free to do as one pleased. America is also, in its own way, a land of bell jars, where loyalty to the wider society depends on its inhabitants being allowed to live as they wish, as groups or individuals. The United States – on the fourth continent and in the third empire in my family's history – allowed its citizens to cultivate their own distinct personality, while simultaneously feeling like part of a whole.

"I only discovered the concept of identity when I arrived in the U.S.A.," one of my uncles told me.

Away from home for the first time, alone in a new country, he had to explain who he was to people who generally assumed he was an Indian. In East Africa it was imperative to distance oneself from other races and religions; in the U.S.A., multiculturalism offered an alternative. Here they could find the balance between belonging and freedom, and I can't help but think that this must have come as a huge relief, an opportunity to process their colonial past, to discover their individuality and develop their own sense of humanity, without the leaden pressure of an imperial order. They were proud of their Goan roots, but was it really so dangerous to be taken for an Indian? Dad's youngest sister loves The Beatles, practices yoga and meditation, and believes that many postcolonial Indian authors give expression to her story too.

I imagine that Dad might also have made an exemplary American. His father and siblings certainly encouraged him to join them, especially after the divorce. But something tells me that it would have been impossible for him to return to the family unit, that he'd have found the obligatory intimacy cramping. He had no inner calm, no intention of adapting, and remained the black sheep of the family, even though nobody ever pushed him out. Besides, his sons lived in Norway, and he never gave up hope of winning us back.

When all is said and done, Savio probably has a point. I am the son of a homeless man. As indeed were all the migrants in my family, in that they broke with their origins and lived fragmented and scattered lives for years as they searched for a new homeland. Eight or nine years could pass without the siblings and their parents seeing each other. You can live like that for a while, as long as you maintain ties to *something* greater than yourself. For my family this greater thing was the family itself. Roots can be torn, but blood-bonds are surprisingly elastic. And I am not thinking of the family as an abstract, authoritarian entity, but of the bonds created between family members who share a history. Through the Curry Triangle they succeeded in preserving their community outside the land of bell jars.

In recent years, Skype and Facebook have kept us together in ways that only emigrant families can understand the true meaning of. And even Dad is part of the community again, whether his family visits him at the nursing home in Spain or he sits in front of the computer singing old hits with his guitar-playing brother in Holland over Skype.

Which is why I still can't quite do away with the myth and the dream. Because this family itself has something dream-like about it, or to be more precise, something imagined, brought about by years of homelessness and distance. Whether or not their sense of oneness is based on their mythical origins in Goa is of no matter. Their little community is founded on mutual experience, not on anything imposed on them. It is something both given and chosen. And the striking thing is how real this idea of family must have been for my grandparents, for Dad and his siblings in the years they spent apart. Familiar faces on a screen, a parcel of pickles or a blue letter in the mailbox. Pictures, words and tastes that are infused with memories of a childhood in a lost East Africa, an emotional experience as real as the moment of waking from a dream, the split-second when the final frame of a home movie in Grandfather's projector flares up and dissolves into white.

I think Dad's tragedy was that he never really understood the family pact. Or what it required of *him*. Sacrifice, patience, kindness. Nothing more, nothing less. Qualities that are important for any person in any family, but which I imagine must have been crucial in the world in which he and his siblings grew up. A world where family was their real homeland, the only thing that was solid, when everything else was fluid.

The fact that I lacked any understanding of the family ideal Dad craved, was probably largely his fault. But it has also crossed my mind that the explanation may lie in my growing up in Norway. As a Norwegian, born in a welfare state at a time of unprecedented affluence, I was freed from any sense of a shared fate the day I turned eighteen and was awarded a generous student loan. I needed nobody. And this independence, which is historically quite unique, was perhaps fundamental in the Freudian vendetta I have waged against my own childhood and the two people who were responsible for the embarrassing success that is my life. With the noble intention of being myself, I have supped on the remains of their inadequate parenting, fed upon my own self, sucked the marrow out of my memories. Unlike Dad and his siblings, I have never needed to cultivate memories of a happy childhood; instead I considered it my right *not* to have had a happy childhood.

I could smash every lie because I was not dependent on any truth. I could afford to let go at any moment.

Dad and his siblings could not.

And when it comes down to it, nor can I. Not now, not after this trip. And with that recognition I finally decide to go home. I am leaving Saligão, as Aleixo once did. I will travel too fast, of course, much faster than he did when he boarded the ferry that would take him to Bombay at the end of 19th century. I get into a taxi and ask the driver to take me to Mapusa. Darkness is falling; as I turn and look out of the back window, the last houses in Saligão have already been swallowed up by the night. My gaze turns forward, toward the dusty country road that dances in the restless beams of light before me. At the bus station in

Mapusa, I secure myself a place along the wall where I'm not at risk of being run down by passers-by. I sit on my luggage and look vacantly into the eyes of the street kids with their out-stretched hands. When my coach finally arrives, I find my cubical, pull the curtains and fall asleep with the landscape drifting past in the dark outside.

Whereas my great grandfather's first glimpse of Bombay was from the deck of a ferry, I get off the coach on a busy highway into the city. Whereas I take a taxi straight to the airport, he probably spent some days with Ermelinda and their fellow emigrants in the Goan hospices in town. From there they boarded a steamship and spent three long weeks crossing the Indian Ocean, a journey that took him from everything he'd ever known; the village and his house beside the spring. Somewhere out there on the open sea, a moment must have come when Aleixo's roots snapped. Did he feel it happen? As if something inside him was ripped? I, for my part, glide through the sky from one time zone to another. It takes just a few short hours. And I feel nothing.

Benidorm, June 2015

THE FAMILY IS A PULSE THAT never stops beating. We live together across the world's oceans. The Curry Triangle is still intact, transformed into a floating global cyber-community. But these days we are closer physically too. In the 1960s it was too expensive for a son or daughter in the West to pick up the telephone and call their parents in Nairobi; today flights are so cheap that we can meet whenever we want. In Egypt one year, in London the next, it's not important where, as long as we can be together. This year the vote was for Benidorm, so that Dad could come too.

We sit, all thirty-one of us, on a balcony on the twenty-third floor of a holiday apartment block in Benidorm. The youngest is six months old, the oldest over eighty. Uncles and aunts, cousins and nephews are all here; the more distant relatives are simply "cousins." Some have come from the United States, others from Canada, the Netherlands, England, Norway. There should have been more of us, but our "cousins" from Goa and Portugal have been prevented from coming. Mum was invited too, since she and Dad's family only ever had warm feelings for each other. Mum declined politely; it's been more than thirty years since she and Dad saw each other, her life took other paths long ago, none of which lead back to him. My aunts and uncles have prepared masalas and dishes at home, now they're stirring various pots and pans in the cramped kitchen. Sofas, beds and chairs are pulled out onto the balcony. As the day draws to an end it cools, the sky grows red behind the rows of pastel-colored hotels that lie between us and the sea.

The minute we've emptied the plates of food, the guitar is brought out. The balcony fills with laughter and old songs: "Moonlight Bay," "Baby Face," "Guantanamera." Dusk falls, the lights come on in all the high-rise blocks around us, until the entire city looks like a forest of luminous columns against a black sky. One of my aunts hands out the text of Saligão's village song; I sit and watch my wife and daughters spelling out the words in Konkani. They too are part of this now.

And Dad. He sings along, a fraction behind the rest of us, but solemnly, just as when he used to sing in the church choir in Porsgrunn. He is sitting on my right, facing Uncle J.'s guitar, his back turned slightly toward me. He is in astonishingly good shape. But thin, his checkered shirt hanging loosely from narrow shoulders. He doesn't recognize all the faces around him, there are new grandchildren, new boyfriends and girlfriends, and nephews and nieces he hasn't seen for years. But he recognizes his close family, his sons and his brothers and sisters.

Dad's world is small nowadays, but the smile that never leaves his face tells me that he is content. It's strange how easy it is to sit here alongside him. I have not forgotten the past; the damage he inflicted on us. But it is no longer active in me. I can't find a better word for it; but ever since I found him close to death in his apartment in Alfaz del Pi, I've felt this way (although, not quite – occasionally when I leaf through his letters and read those brutal words, or when I'm rooting about for a new childhood memory to complete a gap in this book, a flame of anger flares up in me. But it is always quick to subside, as though there were no longer enough fuel in me to sustain it). Am I reconciled? Or have I just given in to what may be the siren song of my nature: a compulsion to smooth things over, to sweep any conflict under the carpet? Like a true Goan. It's an interesting idea, although I'm probably being too generous with myself. Since I cannot deny that I have grown somehow harder as I've journeyed through my family's history, in and out of the bell jars. In searching for my own tribe, I have turned my back on others. And what kind of reconciliation is there in my ruthless determination to write the story of my father? I tell myself that I am doing this because I must, but I see too that I am doing it because I *can*. His life is in my hands. That's how it is now. Reconciled, but harder. I can live with that. I'll have to. I probably wouldn't even have found an ending for this story if life itself hadn't delivered the solution. Dad's illness has been like the finger of God, *dementia ex machina*. And if life itself has offered an ironic conclusion, who am I to reject it? The phrase that has almost been a mantra for me – that nothing disappears, we carry our burdens for all time – no longer has the same meaning for me. Dad weighs so little now, and the road that remains, is not long.

When we get to the scouts' song that Dad sang to us as children, I catch his eye. But there's nothing there. That is, he nods at me contentedly, but his gaze doesn't express anything uniquely meaningful. There's no sign that he is thinking, as I am, that this is *it*; we're together now like a true Goan family, like the family he grew up in, but which we, his sons, neither could nor wanted to be for him. He looks at me with this uncomplicated smile now, as though we'd always been like this, as though we'd always sat together singing these old songs.

There are thirty-one family members here on the balcony, but I feel as though there were more. I may be the only one who feels it, the past is so close to me now; but don't Michael Joseph, Herminia, Aleixo, Ermelinda, Elizena and Ti Filu belong here too? It's cramped, but the dead don't take up much space. I see my grandfather sitting among his children singing *My Girl's a Yorkshire Girl* in his sentimental vibrato filled voice. There are more children than Herminia's lap could hold, though she'd have found a solution and picked them all up one by one, put her arms around them, while discretely checking that their ears were clean.

In fact one of the dead is among us, quite literally. Earlier this year Uncle Lionel passed away, and his daughter has brought an urn containing some of his ashes. Early next morning we gather at a small white pavilion on a rock facing the sea just below Benidorm's old town. The tourists and café owners are not yet up, and we are quite alone. To get to the pavilion we had to go down a long, steep set of steps. The city is not visible from where we are now, all we can see is the sky and sea. We stand in a semicircle, and my cousin brings out the urn and says a few appropriate words. Some of us cry. Then we walk toward the railings that separate Europe from the Mediterranean. Behind lies the ocean that disappears into the hazy horizon, and behind that again Africa, India, all that is and has been.

No one says a thing, all that is heard is the wind as my cousin removes the lid of the urn and empties its contents over the ocean. A cloud of white billows forth and dances briefly in the air before it dissolves and disappears.

Dear Ivo,

You cannot become a Ganvkar of Saligão. Unless your Dad was a Ganvkar and his name is in our books, you cannot even entertain the thought of becoming a Ganvkar. So please forget about it. In any case you are a foreigner now and that debars you. You can visit us when you are in Goa sometimes and we can have a chat. God bless you. Yours as ever.

Brig. Ian da Costa

ACKNOWLEDGMENTS

Many people have helped me in the writing of this book, sharing their stories with me, allowing me to interview them, pointing me toward useful sources, or reading my manuscript while it was still in the making. They all deserve my sincerest thanks and enormous credit, although I alone must bear the responsibility. This has to be particularly emphasized in relation to the members of my family who shared their stories with me so generously. *A Stranger at My Table* is only my version of our family history; as always, there are many varying interpretations and narratives.

As far as my father is concerned, he was among those who allowed me to interview him and gave me access to correspondence, etc. As this book reveals, he was struck down with dementia before its completion and has therefore neither read nor approved the contents of this book.

I have generally used the real names of the people featured in this story. However, most of my aunts and uncles are represented by their first initial, and the people I met on my travels in Africa and Goa have been given pseudonyms.

CITATIONS AND BIBLIOGRAPHY

See the literature overview below for full reference to individual articles and books. The dates given refer to the edition I have used, not that of the first edition.

p. 49 *"The city does not tell its past..."*: Calvino (1992: 14).

p. 50 *"... direct, rule and instruct..."*: Harry H. Johnston in *The Newcastle Weekly* in 1894, quoted by Carvalho (2014: 22).

p. 51 *"However altruistic we may be..."*: Letter to Chief Secretary, August 10, 1925, AB 82/459, National Archives of Zanzibar.

p. 51 *"This is because we owe a duty..."*: Letter to Chief Secretary, J une 12, 1925, AB 82/459, National Archives of Zanzibar. Own translation.

p. 52 *"I was fond of Dominguez..."*: Greene (1956: 144).

p. 69 *"It's pretty, but quite unremarkable..."*: Waugh (2002: 128).

p. 88 *"The white man and all that he brings with him..."*: Churchill (1962: 2).

p. 90 *"The airplane is faster than the heart..."*: Naipaul (2011: 130).

p. 102 *"Come on, let's get the blacks and the coppers!"*: Philips (1999: 176).

pp. 102–103 *"Are we to saddle ourselves with color problems?..."*: Quoted by Toye (2010: 290).

p. 104 *"It never occurs to us that we might contribute to it ourselves.":*
Naipaul (2011: 165).

p. 104 *"... almost the same, but not quite.":* Bhabha (1994).

p. 141 *"Living in Sin...":* Waugh (2000: 269)

p. 143 *"Be calm and brave...":* quoted by Rao (1963: 164).

pp. 147–148 *"No bacon...":* Greene in *Pinto* (2006).

p. 159 *"... a kind of place...":* Selvon (2006: 27)

p. 174 *"The promenaders were all Indian...":* Moravia
(1972; English edition 1974).

p. 175 *"We came to establish a Christian civilization...":*
Waugh (2002: 128).

p. 175 *"They only see us when they want to hate us...":*
Naipaul (1980: 109).

p. 175 *"The white man versus the black; the Indian versus both.":*
Churchill (1963: 14).

p. 175 *"... black and white love affair.":* Naipaul (1980: 113).

pp. 175–176 *"A Patel remained a Patel...":* Naipaul (1980: 117).

p. 184 *"... belongs to the gravy...":* Menez (2000: 200).

p. 210 *"Like the Roman, I see the Tiber foaming with much blood...":*
quoted by Phillips (1999: 245).

p. 279 *"We're Christians...":* Somerset Maugham (1949: 283).

p. 281 *"Their superiority to the heathen...":* Burton (2001: 73).

p. 281 *"Lifting across the Orient waves they came ...":*
Camões: *Os Lusíadas* translated by Bacon (1966).

LITERATURE

This book is largely based on my own travels, family correspondence, documents, photographs, as well as a large number of interviews. But I have also consulted many articles and books, many of which are listed below. Where I give two publication dates, the first refers to the first edition, the second to the edition I have used.

Portugal and Portuguese India: Unfortunately, I do not speak Portuguese, but I found the following books particularly informative on the history of Portugal: A.H. de Oliveira Marques' *History of Portugal* (1972, 1976) and David Birmingham's *A Concise History of Portugal* (1993, 2003). Michael Pearson also provides an excellent introduction to life on and around the Indian Ocean in *The Indian Ocean* (2003).

Goa: Michael Pearson also writes about Goa's history after the arrival of the Portuguese in *The New Cambridge History of India: The Portuguese in India* (1987, 2006). There are very few academic studies of earlier and ancient Goan history, leaving a vast field open for future historians to explore. However, Teotónio R. de Souza's *Medieval Goa: A Socio-Economic History* (1979, 2009) offers some valuable insights. Worthy of note too, is the Marxist historian Damodar Dharmananda Kosambi's groundbreaking work *An Introduction to the Study of Indian History* (1956) and his article "The village communities in the Old Conquests of Goa" in the *Journal of the University of Bombay*, XV, no. 4 (1947). It should be generally noted that much of the available literature about Goa's history retains certain mythical undercurrents, reinforcing an historical perspective founded on the Parashurama myth and affirming the traditional power of the Catholic Brahmins. An example of such a mythical-historical work is Anant Ramkrishna Sinai Dhume's *The Cultural History of Goa from 10,000 BC–1352 AD* (1986).

Other works I found useful include Stella Mascarenhas-Keyes' dissertation *Colonialism, Migration & the International Catholic Goan Community* (2001) and Jerry Pinto's [ed.] *Reflected in Water: Writings on Goa* (2006). The latter is a colorful anthology of historical, literary and personal articles and essays about Goa, and I refer to several of the essays below.

Among the many guidebooks on Goa, I found Maurice Hall's *Window on Goa: A History and Guide* (1992, 1995) of particular interest. Teresa Albuquerque's short book *Goan Pioneers in Bombay* (2012) tells the story of the Goan population in Bombay, while Scottish travel writer William Dalrymple portrays the Goanese Catholic upper class in his book *The Age of Kali – Indian Travels and Encounters* (1998).

Saligão: J.M. Richard's travel guide *Goa* (1982) mentions the village of Saligão, but I have generally relied on oral sources and a memoir set in the time of my father's generation by Mel D'Souza: *Feasts, Feni and Firecrackers. Life of a Village Schoolboy in Portuguese Goa* (2007). The elderly priest who told me the mythical story of Saligão and its people is Fr. Nascimento J. Mascarenhas, whose book *Land of the Sal Tree* (2012) covers much of the same material he shared with me.

Recent research on Goa: Mascarenhas's book belongs to the mythical tradition that confirms the historical right of the Catholic Brahmins in Goa. Recently, however, more works have appeared that challenge this tradition, partly on historical grounds, partly with a view to representing other communities and groups, including the Hindus and lower castes. I have borrowed the distinction between Goa Dourado and Goa Indica from Caroline Ifeka's article "The Image of Goa" in T.R. de Souza's (ed.) *Indo-Portuguese History. Old Issues, New Questions* (1984). Furthermore, there is an interesting investigation of "the other Goa" in American anthropologist Robert S. Newman's *Of Umbrellas, Goddesses & Dreams: Essays on Goan Culture and Society* (2001) and Parag D. Parobo's relatively new book *India's First Democratic Revolution: Dayanand Bandodkar and the Rise of the Bahujan in Goa* (2015, 2016). While the latter has a certain bias toward the Hindu Bahujan movement, it offers an interesting and well founded counter-history to that accepted by the Brahmins.

Goa 1961: The liberation (or invasion) of Goa in 1961 is mentioned in several books. Narratives written from the Indian perspective are to be found in R.P. Rao's *Portuguese Rule in Goa 1510–1961* (1963) and D.R. Mankekaar's and Aparna Mathus' essay "The Goa Action" in Pinto (2006). The liberation as seen from East Africa is discussed in Margret Frenz's article "Transimperial Connections. East African Goan Perspectives on 'Goa 1961'" in *Contemporary South Asia* (no. 3, 2014). For views on Goan identity in the postcolonial era, see Alito Siqueira: "Postcolonial Portugal, Postcolonial Goa. A Note on Portuguese Identity and Its Resonance in Goa and India," *Lusotopie* (9, 2002) and Nishta Desai's "The Denationalization of Goans: An Insight into the Construction of Cultural Identity," *Lusotopie* (7, 2000).

Goan food: Nobody who has read this book could doubt the importance of food to the Goans. I have had great pleasure in reading food-historian Lizzie Collingham's *Curry. A Tale of Cooks and Conquerors* (2007). This unique book is a collective biography of curries; her chapter about the Goan signature Vindaloo was of particular interest to me. Two Goan cookbooks with fascinating introductions are Fátima da Silva Gracias' *Cozinha de Goa. History and Tradition of Goan Food* (2011) and Maria Teresa Menezes' *The Essential Goa Cookbook* (2000). Finally, Antoine Lewis' article "No Blood in the Snake Oil" and Frank Simoes' "Everything You Ever Wanted to Know About Feni But Were Too Drunk to Ask," both published in *Pinto* (2006) proved useful.

Catholicism: While food has always been important to Goans, religion has been equally, if not more, important. Pamila Gupta's book *The Relic State. St. Francis Xavier and the Politics of Ritual in Portuguese India* (Studies in Imperialism MUP) (2014) has been my main source of information about the story of St. Francis Xavier's body, cf. the article "Relics of St. Xavier Still A Draw" in *The Times of India*, December 3, 2009. Naresh Fernandes is the journalist who has investigated what happened to the saint's right elbow, cf. his essay "Tomb Raider. Looking for St. Francis Xavier," published in *Pinto* (2006). Evelyn Waugh's novel *Brideshead Revisited* (1945, 2000) offered me the opportunity to reflect on Catholic guilt, while my main sources on the subject of Catholicism in Norway included John W. Gran's (ed.) *Den katolske kirke i Norge. fra kristningen til i dag* (The Catholic Church in Norway. From the arrival of Christianity to Today) (1993) and *Den norske ordensprovince* (The Order in the Norwegian Province) Vols. I–III (2009) issued by the St. Joseph's Sisters of Chambéry.

East Africa, Zanzibar and Pemba: Two works offered me a broad view over of Britain's presence in East Africa; from Oxford University Press: *The Oxford History of the British Empire*, Vols. III and IV (1999), and the four-volume *History of East Africa* (1963–76). For the history of Zanzibar and Pemba, I enjoyed reading both W.H. Ingram's classic study *Zanzibar: Its History and its People* (1931, 2007) and Esmond Bradley Martin's *Zanzibar: Tradition and Revolution* (1978). The local historian Abdul Sheriff showed me around Stone Town during my visit. Sheriff has also written many articles and books, of which his small architectural guide book *Zanzibar Stone Town. An Architectural Exploration* (1998, 2008) also proved very useful.

I sought additional advice from the Norwegian social anthropologist Anne K. Bang, and consulted her book about Zanzibar and the island's most famous Norwegian, Oscar Christian August Olsen: *Zanzibar-Olsen: Norsk trelasthandel i Øst-Afrika 1895–1925* (The Norwegian Timber Trade in East Africa) (2008). In regards to more recent research on Zanzibar's social, political and cultural structure viewed in light of city planning and development, William Cunningham Bissell's book *Urban Design, Chaos and Colonial Power in Zanzibar* (2011) proved particularly interesting, as did his short article "Camera Zanzibar," in Dilip Parameshwar Gaonkar's (ed.): *Alternative Modernities* (2001), in which he describes British oriental architecture on the island, including the John Sinclair Peace Museum, Beit el Amani. I found additional information about the Pemba mission station and the cemetery where my grandmother is buried in *Zanzibar Slave Memory* (2005) by Salim Khamis and Abdurahman Juma.

Kenya: Bruce Berman's and John Lonsdale's two-part work *Unhappy Valley: Conflict in Kenya & Africa* (1992) offered excellent insights into Kenya's history. The standard work on the British handling of the Mau Mau rebellion is David Anderson's *Histories of the Hanged: The Dirty War in Kenya and the End of the Empire* (2005). Caroline Elkins' *Britain's Gulag: The Brutal End of Empire in Kenya* (2005) is interesting, although somewhat biased. It is worth mentioning here that debate about Britain's conduct in Kenya and other colonies continues, not least after the extensive archival finds of the last years; see Marc Parry's "Uncovering the Brutal Truth About the British Empire" published in *The Guardian*, August 18, 2016. For information about Nairobi's history and social geography, I have consulted Rashmi Varma's *The Postcolonial City and Its Subjects. London. Nairobi. Bombay* (2012), Shadi Rahbaran's and Manuel Herz's *Nairobi, Kenya: Migration Shaping the City* (2014) and O.A. K'Akumu and W.H.A. Olima "The Dynamics and Implications of Residential Segregation in Nairobi," in *Habitat International* (no. 31, 2007).

Asians in East Africa: Of books on the subject of Asians including Goans in East Africa, the two that stand out are Hugh Tinker's *The Banyan Tree. Overseas Emigrants from India, Pakistan and Bangladesh* (1977) and Jagjit Singh Mangat's *A History of the Asians in East Africa c.1886 to 1945* (1969, 2012). On the subject of building The Uganda Railway from Mombasa to Kampala, which brought so many Indians and Goans to East Africa (and took my father out of the country in 1958), a great deal has been written, the book which describes the madness of this project most amusingly perhaps being Charles Miller's *The Lunatic Express* (1987).

Goans in East Africa: By a stroke of luck, while I was working on this book, Margret Frenz's extensive research on East African Goans came out with the Oxford University Press. Her *Community, Memory and Migration in a Globalizing World: The Goan Experience, c.1890–1980* (2014) has been my most important source in developing my chapters on the history of the Goans on this continent. She also writes in depth about the relationship between the Goans and the Portuguese in British East Africa, in her article "Representing the Portuguese Empire. Goan Consuls in British East Africa c.1910–1963" in Eric Morier-Genoud's and Michel Cahen's (eds.) *Imperial Migrations. Colonial Communities and Diaspora in the Portuguese World* (2012). In addition to Frenz, I have especially enjoyed the work of Selma Carvalho and Cliff Pereira. Carvalho has written two books on the Goan diaspora, *Into the Diaspora Wilderness* (2010) and *A Railway Runs Through: Goans of British East Africa, 1865–1980* (2014). The latter, in particular, gives a broad picture of the Goans in East Africa. Pereira is the author of two articles: "Goans of the North Atlantic. A Transnational Study of Migration, Technology Adaptation and Neo-Culturation across Six Generations," in Myna German's and Padmini Banerjee's (eds.): *Migration, Technology, and Transculturation. A Global Perspective* (2011); and "Cogwheels of Two Empires. Goan administration within the 19th Century British Indian Ocean Empire" published online at academia.edu. (2012).

Goan freedom fighters in East Africa: There is a great deal of information about Fitz de Souza, Joseph Murumbi and Pio Gama Pinto, in Frenz (2014). *Battles Waged, Lasting Dreams. Aquino Bragança; The Man and His Times* (2011) written by Silvia Bragança, the widow of Aquino de Bragança, reviews his involvement as a Goan activist in Portuguese East Africa, as well as others there, including Sita Valles. Meanwhile Leonor Figueiredo has written the biography Valles: *Sita Valles – Revolucionária, Comunista até à Morte (1951–1977)* (2010), which, to my knowledge, is only available in Portuguese.

East African memoirs and novels: Personal accounts by East African Goans that I have referred to in my research are: Mervyn Maciel's *Bwana Karani* (1985), in which he describes his time as a functionary in several British provinces in Kenya during the period of the Mau Mau; Braz Menezes' two novels about life in Goa and East Africa after World War II, *Just Matata. Sins, Saints and Settlers* (2011) and *More Matata. Love After the Mau Mau* (2012). From Zanzibar I have supplemented the childhood memories of my own family with

George Pereira's essay "Why I Miss Zanzibar" in *Goa Masala: An Anthology of Stories by Canadian Goans* (2010). It is also worth noting that the most famous Goan novels to come out of East Africa are Peter Nazareth's *In a Brown Mantle* (1972) and *The General Is Up* (1991).

Travel writings: Of all Europeans who traveled the colonial world and wondered at all those who were different than themselves, the most interesting character is undoubtedly the explorer Richard Burton (1821–1890). Burton traveled to both East Africa and Goa, but of his own books, I have largely used *Goa, and the Blue Mountains. Or, Six Months of Sick Leave* (1851, 2001). Otherwise, I have read two biographies about him with especial interest: Thomas Wright's *Life of Sir Richard Burton* (1906) and Byron Farwell's *Burton: A Biography of Sir Richard Francis Burton* (1963, 1990). In the chapter where I visit Velha Goa, I mention that Burton translated the Portuguese national poet Luís Vaz de Camões' epic poem *Os Lusíadas* (1572). The quotes given here, however, are not from Burton's translation, but from Leonard Bacon's in his *The Lusíadas of Luís Vaz de Camões* (1950, 1966).

Of other European travel writings, I have come across new editions of two early-20th century portraits of Zanzibar: Robert Nunez Lyne's *Zanzibar in Contemporary Times* (1905, 2011) and F.B. Pearce's *Zanzibar Island: Metropolis of Eastern Africa* (1919, 2006). Of these two, it is Nunez who claims that Goan chefs had a habit of getting drunk during dinner parties.

I also consulted one solitary Norwegian travelog, that of P.B. Holte *Fri fants reiser* (Travels of a Vagabond) (1944), based on a trip he made to the island in the 1920s.

But returning to the British travel writers who feature in this account: I could not have predicted that Evelyn Waugh would become one of my "companions" in the writing of this book. But Waugh proved of use in many ways: his descriptions of Pemba and Zanzibar appear in his travel book *Remote People* (1932, 2002), while those of Velha Goa are taken from "Goa. The home of a saint," *Month*, (December 1953) and his correspondence with his wife, published in *The Letters of Evelyn Waugh*, edited by Mark Amory (1981). William Somerset Maugham and Graham Greene also portrayed Velha Goa and Maugham in *A Writer's Notebook* (1949), Greene in his essay

"Goa the unique" published in *Pinto* (2006) and elsewhere. Greene's portrait of the Goan servant appears in *The Quiet American* (1955). Last, but not least, Winston Churchill set down his views on Africans, Indians and Europeans, as well as the future of British East Africa in *My African Journey* (1908, 1962).

That all of these historical travel sources exude orientalism and prejudice against Africans and Indians should be of no surprise. One work that does not is by the staunch critic of imperialism, Italian author Alberto Moravia: *A quale tribù appartieni?* (1972) Additionally, an interesting and provocative West Indian perspective on East Africa can be found in Shiva Naipaul's travel book *North of South. An African Journey* (1978, 1980).

Postcolonial fiction: As my aunt M. says, global colonial and postcolonial history also reflects much of our own family history. Not least, there are striking parallels between my father's encounter with Great Britain and that described in V.S. Naipaul's novel *A Bend in the River* (1979). Naipaul's term "half-and-half life" is found in his autobiographical novel *Half Life* (2001), while his meeting with India is depicted in *An Area of Darkness* (1964, 1968). Meanwhile, J.M. Coetzee gives us a young white man's perspective in *Youth* (2002), Abdulrazak Gurnah gives an excellent description of Zanzibar and its meeting with Britain in the novel *By the Sea* (2001), and the Trinidadian author Sam Selvon depicts West Indian immigrants in 1950s London in *The Lonely Londoners* (1956, 2006). The terms "almost the same, but not quite" and "mimetic people," which I use on pages 104 and 282 are borrowed from the critical theorist Homi K. Bhabha's *The Location of Culture* (1994).

Britain and immigration: Details about colonial and postcolonial immigration to the U.K. have largely been taken from Randall Hansen's *Citizenship and Immigration in Post-war Britain: The Institutional Origins of a Multicultural Nation* (2000) and Dilip Hiro's *Black British, White British: A History of Race Relations in Britain* (1992). Interesting too is the book *Windrush. The Irresistible Rise of Multi-Racial Britain* (1999) by Mike Phillips and Trevor Phillips, which looks at the first wave of immigrants from the West Indies. Winston Churchill's skepticism about immigration is plotted in Richard Toye's *Churchill's*

Empire: The World That Made Him and the World He Made (2010). Goan immigration to the U.K. is also discussed in Selma Carvalho's books (mentioned above) and in Stella Mascarenhas Keyes' *Goans in London – Portrait of Catholic Asian Community* (1979). The latter was published in London, but is extremely difficult to get hold of; I finally tracked a copy down in the Goa State Library in Panaji.

Knut Kjeldstadli's standard work *Norsk innvandringshistorie* (Norwegian Immigration History) (2003) has been a useful reference on the subject of immigration to Norway.

And finally, the ideas explored in connection to the photograph on page 299 are based on the writings of the French philosopher Roland Barthes in his *Camera Lucida: Reflections on Photography* (1980). The lovely quote about cities on page 49 is taken from *Invisible Cities* by Italo Calvino (1972, English edition 1974).